WIN ALL YOUR BATTLES

Readers' Praise for *Kar Har Maidan Fateh*

'Very useful for UPSC aspirants not only from Maharashtra but also from the other parts of India.'

—Shushrut Jhadav

'An inspirational book. A must read. Kudos to Mr Vishwas Nangre Patil.'

—Sarweshwar

'A must buy. Awesome book.'

—Vivek Gosavi

'Inspirational book. It gives you goosebumps while reading the journey of the author.'

—Omkar Phatangare

'It is the best book for anyone who wants to clear their mind from negative thoughts. It motivates to pursue your dreams.'

—Shardul Gayake

'Best book for all the UPSC aspirants.'

—Kiran Daf

'It is a good read, especially for those who are preparing for competitive exams.'

—Aditya P. Bhavar

FOREWORD BY **AKSHAY KUMAR**

WIN ALL YOUR BATTLES

VISHWAS NANGRE PATIL

Translated from the Marathi by **Subha Pande**

HarperCollins *Publishers* India

First published in English in India by HarperCollins *Publishers* 2022
4th Floor, Tower A, Building No. 10, Phase II, DLF Cyber City,
Gurugram, Haryana – 122002
www.harpercollins.co.in

2 4 6 8 10 9 7 5 3 1

Published in arrangement with Mehta Publishing House.
Originally published in Marathi by Mehta Publishing House 2021.

P-ISBN: 978-93-9440-781-7
E-ISBN: 978-93-9440-786-2

Typeset in 10.5/13.7 Adobe Caslon Pro at
Manipal Technologies Limited, Manipal

Printed and bound at
Thomson Press (India) Ltd

MIX
Paper
FSC® C010615

This book is produced from independently certified FSC® paper
to ensure responsible forest management.

Contents

Foreword

It rarely happens that when two people meet they instantly connect. It is human nature to judge most of the time, to evaluate a person based on your own IQ and form opinions about them. But none of this happened with Vishwas and me. Our wavelengths matched instantly, we formed a deep connection, and our friendship was inevitable. Taking that connection forward, over the years we have interacted on diverse subjects and have taken numerous initiatives for the welfare of our farmers, drought-affected people of western Maharashtra, and families of martyrs and policemen working as frontline warriors during the COVID-19 pandemic. We have shared our life experiences with each other, and we both have the same dream of serving and giving back to society.

Of course, for who he is, in such a high place, there are always people who want to know him, befriend him, flaunt that they know Vishwas Nangre Patil, and sure Vishwas too has friends in high places and contacts to reach, whichever office of the country he chooses, but he is one of those rare individuals who if needed, will use all of his networks only to help someone or guide someone and also to solve the cases he works on to see justice is done where it is deserved. I can give you many such examples but as you read the book, you will understand the underlying subtext, of what the man is. On a lighter note, I'd like to add that I modelled my character of Veer Sooryavanshi, in the movie *Sooryavanshi,* on Vishwas. He looks good in the uniform, and I thought if I could carry the police uniform, which I hugely respect, I'd have done at least the physical appearance of my character right.

I've had the privilege of knowing Vishwas Nangre Patil for over a decade now, and it is with absolute pride that I write the foreword for the English edition of his book *Kar Har Maidan Fateh* [*Win All Your Battles*]. This book is about the moulding and building of an IPS officer, just like the transformation of raw material into the final, refined product. It's about the journey of a young lad who, with his serious determination, relentless consistency and ironclad dedication, is groomed into a seasoned policeman. It is a book about how a young boy with limited means from a humble village got selected for the elite police service, and how the training process at the academy strengthened his abilities and instilled a spirit of service in him.

Vishwas, in *Win All your Battles,* talks about his encounters with unforeseen challenges that life presents. He describes elaborately the training he received at the Lal Bahadur Shastri National Academy of Administration in Mussoorie and the Sardar Vallabhbhai Patel National Police Academy in Hyderabad. He talks about the crucial lessons he learnt during his training period and how these lessons helped him in tackling mobs, handling law-and-order situations and solving some serious crimes later in his career. He speaks in detail about how the rigorous indoor and outdoor training moulded him and helped him imbibe the qualities that were necessary to overcome challenges in his personal and professional life. The part that really caught my attention is when he speaks about the field tactics and the presence of mind, that he learnt during his training period, which helped him immensely in combating the terrorists at the Taj Hotel during the deadly Mumbai terror attacks on 26 November 2008. A day no Indian can forget …

This book is also an essential read for every youth in this country wishing to serve the nation, as Vishwas explains through his own example the importance of self-discipline, perseverance and hard work. He tells the youth how they can equip themselves to face any challenge in life, develop courage, and walk that extra mile for the benefit of society—virtues that are dear to my heart as well.

I especially want to call out two portions from the book. One, where Vishwas speaks about how he started worshipping his profession after his encounter with an old lady in an Uttar Pradesh village. In his words, 'From then on, I pledged that every person who walks into my office is my God. Working became really easy after that. There remained no difference between my professional duties and service to God.'

And the other is Shri Ajit Doval's speech during the IPS passing out parade that Vishwas quotes in the book. Mr Doval said that it is essential for each one of us to develop our own personal 'brand' that epitomizes our values, beliefs, upbringing and ethics. The youth must follow this life mantra. Vishwas has, over the years, exemplified this mantra and has succeeded in making his 'brand' an inspiring one. Today, every young person in Maharashtra knows about Vishwas and many try to emulate him. They consider him a role model.

But not everything is just about only the good. In *Win All Your Battles*, Vishwas candidly talks about his failings and weaknesses, his inferiority complexes and how he managed to overcome them. I would personally like to add that no two situations will be the same for you in life, and life will keep throwing both good and bad, triumph and failure, love and hate to you. Being prepared for all situations, one should consciously work on and try to imbibe the mental strength, physical fitness, discipline, commitment and enthusiasm that the author himself embodies. He also emphasizes taking charge of one's own life—not letting astrology or palmistry decide your future! One should 'take life head-on! Look into the other person's eye and not be cowed down! Who were the constellations—Amavasya, Rahu, Ketu, and Shani—to come in my way?' says the author. The life of a police officer is not an easy one. One needs to cultivate 'physical, mental and spiritual capabilities' to become a successful public servant, as Vishwas rightly mentions.

Over his decades of service, Vishwas put all his learnings into practice: initiatives like the Nirbhaya Squad, banning of Dolby systems during Ganesh Chaturthi to curb nuisance to people, youth parliament to give the young a taste of policymaking and a host of other welfare schemes for the employees of the police department and their families. And more recently, his work during the COVID-19 outbreak, curbing its spread in Maharashtra. He speaks of that in the book.

The love and care Vishwas has towards his 'police family' is remarkable. I have seen him going to great lengths to bring about changes in the police subculture, so his fellow officers feel less pressurized at work, and spend more quality time with their families.

I would like to sum up this foreword by saying this book is straight from the heart. It is written with utmost sincerity. It is not a sermon on morality, but something for everyone to read and ponder. It educates you about various social evils such as the negative effects of social media, cybercrime, online abuse and drug addiction. It offers valuable counsel on how youth can safeguard themselves from these challenges. It tells parents to ensure that their children don't fall victim to such crimes. It provides guidance to girls and women on protecting themselves from harassment at home and elsewhere.

I congratulate all those who have put their efforts into making this book possible. I hope it reaches as far as it can go in inspiring and guiding anyone who wants to serve their country.

In the end, I will just say, 'Vishwas, I am so happy for you, my friend.'

To serving more,
Jai Hind!

Mumbai **Akshay Kumar**
27 March 2022

Preface

The time between my selection for the Indian Police Service (IPS) and the commencement of training passed in a blink. There were felicitations, garlands, processions and celebrations galore, and it looked as though I had won an election. I, too, visited schools and colleges patiently and guided students on the Union Public Service Commission (UPSC) exams and the preparation methods and techniques. They crowded around me for my autograph! Because I explained the way to crack the tough UPSC exam in simple terms, they felt confident and saw a ray of hope. We, too, had been motivated by the words of Vikas Kharage (IAS) and Bhushan Gagrani (IAS). And owing to that inspiration, and our energy and hard work, Anand, Hemant and I were selected at the same time.

We took it upon ourselves to spread that energy in our village Kokrud and the surrounding areas. Students began coming to the study centre we had established. It became a movement of sorts, as several people joined in and started preparing for the UPSC exams with renewed optimism and vigour. Students from rural areas began clearing these exams and reached great heights.

Sugandh Chougule from the neighbouring Sarud village got selected for the Indian Foreign Service (IFS). Shridhar Patil from Kotoli got into the IPS. Abhinay Kumbhar from Shirala and Yogesh Kamat from Sarud got selected for the Indian Revenue Service (IRS), while Sandeep Diwan from Mangle and P.R. Patil from Sarud became deputy superintendents of police (DySPs).

The context of our lives changed after our selection into the IPS. Felicitations and ceremonies carried on for quite a few days. All the questions that had plagued us vanished, and new challenges raised their heads. Marriage alliances from reputed and well-to-do families began to pour in. The number of visitors also increased, and the expectations of people at home and in the village were sky high. But I had turned inward, introspecting deeply about what the uniform would mean to me; the transformation of a simple village boy into a high-flying bureaucrat seemed like a huge challenge. I needed to understand and absorb this new lifestyle and the requisite personality traits.

In life, it is these changes that expose us to new ways of living and give us opportunities to learn every day. Training was the first phase in this process. It began with the initial sixteen-week foundation course at the Lal Bahadur Shastri National Academy of Administration (LBSNAA). This was followed by a tough fifty-four-week training for IPS trainees at the Hyderabad-based Sardar Vallabhbhai Patel National Police Academy (SVPNPA; henceforth NPA or academy for short). After completing the training at NPA, we had to further undergo practical field training. The entire training period completely transformed the personality of several trainee officers like me. I realized that this must be the reason the British had set a very young age for joining the police service. The value systems, attitudes, and professional skills that youth learn in their early twenties are difficult to learn at a more advanced age. I, too, entered that environment with optimism, a keenness to learn and a will to achieve great things.

Initially, I was blinded by the majesty and luxury of the environment that I found myself in. The Anglicized ambience sent shivers of fear through me. The difficult practicals made my head spin. Mussoorie's bone-chilling cold froze my arrogance, and Hyderabad's blazing heat singed my inferiority complex and physical weakness. I changed completely under the tremors of these fluctuating, shocking and tough mental challenges. This transformation process was a prelude to personality development, education, progress and change. I have tried to describe this process in the book.

The main objective of writing this second book is to explain in simple terms the mental, physical and spiritual aspects learnt during training, to all those people who are not fortunate enough to get into the academy. Another purpose is to clearly express the positive changes that training wrought in me, and the healthy habits that I could inculcate in myself. I wanted to narrate how all these positive habits transformed all the bitter challenges into interesting and inspiring ones. I wanted to share how my educated mind and body worked in sync with the personal and professional changes I underwent. I wanted to elaborate on experiences that helped me enhance my skills at every step, led to my constant progress and have formed my journey till today. I wanted to write this book to guide my younger brothers and sisters in their lives. My desire is that this book will give them the right impetus and hope at the right time in their lives and channel their immense energy in the right direction. I believe that the knocks I faced and the solutions and cures I found for them will aid the new generation in the development of their personality.

The fundamental purpose of this book is to develop their skills, eliminate their inferiority complexes, and build their self-confidence and proactive nature. The youth from rural backgrounds faces a lot of suffocation once they enter the steely framework of the Indian bureaucracy established by the British. They will face conflict once they take over their roles and enter the unrestrained and independent existence that is on offer. My intention is to draw their attention to this important aspect.

You will find on every page of this book how I cultivated my physical, mental and spiritual capabilities and the self-confidence that I got as a result. Training was just one aspect; but the new places I worked in, the people I met and the emotional connections I made, were all my own. In my autobiography, *Man Mein Hai Vishwas*, I have presented the initial struggles I went through. My selection into the IPS is its high point.

This second book is an attempt to describe how a young man is transformed into an officer once he joins the service. Of course, this kind of positive and constructive transformation is expected of every educated young person in their early twenties and is constantly shaped by their career choices and lifestyles. But in my case, it was a swift process and more effective, because all the necessary resources and training were made available to IPS trainees by the government. That is why I have made a sincere attempt to share here in simple terms the knowledge, behavioural facets and scientific aspects necessary in our personal and professional lives.

I recall a conversation with former NPA director and decorated IPS officer, Shri K. Vijay Kumar, when he spoke of the characteristics of a good leader. According to him, a good leader should be a motivator, and optimistic and enthusiastic. We cannot make this world heaven, but we can certainly remove a few thorns from our path to make the journey more comfortable and meaningful.

Last year, I made it a point to attend the felicitation of a girl in Beed who had scored 98.5 per cent in her class ten board exams. She belonged to a family that worked on the cremation ground. When there would be no lamps lit at home, she would study sitting by the light of the burning pyres, oblivious to everything around her. She was neither afraid of ghosts, nor affected by the smell of burning dead bodies. She was focused only on her goal and was going through intense struggle to build a bright future. When she told her mother that she had scored 98.5 per cent marks, her mother couldn't understand what that number meant. Salute to this brave girl! She was moved to tears while accepting a cheque for one lakh rupees that the people of her village had collected for her. She said in a voice quivering with tears, 'I, too, want to go to Hyderabad Sahib, but not like Parsha and Archi in *Sairat*, who eloped to get married.[1] I want to go to the police academy to get trained like you and become a police officer. And for that I need your support and my parents' blessings!' I am certain that this brave girl will succeed with flying colours. However, alongside this, I was unfortunate enough to witness a sad incident when I was the inspector general (IG) at Aurangabad.

Marathwada had suffered a severe drought and all the crops had been destroyed. People and animals were starving and many families were suffering untimely deaths. People were devastated. I was witness to one such unfortunate family tragedy in Kingaon, close to Latur. This family's crop of tomatoes on three acres of land was lost to the famine. There were five mouths to feed, and since they had no way to earn their living, the father

1 *Sairat* (Wild) is a Marathi movie made in 2016.

left for Karnataka and the son for Pune to work as daily-wage labourers. The eldest sister was of marriageable age while the younger sister, who was a good student, had taken admission in science in class eleven and was now in class twelve. The mother worked as a maid and earned money to buy her daughter books and a monthly bus pass.

Since the mother couldn't get any more work during the drought, the daughter had to miss fifteen days of school. The class twelve board exams were close and the child was extremely stressed. As the days went by, she lost all hope and ended her life by hanging herself. That was her final solution. She left behind a letter to her parents in which she said:

> Baba, please forgive me! I couldn't take it any more and that is why I decided to end my life. But don't lose hope. I did this because I wanted to reduce one burden from your shoulders. You will now have only one daughter to get married. And Baba, I have a sincere request to you, please don't host a feast on the thirteenth day of my death for our relatives and the villagers. Please save that money and use it for Akka's wedding. Baba, please forgive me!

I wonder why even after seventy-three years of our independence, we have to witness such despair and hopelessness. Such tragedies occur every single day in some corner of our country. My stomach churns, I get angry and feel numbed. Do such incidents affect my personal life in any way? Does anything in my life stop? These heart-wrenching incidents do not affect our selfish, narrow-minded and defeated society. True revolution and change are possible only when our general public expresses its sensitivity, when people shed their indifference and silence, speak out about the evils in society and suggest constructive plans. For this to happen, a small flame is not enough; what is needed is a raging volcano. I have come across several such flagrant and intense situations in my life that have ignited and enthused me. The purpose of this book is also to help our youth face their emotional challenges, give them the ladder of support they need, mentor and advise them and—for me as an elder brother—to reach out to their tender minds and also warn them when needed.

Like Confucius said, 'I hear and I forget. I see and I remember. I do and I understand.' I have followed this and have attempted to present clearly and simply whatever I have experienced, understood and done in my life.

Life is like a balance sheet. Our birth is our opening stock, death the closing stock. Whatever we receive is credit and what we lose is debit. Our ideas are our deposits and our bad habits are our debts. Happiness and pleasure are our profits and sadness is our loss. Our soul is our credibility and our hearts are our stability. Our character is our capital. The education and knowledge we gain in our lives are our investments. Our advancing age and health condition is depreciation with time. Lastly, there is a strict and tough auditor sitting above who maintains all our accounts and records everything with his CCTV camera.

That is why I planned how I would ensure that my balance sheet remained exceptional during my training period. My physical and mental training was taken care of during the outdoor training. However, remaining healthy over the years and restricting the deterioration that happens with age and stress is possible only with strict discipline, regular exercise and proper diet. The day should be divided into three equal parts. We should work sincerely and hard for eight hours, in my case for the IPS. We need to sleep well for eight hours and the remaining eight hours should be reserved for the 3 'F's (family, friends and faith), the 3 'H's (health, hygiene and hobbies), and the 3 'S's (soul, service and smiles). Once this is done, our balance sheet will be vibrant and easy. I have expressed my life's balance sheet in the pages of my book. Everyone makes mistakes in life, but they can be avoided by being aware of our own and other people's mistakes. However, we certainly should be careful not to repeat the same mistakes. I came across a letter a father had written to his young daughter that expresses all this rather well:

> I am writing this letter for three reasons. One, our life, destiny and accidents are not in our control. No one can predict how long we will live. The second reason is, who will tell you all this, if not me? The third is, whatever I am telling you is from my bitter experiences and can help you prevent a lot of headaches in your life. You must remember these throughout your life journey. Don't get bitter with anyone who doesn't treat you well. Nobody other than your mother and I are bound to be good to you. Be careful when someone tries to come too close and tries to be too sweet, because such people always have ulterior motives. Do not blindly believe that they are your well-wishers.
>
> Secondly, nobody is indispensable in this world, and there is nothing that you should compulsorily have. The sooner you understand this, the better for you. Whenever someone spurns you, cheats you or ticks you off, or you lose someone or something very dear to you, it will become easy for you to stand up again strongly.
>
> Thirdly, remember that time passes very fast and life goes in a flash. You can't waste time, you can only waste life. The earlier you realize this, the more you can enjoy life.

> The fourth point is, of course, about love. Love is a relative and ever-changing emotion. It fades with time and mood. Don't despair if you fall in love and then have a break-up. With time and patience, your pain and wounds will heal. Hence, don't get carried away by the beauty of love nor the sorrow caused by separation.
>
> The last piece of advice is that there are innumerable successful people in the world who did not get educated. This doesn't mean that one can be great without studies and hard work—the knowledge you gain is your weapon. To climb a hill, you have to start from the bottom.

These words are so telling! I have expressed the same words more or less in this book. I have written in simple terms the problems faced in society that are not mentioned in our school education and not spoken about in colleges. I have tried to make the boring and banal topics like cybercrimes, policing methods, addictions, safety and public security, personal and professional management, time management and prioritization of tasks, interesting through my own experiences and personal anecdotes. In summary, this book is an accumulation of my experiences, training and duties.

I hope the youth will love this book, just as they did my first one. This is certainly not a self-help book or a serious text on personality development and self-management. I have tried to include a lot of well-known poems, sayings and some impressive and useful information from our WhatsApp and Facebook University! Please pardon me if I have got the names wrong or have left any out. Whatever daily experiences, information and knowledge that I have come across, liked, and found useful, I have presented in this book for the youth of today.

Recap

I was born in Kokrud, a small, picturesque village nestled in the Sahyadris, where the river Warana meanders around the district of Sangli. My village was the centre of my universe till the age of twenty-three. I had dived headlong into intense studies while growing up, as I wanted to make a name for my family and build a bright future. It was only when I got selected for the IPS that I felt I was settled. I have written about this journey in my book *Man Mein Hai Vishwas.*[2] But life came to a standstill only for a short period with my selection; I had set larger goals for myself and the baby steps I had taken thus far would not be enough for my survival. A frog's jump would not do; what I needed was to propel myself with all my energy, like a pole-vaulter. The days of theory were over, it was time for the practicals. The preparation for my pole-vault leap was to take place at the academy. As I write this, I have been in the IPS for the past twenty-three years, working my way up constantly.

2 Patil, Vishwas Nangre, *Man Mein Hai Vishwas* (Rajhans Prakashan, 2016).

What I present in this book is the confluence of my training and my experiences over the years.

Rural Maharashtra became aware of civil services exams during the '90s in a major way. Some students from the villages around Warana succeeded in clearing the UPSC examinations and found their names on the list of successful candidates. My name figured in that list in 1997. That year, I cleared twelve consecutive exams and got selected as the deputy collector, as well as a sales tax inspector through the Maharashtra Public Service Commission (MPSC) exams. It was after clearing the UPSC exams that I got selected for the IPS, and now I had three options before me. This was not a stroke of luck but a fool-proof plan that I had made and followed sincerely since 1990, that helped me in my success. I had achieved what I had aimed for.

A mud house, a wrestler father, a joint family and a rice field—that was the background I grew up in. I spent my days ploughing the fields, plucking and eating mangoes and blackberries, swimming in the river and ponds and hunting at night with the village dogs for company. My elementary education was in the village primary school and I moved to New English School in the taluka to complete middle school. I initially stayed with my Buva, my father's sister, whose discipline and encouragement helped me develop an interest in studies. But it picked up speed thanks to the encouragement I got from Gaekwad Sir while I stayed in his house as a tenant during my class ten board exams. As the poet Longfellow wrote: 'The heights by great men reached and kept were not attained by sudden flight, but they, while their companions slept, were toiling upwards in the night.'[3] Something similar happened to me too. Gaekwad Sir

3 Longfellow, Henry Wadsworth, *The Ladder of St Augustine.*

got me into the habit of getting up at three in the morning, and that helped me clear the tenth board exams with 88 per cent marks. I stood first in the taluka.

I then took admission in New College at Kolhapur for my higher secondary education. For the first six months, it was a struggle as science subjects were taught in English, and even later I just did not enjoy studying these subjects in English. Meanwhile, when I reached class twelve, Bhushan Gagrani of Kolhapur stood third (all-India) in the IAS exam that year. He had opted for Marathi literature and History as his optional subjects. I had been keen to drop the science subjects but had not found the courage to do so until now. I consulted my father and decided to choose civil services as my career. Despite scoring well in the class twelfth board exam, I chose BA History at Rajaram College instead of opting for the popular engineering course. Quite naturally, my teachers, relatives and friends felt my decision was suicidal, but my father stood firmly by my side and sacrificed everything for me. I still remember the postcards he wrote to me in his broken Marathi whenever I travelled to Delhi for my exam preparations. He never wrote about the problems in the village lest I worry, and he avoided giving me any unsolicited advice. He always ended his letter with blessings and love, with his favourite line that motivated me at all times. My pet-name was Bhavdya. He would write, 'Bhavdya, my lion! Before I die, I want to see you arriving at our home in the collector's car with its red beacon flashing on top!' I would get inspired reading that line and my body would feel electrified as if a thunderbolt had passed through it. A million suns would rise within me and energize me.

However, having taken an arts course in college after class twelve, getting through the UPSC was a 'do or die' situation for me. Though I was determined and worked hard, I was not getting the right path. I was ignorant and didn't even know when and where the civil services exams took place. At college, the BA classes were rarely held and the huge campus of the college became a perfect excuse to just waste time. Fortunately, I came across a pre-IAS centre, which turned out to be hugely beneficial getting me into contact with the candidates and teachers there. They helped familiarize me with the scope and landscape of competitive exams. It would not be an exaggeration to say that the director of the institute, Gholkar Sir, guided me through this difficult journey. Apart from taking part in the activities of the National Cadet Corps (NCC) and the National Service Scheme (NSS), in shooting competitions and other co-curricular activities in college, I also spent a lot of time in the library.

I ended up doing well in college and went to Mumbai for higher studies. The 'hi-fi' environment of Mumbai was stifling, and my inferiority complex made things worse. I found no meaning in pursuing the MA course. Luckily, I got selected by the State Institute for Administrative Careers (SIAC), as a full-time trainee. SIAC prepares aspirants for the civil services exams. There I worked hard but failed the preliminary exam of UPSC, though I managed to clear the preliminary MPSC state services exam. Working hard for another month, I cleared the finals too, but scored a poor 75 out of 200 in the interview. With such marks, I could not get a Class II appointment. I was stressed and anxious; nothing was working in my favour. The first half of 1995 was thus full of disappointment and dejection for me.

I thought it would be best to get out of the slippery world of competitive exams and return to farming in my village, but my father's dream stopped me from taking that step. There was no way I could give up or accept defeat so easily. It was not easy to stumble, fall and try to walk again. I did everything I could to stay on track. My mind wavered like a kite whose string had been cut and which now drifted aimlessly. All kinds of thoughts rattled my mind.

But I had my own magic mantra, 'Shivaji, Shivaji, Shivaji!' He is my ideal and his story always inspires me. I had studied at Shivaji University for a while, and the rural atmosphere, the scent of the flowers in the garden and the company of the simple rural folk energized me. I remember spending nights sitting on a bench near the Shivaji statue absorbed in my books. Whenever I was sucked into a whirlpool of negativity and despair, I would start chanting 'Shivaji, Shivaji, Shivaji…' and a wave of positive energy would course through my mind and body, and my self-confidence would soar. There is a saying in Marathi '*Pratipchandralekhev Vardhishnurvishwavandita Shahasuno Shivsyaesha Mudra Bhadray Rajate*', which means, 'The glory of this seal (mudra) of Shahaji's son Shivaji will grow like the new moon. It will be worshipped by the world and it will shine only for the well-being of people.'

Like the growing crescent of the moon, the trajectory of my studies continued to grow. I was becoming more and more confident by the day. I did not sit and stare at the skies but dived into the challenging world of competitive exams. I decided not to complain or blame anyone or anything. I knew that playing blame games and making excuses was a recipe for disaster. I backed my dreams with my efforts and hard work. I believed in myself fully and ensured I kept away from negative thoughts and people. I embraced my failures wholeheartedly. The only mantra for me was 'hard work and more hard work'.

Fully charged, I came to Thane and stayed at a friend's house to start my studies in earnest. I appeared for the IAS prelims and, as a fall-back option, took the MPSC exam as well. I cleared both and my excitement knew no bounds. My exhilaration was cut short when the finals for both the exams got scheduled close to each other. However, I didn't allow the situation to get the better of me and distract me from my focus. I kept my presence of mind and made a perfect timetable for the finale. I followed my plan to the 'T' with utmost discipline. I was enjoying my hard work and putting in sixteen hours of effort daily.

The IAS exam is a tough one and often the questions asked are out of context. The syllabus is vast and wide. It is crucial to focus on *how* and *what* one has to study rather than *how much*. Hence, it is important to understand what *not* to study. Merely working like a donkey is not effective at all. I studied keeping all this in mind, with precise and focused efforts. While writing the exam, it is crucial to answer the questions in a comprehensive manner, without deviating from the main points. It is also important to write clearly and neatly, because a clean answer sheet impresses the examiner.

With my bag of tricks and a well-planned study plan, I was ready for the baptism by fire. I had prepared in advance for the alternate subjects. I was fully ready to use the arrows in my quiver and hit the target. My deep analysis of the syllabus proved right, and I did not find the questions difficult at all. I aced the exam, doing better than I expected in all the papers. After clearing both the prelims and the finals, it was time for me to face the personal interview. I had a month's time for it. I prepared my biodata and focused on keeping myself updated on current affairs. I didn't want to hide my humble and rustic rural background, my frank nature and the authenticity that defined me. I had been involved in social welfare and in creating general awareness among the public at large, and planned to share that too if asked. Fortunately, the questions in the interview were related to such topics. Lt Gen. Surendranath, the then chairman of the interview board, asked me some incisive questions on my involvement in the NCC and participating in the shooting competition. I was a little conscious about using Marathi in the interview, but I answered all the questions confidently using a mixture of Marathi, Hindi and English. Finally, Lt Gen. Surendranath asked in Hindi, *'Aap is duniya mein kyon aaye ho?'* [Why have you come into this world?]. It was a tricky question, but I managed to give an impressive answer. I replied by quoting a song from a popular musical *Man of La Mancha*:

To dream the impossible dream
To fight the unbeatable foe
To bear with unbearable sorrow
To run where the brave dare not go
To right the unrightable wrong
To love pure and chaste from afar
To try when your arms are too weary
To reach the unreachable star
This is my quest
To follow that star
No matter how hopeless
No matter how far
To fight for the right
Without question or pause
To be willing to march
Into hell for a heavenly cause
And I know if I'll only be true
To this glorious quest
That my heart will lie peaceful and calm
When I'm laid to my rest
And the world will be better for this
And one man, sore and covered with scars

Still strove with his last ounce of courage
To fight the unbeatable foe
To reach the unreachable star

I confidently stated that I wanted to make positive and creative changes while being part of the system. I said, 'It is not my intention to create chaos or disruption, but my whole effort is to bring about change. The fire should burn, be it in my heart or yours; it doesn't matter where, as long as it continues to burn.'

I was more successful than I had expected. I got selected for three posts—deputy superintendent of police or DSP (IPS), deputy collector or DC (IAS), and as sales tax inspector or STI (MPSC). I was always attracted by the uniform and decided to join the IPS. The training for IPS is considered one of the most vigorous and rigorous in India. All police officers have to lead their teams in the state they are assigned to. The training is challenging but builds confidence and the ability to win. Lines from one of Tagore's poems in *Gitanjali* (1910) echoed in my mind as I waited for the training to begin:

That You protect me in danger
this is not my prayer,
Let me not know fear when in danger.

I do not ask You to comfort me
in the heat of sadness,
in an aching state of mind,
Make me victorious
over sadness.

Let not my strength break down

when I find myself without a refuge.
If I suffer any worldly loss,
if I'm repeatedly frustrated,
Let me not consider this harm irreparable.
That You come to save me
this is not my prayer,
I ask for
strength to overcome.

You need not comfort me
by lightening my load,
I ask for strength
to carry my burden.

On days of joy
with humble head
I will remember You.
I will recognize You.
On a dark sad night
full of frustrations,
O then may I not doubt You!

1

Lal Bahadur Shastri National Academy of Administration

Before IPS training starts, one has to undergo a four-month foundation course at Lal Bahadur Shastri National Academy of Administration (LBSNAA) which is located in Mussoorie, Uttarakhand. The only thing I knew about Mussoorie was that it was a beautiful hill station. My training began on 7 September 1998. As the training period was during peak winters, I bought enough warm clothing in Delhi and boarded a bus for Mussoorie. I had read *English August*, and I remembered the protagonist being confused about whether or not to take a cycle rickshaw driven by the labour of another human being.[4] It was a moral dilemma, but I realized it was the best way to reach the academy from the bus stand. I hopped onto one, along with two big suitcases, and began the 3.5-kilometre (km) journey to the academy.

My mind was in turmoil. I was going to meet all the trainees who had been selected for the Group A services—the IAS, IPS,

---

4 Upamanyu Chatterjee (1988), *English August: An Indian Story*, London: Faber and Faber.

IFS and IRS—and would undergo the four-month foundation course. The academy was meant to train IAS officers, and the toppers who were selected for the IAS would stay on for the year-long course, once the common foundation training course was over. I entered the charming LBSNAA campus after registering my name at the gate. An orderly followed me with my suitcases.

It was (and is) a stunning and modern campus with brick-red buildings against the backdrop of the mighty snow-clad Himalayan peaks. It felt dreamlike—the kind of place I had seen only in movies. So far, I had stayed in a village house or in a dirty, suffocating room in Mumbai. The academy and its environs were heaven to me! I was assigned a room in Ganga Hostel. Every room was meant for two people. My roommate answered the doorbell. He was tall, had a dominating personality and looked like an antihero from a Hindi movie.

'Hello, I am Surinder Pal, IRS, Income Tax!' he said introducing himself. The IRS had two branches—Income Tax, and Customs & Excise. I, too, introduced myself but somehow felt that I would not be able to get along well with this man. I unpacked my suitcase. It was stuffy because there was no air conditioner or fan in the room. A lone heater stood in one corner to drive away the cold. I lay on my bed wondering what the next day would bring. A cousin of mine living in the slum area of Jogeshwari had gifted me a blazer. I took it out and hung it in the cupboard. I was tired. After a quick meal of parathas and curd at a nearby dhaba, I went to bed early.

Be open, be positive

Training began at 7 a.m. the next day. Despite my warm clothes I had shivered the whole night as Surinder did not allow me to set the heater to maximum heat. I woke up at 5.30 a.m. after a disturbed night. Then Surinder and I had an argument about who would use the bathroom first. Eventually, we managed to get ready in a hurry and reached the auditorium. Our course director was Shri K.N. Kumar, IAS, a slim gentleman.

The motto of our foundation course was 'Be open. Be positive.' The logo of our 64th Course was designed in the shape of a half-opened skull to resemble the alphabet 'B' and a few other images to show positivity. Along with the study material, there was a 120-page compilation of daily thoughts: one thought for each of the 120 days of training. Director Kumar addressed the gathering with a simple and concise speech in a voice filled with energy and excitement:

> Hello friends, your sixteen-week foundation course begins today. It is the academy's desire to transform you during this period. Great changes in life do not happen over time, but through the crucial decisions you consciously take at certain moments. These are decisions not taken in haste. These are decisions that deeply affect you and shake you up. And when do these changes take place? The moment you decide, my friends! This is the time and place for you to take that oath—at your alma mater, the academy!
>
> All we need is a firm commitment from you and you alone. Once you decide to commit yourself, you will not believe the kind of energy and strength that will course through your veins. Your personality, professional life, mind and body, relationships, and your way of seeing things, everything will change. Your josh will increase.
>
> How is the josh?

'Very high, Sir!' we all shouted in unison.

> Nothing changes or happens till you decide for yourself. We will make attempts in these 120 days to change your thoughts, behaviour, habits and your way of thinking. Are you ready for it?

'Yes, Sir' we cheered.

> This is the reason the motto for your course is 'Be open. Be positive'. The biggest decision you have to take is to be willing to undergo this transformation. You might say that you have already taken several such decisions while studying for the civil services examination, but they didn't bring about any fundamental changes in you. Why does a mountaineer, who has failed to climb Everest thrice, try once more? Because the determined climber knows that he will succeed one day. He challenges the mountain saying, 'You defeated me once, the second time you subjugated me and the third time you made me lick dirt. But one day, you will be beneath my feet. I will overcome you. You cannot grow in size, but I can scale higher. No more baby steps for me! I will pole vault over you and be victorious.'
>
> You all have to walk forward with an innovative mind, a sensitive heart and a fire in your belly. What you choose to do in your life may be your decision, but the results are not in your hands alone. If you have an intention to do good for society and a willingness to change, you can use your position and your authority for good causes. However, remember that you need to keep your mind alert, eyes open and remain optimistic!

K.N. Kumar's face looked serene. He was a powerful speaker whose words touched the audience.

> Our mind and body undergo change every day. We see the water in a river, but the river you see today is not the same tomorrow. Many waters would have flowed into it since then. One should not fear change because change is a sign of being alive. If the human's cells stop replacing the dead ones, we will soon be lifeless. Nothing is permanent. Your emotions, feelings, personality, and outlook—everything is constantly changing. For most people, this happens in a directionless and uncontrolled manner. If we don't hold the reins of change in our hands and don't take charge, we end up in failure and disappointment. We blame it on our fate.

The preparation for the UPSC exam challenges a person to the extreme. My personality, too, had become fragile owing to the uncertainty of the results and having gone through the highs and lows of success and failure. I had become fatalistic and surrendered to God every time my hopes were shattered and I was in sorrow. Whenever difficult questions arose, obstacles crossed my path and troubles appeared on the horizon, I would resort to superstitions, only using the telephone booth near the Siddhi Vinayak temple to enquire about my results. I had searched for answers through fasting, pious observations, astrology and palmistry. But I had also looked for motivation in inspirational articles and self-help books. I had muscled my way to Mussoorie through such rugged, confusing and tortuous paths.

I had taken small but creative steps to improve myself throughout my journey. It was not easy to stay away from temptation despite constant reminders to shun all earthly, carnal and materialistic desires. Although the materialistic world pulled me towards it, and I sometimes fell prey to it, I managed to keep the internal struggle alive. I never let go of my sagacity and efforts. I constantly thought about ways of improving myself and tried to imbibe good habits. Yet, cynicism and envy refused to leave me. I was at times very nice, and extremely bad at other times! I was a gentleman one day and a rogue the other. I did constructive things one day and succumbed to self-destructive thoughts and behaviour the next. It was a clash of character, and I grappled between right and wrong. I realized that I changed a bit every day, and my ambitions took on new forms constantly.

While preparing for the UPSC exams, there is a constant clash of mind and intellect. While the intellect wants one to remain calm, think of the future and be practical, the mind is a free bird that wanders. It revolts and urges one to be daring and take risks. It complains all the time, making noises, wailing and screaming for attention. The mind does not accept injustice or prejudice, and starts itching for action. It affects the body; the heart starts pumping faster and stress leads to aches and pains. It is tough to keep such a mind under one's control.

I had to learn to take charge of my monkey-like mind during my training period. I had to learn to meditate and look within myself. I had to touch my consciousness. I had to kill all the viruses poisoning my mind. I had to keep my mind cheerful and fresh, and meditation was the best way to do that. I had to become aware of the fact that most of my needs were unnecessary, and I had to impress upon my mind that most of the stresses were meaningless. I had to strive to become one with the Almighty and constantly instruct myself to focus on my inner self.

I needed to segregate my long-term, medium-term and immediate goals and work on them accordingly. As they say, 'The whole universe conspires to make things happen if you focus on something and wish for it sincerely.' The intent was to be positive, have good thoughts and get satisfaction by doing good things with the right efforts. I had heard that sportspersons participating in the Olympics are trained to visualize themselves winning the gold medal. A divine strength is generated with such visualization techniques, and one experiences success twice—once in the mind and then in reality! I had to imagine that I had already realized my dreams.

As we are aware, a healthy mind resides in a healthy body. I had to get rid of my lethargy and fill my body with energy. Exercise and yoga were a must. I had to stay away from carnal desires and not become a slave to them. Bad habits are a curse to consciousness. They destroy the power of focus. Happiness gradually slips away, giving place to creeping fears. It was therefore important to keep the body fit and the mind cultivated. Reading and writing are imperative. This makes the person fresh and opens the mind. I was conscious of this while I was preparing for the exam. In the academy, I had to ensure that I moved forward with excellence. My horizon had expanded, and I no longer belonged to myself. I belonged to society! I had to take on huge responsibilities and duties in future.

The first thing was not to be fatalistic. I had to create my future based on my actions, accept challenges and not shy away from problems. I had to take life head-on, look into the other person's eye and not be cowed down. I would not decide about my future based on astrology or palmistry. Who were the constellations—Amavasya, Rahu, Ketu, and Shani—to come in my way? I was not going to allow saade saati, the seven-and-a-half-year period of Shani, to thwart my dreams. Why should I waste precious time waiting for the 'auspicious moment'? Why should I worry and get drowned in anxiety? *Where there is a will, there is a way.* I had to keep my will strong and my capabilities high. I had to remind myself that to attract good fortune, I needed a smile on my lips, a cool head and my feet firmly on the ground. I resolved to ensure that my future journey would be full of humility and that I would constantly remain true to myself. I promised to take responsibility for myself and my team members.

I recall a lovely anecdote narrated by Dr APJ Abdul Kalam Sir.[5] He was the director for the SLV 3 satellite mission in 1979. His job was to ensure that the satellite reached its orbit as per plan. Thousands of technicians and scientists had worked on the project for ten years. The time had come for lift-off. The timer at Sriharikota began its countdown '…T minus 5 minutes, T minutes 4…'. At T minus 40 seconds, a warning bell rang. The decision to abort the mission rested on Kalam Sir. There were six scientists with him on the mission who studied the data and the signals and concluded that the problem was indeed critical. There was a leakage in the control system. Kalam Sir estimated that despite the leakage, there would be enough fuel to propel the satellite into orbit. He decided to go ahead against the opinion of the six scientists. The rocket passed the first stage successfully, but failed in the second stage and fell into the Bay of Bengal. It was a disaster.[6]

It is easy to handle success but a challenge to face failure. The then director of the Indian Space Research Organization (ISRO), Satish Dhawan, said, 'Let us inform the press.' A shiver ran through Kalam Sir's spine. The press conference was being attended by reporters from across the globe. Kalam Sir's worry was justified, he would have to bear the brunt of the failure. Satish Dhawan addressed the press saying, 'Friends,

---

5 Dr APJ Adul Kalam, rocket scientist and later President of India.

6 What Dr Abdul Kalam said on failure after ISRO's SLV-3 mission crashed, *Indian Express*, 2019, https://indianexpress.com/article/india/chandrayaan-2-dr-abdul-kalam-on-failure-after-isro-slv-3-mission-crash-5974097/

we have failed today, but at this moment I stand firmly behind my engineers, scientists and staff because I am certain we are going to be successful next year.' Satish Dhawan took the entire responsibility for the failure!

As expected, the press severely criticized ISRO for having lost hundreds of crores of rupees in the failed mission. But Satish Dhawan was clear, he and his team would succeed the following year. And as he had confidently proclaimed, on 18 July 1980, the team did succeed in putting the satellite into orbit. It was a crowning glory for ISRO. But look at the large-heartedness of the leader! Dr Satish Dhawan told Kalam Sir, 'You must address the press conference today. Let the world know of our success!'

What does this mean? A great leader takes full responsibility for the failure of the team and lets the team members take credit for the success. I, too, resolved to create camaraderie with responsibility, harmony and accord.

While in the academy, I promised myself that I would be committed to my work and that every step I took would be action-oriented. Most importantly, I would remain a student for life and learn continuously and uninterruptedly. I would learn the tricks of the trade and absorb them sincerely. To begin with, I would have to learn the art of public speaking. I was weak in English and decided to sincerely make an effort to improve it. Punctuality, and good planning would be the other two guiding principles of my life. I would be enterprising and would make sure that the quality of my work kept improving. My mantra would be optimism and responsiveness. I would be available for people at large, without caring for my own comforts. I resolved to do administrative and social work in such a manner that it would become an ideal example for others and be contextually appropriate.

I remembered a poem I had read in childhood, where the poet describes an ant trying to climb up a wall carrying a sugar crystal. It climbs a little and slips back to the floor again and again, but with each failure, its resolve increases and it finally succeeds. Similarly, a diver diving into the ocean searching for pearls comes up empty-handed most times. It is not easy to search for pearls in the vast ocean. But that is what makes him more determined. There are times when he does find a pearl. One, who tries tirelessly, succeeds. Failure is a caution that one should acknowledge. Identify your weaknesses and work on them. And don't sleep till the goal is achieved. My goal was (and is) to find victory in the battleground of life and its challenges. One has to make miraculous efforts to earn public trust. Sincere efforts are always rewarded in the end.

The period following my college days when I was preparing for the competitive exams was when my mental, conceptual and philosophical make-up evolved. During the training period at the academy, I was constantly aware of the influence of my mental, conceptual and philosophical make-up on my value systems and moral causes. To achieve success in my professional career, my fundamental mantra had to be selflessness. At the same time, compassion, a neutral and balanced attitude, and a readiness to put in hard work were crucial ingredients.

That first day's morning session was only brainstorming. Over 300 of us, from eleven different services, mingled with each other. I was looking for a group I could relate to. The fifteen of us from Maharashtra were quite identifiable. We went to the splendid mess for lunch. For the first time in my life, I had unlimited ice cream and fruits on offer. I ate to my heart's content, but was in for a rude shock when I heard that the mess bill could be as high as Rs 3,000 a month. My salary was Rs 8,000, and if I were to spend so much on food alone, I wondered how much I would be able to send home.

Rules and training

I had studied the law in the context of politics, fundamental rights, directive principles of state policy, system of union of states, division of rights, citizenship, and the judicial system. I had studied all these in detail for the exam and almost knew them by heart. India had adopted the British form of Parliament. The makers of the Constitution took ideal concepts from across the world. We adopted fundamental rights from America and directive principles of state policy from Ireland. The method of amending the Constitution came from Africa while the principles of emergency were based on German concepts. Our Constitution was greatly influenced by the Government of India Act, 1935. The essence of the Constitution is its preamble itself. It goes as follows:

> WE, THE PEOPLE OF INDIA, having solemnly resolved to constitute India into a SOVEREIGN, SOCIALIST, SECULAR, DEMOCRATIC REPUBLIC and to secure to all its citizens;
> JUSTICE, social, economic and political;
> LIBERTY of thought, expression, belief, faith and worship;
> EQUALITY of status and of opportunity;
> and to promote among them all
> FRATERNITY assuring the dignity of the individual and the unity and integrity of the Nation;

IN OUR CONSTITUENT ASSEMBLY this twenty-sixth day of November, 1949, do Hereby Adopt, Enact And Give To Ourselves This Constitution.

All our rights originate from the people of India. Our democracy, in essence, is a government for the people, by the people and of the people. The core of the Constitution is justice, liberty, equality and fraternity. Our government is welfare-oriented and secular. It is a democratically-elected government, which is also socialist. In the third part of the Constitution, every citizen has been given the freedom of thought, conscience, religion, opinion, expression, association and assembly. A government run with the rule of law and which provides equal protection to all are the two resolutions that have been embodied in the Constitution. It is the duty of the bureaucracy to ensure that these values and principles are protected and followed in practice.

During the morning session, Dr Banerjee spoke about 'Rules and Administration'. Dr Banerjee was tall, fair, with light-coloured eyes like a cat, and in his suit, he reminded me of a British officer. He addressed us in a thundering voice and then went on to explain the origin of laws and the intriguing and colourful story of 'Contradictions in Law' from Greek history. It was about the law expert and philosopher Protagoras and his disciple Euathlus discussing 'Protagoras's Paradox'. Even today, the story is used to debate the issue of logic in law colleges. The story goes that a poor student, Euathlus, goes to a famous law teacher, Protagoras, to learn law. Euathlus has no money to pay the fees, and proposes that he will pay the amount as soon as he wins his first case. Protagoras agrees and starts teaching. Once the teaching ends, Protagoras demands his fees, but Euathlus reminds him of the condition they had agreed upon. Annoyed, Protagoras files a case against Euathlus and tells the court, 'If I win this case Euathlus has to pay the fees, as I filed the case to get the fees he owes me. And if I lose Euathlus still has to pay, since he promised to pay me once he won his first case. So, he has to pay me irrespective of whether I win or lose.'

Euathlus replies, 'The case is regarding payment of fees. If I win, the question of paying the fees doesn't arise. And if I lose, I won't pay the fees as the contract says that I can pay only when I win a case.'

This is a unique example of an unresolved question. The example kindled our curiosity about the field of law. Dr Banerjee explained, 'You will be faced with many paradoxes for which you will have no answers. You will be thoroughly confused. Many times, such situations will be deliberately created to confound you. It is your balance of mind, knowledge of law, decisive mind and the ability to use law correctly that will help you come out of such situations.'

Dr Banerjee had explained the concept of natural justice in law to us in simple words. While studying about natural justice, I realized the importance of two aspects: one, giving the other party a chance to present their viewpoint; and two, if any of the parties have a vested interest in the judgement it should not be granted. The two pillars of the British Judicial system—an opportunity for an unbiased hearing and having no prejudice—form the core of their administration. Dr Banerjee said firmly:

> Whatever you do as an administrative officer should be just, legal, unbiased and in the interest of society. Any fearless officer who follows these rules will never have ideological issues, and every task he or she undertakes will be correct and fair. If one adopts these principles, there will be no arguments or controversies. That is why every administrative officer and responsible citizen should

> adhere to these two terms—honesty and integrity. To stick to our commitments is the lowest form of integrity; not letting go of our values and ideals, the intermediate form; and to act according to our inner being or conscience is the highest form of integrity! We always have the choice of deciding what to accept and what not to, so we need to choose what is just and right. Following these principles will automatically lead to positive results. We need to use our power for social welfare.

Dr Banerjee's fluent speeches laid the foundations of our ideologies. The Latin terms *actus reus* and *mens rea*, developed in English law, define what crime is: 'an act does not make a person guilty unless (their) mind is also guilty'. For example, when a doctor cuts open his patient's body with a sharp knife, it is not a crime because the intention behind the act is good.

This introduction by Dr Banerjee was followed by intense discussions on whether euthanasia and suicide were crimes or not, and other such controversial topics. The Constitution lays down fundamental rights but it also gives guidelines for governance. It takes into account the welfare of the people at the lowest rungs of society, the downtrodden and the deprived while formulating laws. These guiding principles provide direction to the states. There are hundreds of laws that have been passed over the years. And every law is founded on ethics. The legislature framed laws suitable for the times and these became a part of common culture once the people got used to them. And from that came social discipline. Dr Banerjee made us aware of the fundamental concepts of why laws are made, how they are structured and how policies for their implementation are formed.

How a state should be, has been described in the 'Shanti Parv' of the Mahabharat, where Bheeshma tells Yudhisthir: '*na rajyam na rajasit na dandayo na cha dandikah/ dharmenaiva prajassarva rakshanti sma parasparam*' [There is no kingdom nor any king; no criminal nor any judge to give the penalty to the criminal. All the people protect each other by the virtue of Dharma.]

This is a description of an 'Adarsh' samaj or an 'ideal society'. A society that is a 'live' society, in which each and every individual lives completely up to his responsibility. Would there be any need for a police force in such a society? But, in today's social structure, the police has become an integral part of the government machinery. The British gave this force its organizational structure but used it to promote their selfish 'divide and rule' policy. They established the 'police raj' and spread the colonial mindset. Today while the 'police raj' is being transformed into a welfare state, has the police system changed in any real sense? The laws remain the same to date. The Indian Penal Code (IPC) that is in force today came into being in 1860, and the Indian Evidence Act was passed in 1872. That being the case, how is it possible to implement it in the context of the twenty-first century mindset? What has really changed then? How and why did human rights gain importance?

Several laws like the Atrocities Act, Pre-Conception and Pre-Natal Diagnostic Techniques Act or PCPNDT Act to stop female foeticide, Dowry Prohibition Act, Anti-corruption laws, POTA and other new Acts have been passed after Independence, and stringent steps are being taken to control antisocial activities.[7] The IPC, CrPC and the Evidence Act have

---

7 Atrocities Act refers to the Scheduled Castes and the Scheduled Tribes (Prevention of Atrocities) Act, 1989. The PCPNDT Act was passed in 1994, and the Dowry Prohibition Act in 1961. The full form of POTA is Prevention of Terrorism Act, 2002. CrPC stands for the Criminal Procedure Code (enacted in 1973).

been amended from time to time to suit the needs of society. Sections 498-A and 304-B of the IPC have been expanded to prevent dowry harassment and deaths. According to these, if a young newly wed woman dies under suspicious circumstances and a complaint for dowry death is registered, the burden of proof rests with the accused. Following the recent gruesome Nirbhaya case in Delhi, the definitions of acid attacks, outraging a woman's modesty and rape have been expanded through the Criminal Amendment Act. The IPC has been amended and the punishments made harsher.

We had seminars on why laws are amended. In short, the focus in LBSNAA was more on the basic philosophy behind the laws than on the laws themselves.

We, the bravehearts

I came back to my room, pulled out my diary and wrote down my resolutions and decisions. One was to reduce unnecessary chats and the second was to read at least for two to three hours at any cost. I wrote:

> I am determined to shake off my lethargy, speak to the point and behave appropriately. I will behave respectfully and honourably with everyone and be empathetic towards all. I will avoid being overly excited and showy. I will try to lead with humility, discipline and calm. All paths become smooth and the destination is reached once one is determined.
>
> I will try to be happy and enthusiastic in life. Our thoughts decide our mood and we feel sad or happy. I will live each day to the full and with a strong will and determination make the most of the opportunities God has given me. God has given me a conducive

> environment to develop myself physically, mentally, spiritually. This is the time for peace and learning. We stake everything we have during our struggles and achieve our goals; can't we achieve miraculous success if we do the same in our daily life as well?

I recalled reading a story somewhere. A man, in some foreign country, was reversing his SUV when he heard a heart-rending scream. He found to his horror that his own five-year-old son was stuck under the wheels of his vehicle. Without waiting to think, the man who weighed hardly 70 kilograms (kg), grabbed the boot of his car and lifted the monstrous 700 kg vehicle easily, thus saving the life of his son. I wrote:

> We get the strength of ten elephants when we are faced with danger or attack. We must be able to channelize our inner strength at the right time and use the energy to achieve our goals in our day-to-day lives. We need to have routines but we shouldn't become their slaves. We should lead our lives without complaining. We should live like Chatrapati Shivaji—with courage, determination and clarity—a true warrior! A famous military commander once said, 'I am never worried about a platoon of a hundred lions led by a goat, but I will have to think a hundred times before facing a platoon of goats led by a lion!' Shivaji was a man of steel who faced challenges with courage. He was an army in himself. We should follow his footsteps and shape our lives and careers, drawing inspiration from his tremendous achievements.

I used to feel a lot of anxiety in the academy. I was filled with an inferiority complex and felt suffocated in that environment filled with academic excellence and scholarly people. During such times, I would remind myself of Shivaji's war cry, and my veins would burst with energy and pride:

> Had the British not colonized India, the Marathas would have ruled India all the way from Thanjavur to Delhi in the first half of the eighteenth century. Had the defeat in the third battle of Panipat not happened in 1761, India's history would have been different. I need to make a place for myself, create an identity based on my hard work and determination. I must never forget that I am now a part of a national service...

I dozed off while writing my diary: 7 September 1998 had come to an end.

Physical training or PT was scheduled to start from 8 September and we were asked to assemble at the PT ground at 5.30 in the morning. All the trainees in their white PT uniforms looked like egrets on a farm. The booming 'Attention Please' of the short lanky officer broke our chatter. A few trainees came rushing to the field late and were promptly made to stand in a separate line by the officer-in-charge, who now addressed us:

> I am Tarun Shridhar, and will be in charge of your outdoor training. How much you sweat on this cold morning will be the true test for you today. Good exercise, nutritious food and adequate rest form the three cornerstones of health. From today, for the next

> ninety days, you all will have a daily schedule consisting of yoga, PT, horse riding, sports, trekking or cross-country runs. I know it is difficult for you to get out of your blankets early in the morning in this cold weather. But you must drop any ideas of giving excuses like 'It is raining', 'I am feeling cold', 'I am not feeling well', and be present on the field on time.
>
> Make fitness your favourite habit and think about it day in and day out, dream about exercise, perform activities that will make your body tough and will challenge you to the extreme. Each day of exercise can make you stronger, more powerful, and healthy; you will be able to create a better version of yourself. For that you need to eat well, and the best, healthy and nutritious dishes from all over the country will be served to you at the mess. And, remember! There will be no late-night parties that will rob you of a good night's sleep. There will be surprise visits to your hostels and your rooms will be checked without prior notice.

Sir's words were bursting with authority and filled us with apprehension. A young IAS officer from the Himachal Pradesh cadre, Tarun Shridhar was a stickler for discipline, and his personality reflected sternness. He explained the importance of physical fitness to us in a few words. He told us why and how we needed to include yoga and sport in our daily lives. He described to us the importance of reflexes, how fitness could enhance our energy levels and how regular exercise could keep our muscles strong. He reiterated that this was not just for the 120 days of training at LBSNAA but to be followed throughout our lives.

Many trainees made fun of Shridhar Sir's words. They did not change their old habits and made their lifestyles worse. Sadly today, after twenty years some of my batchmates are not in good health. They not only have become out of shape but are also suffering several lifestyle-related health problems. On the contrary, I followed Shridhar Sir's counsel throughout my career and have made exercise and sport an integral part of my lifestyle. I have certainly gained a lot because of it. My weight remained in control and I have been able to keep away from disease. I have become capable of managing stress, maintaining punctuality and giving attention to detail.

We had to do PT and then run rounds of the ground on the first day. My body was stiff and refused to bend but I somehow managed to finish the exercises with great difficulty. Then I went back to the room, got ready within half an hour and reached the spacious dining hall. The daily breakfast was a mix of hot and tasty south and north Indian vegetarian and non-vegetarian dishes. We also had a range of fruits, juices, tea and coffee. We could eat as much as we wanted! After a sumptuous breakfast, we had to reach the hall on time for our lectures, where we would feel sleepy within a few minutes!

We had lectures on different subjects including administration, law and management from 9 a.m. to 2 p.m. Moreover, several senior and high-ranking offices delivered guest lectures and guided us. The afternoons were reserved for hobby classes such as horse riding, learning a language, or computer training. On the whole, we were kept busy the whole day. There were cultural programmes in the evening with music, dance and plays from different states of India.

The trainees grouped themselves on regional affiliations but soon blended together. Days passed in fun! The foundation courses gave us trainees an introduction to administration, the administrative structure and its functioning right from the village panchayat level up to the Central government. There would be discussions on the faults and loopholes in the system, our opinions on them and the possible corrective measures. Field visits and case studies helped us understand the subjects better.

Roop Kund trek, a breathtaking experience

Trekking was something new for me, and I experienced it for the first time at the academy. I used to roam around a lot in the hills and valleys near my hometown, and I remember losing my way while searching for berries and jamuns. Many times, my slippers would tear and thorns would prick my feet. I can't remember the number of times I have fallen from a tree. Everything was so natural and simple. My wanderings had no plan or purpose! One can build physical and mental strength only through tough experiences.

Some people break under pressure while others go on to create records. I had decided to break small records in my life right from childhood, and that is why I chose a high-altitude trek instead of a simple one. I bought warm jackets, gloves, caps, trekking shoes and water bottles for the trek. When I picked up my rucksack packed with all these items, sleeping bag, cooking utensils and food items, it was so heavy that my back bent with the weight, and I was forced to take the support of a walking stick. Dr Swami had come to give us all the information regarding the trek. He gave our group precise and vital information. 'The Roop Kund trek is a challenging one with its dense forests, howling winds, wide expanses of woods, freezing cold and snow-covered paths that you will walk on!'

This trek was going to be full of varied experiences, a mixed bag of good and bad! He further informed us:

> Your goal is to cross Roop Kund at an altitude of 15,750 feet from mean sea level. The vast, beautiful, green meadows of Ali and Bedni await you. The moment you cross these meadows, the tough alpine climb begins. As you climb up and reach higher, the peak of Mount Trishul becomes visible and once you reach Roop Kund, you will experience the biggest thrill in your life. You will be going up from 8,000 feet to 16,000 feet in six days. Always remember that over-enthusiasm and desperation will prove dangerous. Conquer the Himalayas and come back victorious and safe! My best wishes to all of you on this adventurous journey!

Dr Swami's words not only kindled our curiosity but also filled us with a sense of fascination. We had to initially find our way through the dense and widespread forests of the Himalayas and the plan was to cover 30 to 35 km every day. We reached Lohajung after a twelve-hour journey. According to mythology, Goddess Parvati had defeated the demon Lohasur at this place and hence the name Lohajung.[8] The actual trek was supposed to start from a point called 'Wan', an hour away from Lohajung. We reached Wan, travelling by bus over rugged paths.

Soon, we left the villages behind and entered dense forests full of hundred-year-old Cypress trees. The woods were beautiful, fragrant and fresh. Cool winds howled past, greeting us on our journey ahead. The tree trunks were so wide that even when four of us tried to hug them, our hands didn't meet! We saw a temple of Goddess Lata Devi on the way. Our guide told us, 'Please go and seek her blessings; you will return safely only

---

8 Brahmatal Trek Overview, *Himalaya Shelter*, https://himalayashelter.com/trek/brahmatal-trek/

with her grace.' He showed us a mountain called Ranakadhar. When Goddess Parvati knocked down the demon Lohasur, jets of his blood erupted, giving the place its name 'Ranakadhar'. We were getting to hear a lot of intriguing and mystical tales. Also, there were 300 human skeletons waiting for us in Roop Kund!

Filled with a strange attraction coupled with an unnamed fear, our group pushed forward. We came across the gurgling Neelaganga River on the way. We filled our water bottles and rested on the river bank for a while. Our legs were hurting after walking almost 20 km. Lactic acid had begun to accumulate in our muscles.

Focus on the goal

'The woods are lovely, dark and deep/... Miles to go before I sleep/... Miles to go before I sleep'—these words by poet Robert Frost echoed through the forests.[9] The woods are beautiful, peaceful and calm, but I have given my word to someone. I have to reach my destination. No rest, no stops, no doubts, no questions. *'If we rest, we rust'.* Hence get up; we have to reach Roop Kund.

You too will face small and big obstacles just like those faced by Lord Hanuman when he left to fulfil the promise he had made to Lord Ram. If you rest too much, the destination will move further away. Struggles lead to success and miracles happen when there is confidence. When there is undivided focus on the goal, victory is certain. One shouldn't pause or rest during the quest for the destination. Lord Hanuman's story is so inspiring in this context. When he decided to cross a distance

---

9 Excerpted from 'Stopping by Woods on A Snowy Evening', by Robert Frost.

of 900 km to reach Lanka during his search for Sita Mata, three impediments in the form of temptation and danger came in his way. He could overcome all the obstacles, reach his destination and succeed in finding Sita Mata only because of his determined and sincere efforts.

The first obstacle in Lord Hanuman's path was Mount Mainak in the middle of the ocean. This mountain was no less than today's five-star hotels and had all the luxuries and conveniences; it was like paradise! The gandharvas and apsaras (demi-gods and celestial nymphs) requested Hanuman to stop and take some rest. But he refused saying that he would not rest even for a minute till he completed the task given to him by Lord Ram. When our goals are high and our intentions noble, there should be no place for doubts in our mind. Many times, we begin a task or a journey with a lot of enthusiasm, but we stop midway and fall for temptations. Our mind wavers and shakes our willpower. We lose sight of our goal. Once we pause for rest or fall for temptations, boredom and lethargy set in, and our pace slows down. That is why we need to be wise and clever at all times. Being wise means knowing the difference between good and bad, while cleverness means the ability to make decisions based on the situation and its seriousness. These two qualities make our paths easier.

As Hanuman went forward, the second obstacle came in the way. The gods, gandharvas and sages requested Surasa, the mother of serpents, to assume the form of a terrifying demoness and test Lord Hanuman's resolve. She stopped Hanuman and said, 'You are food that gods have provided me, and I am going to swallow you right now.' Hanuman pleaded with folded hands, saying, 'Please let me complete Lord Ram's task of tracking Sita Mata. I promise to return to enter your mouth willingly on my way back.' But Surasa disagreed and said, 'I will eat you right now' and opened her huge mouth wide. She told him that he could pass only through her mouth. Hanuman expanded and grew larger and larger. Surasa was forced to widen her jaw more and more. Once she had opened her jaws really wide, Hanuman suddenly assumed a tiny form—the size of a thumb—and entered her mouth and left it before she could close it. He told Surasa, 'I have entered your mouth and come out as per your instructions. You must let me go now.'

The demoness was impressed by Hanuman's wisdom and presence of mind and sent him on his journey with blessings. This is not just a simple tale. It tells us that we need to be aware of when to use our strength and when to use our reasoning and wisdom. We need to know when to be small and when to be large. We need to be soft at times and tough at others. We should not make every situation a question of our ego and prestige. Unless we drop our ego and sense of 'I', we will not be able to remain focused on our goal and move forward.

As Hanuman moved ahead, an unknown power seemed to pull him towards the ocean. That Shakti or power called 'Simhika' represented envy and grudges. The envious cannot tolerate good things happening to other people. They can't bear to see others succeed. Envy is one of the root causes of the downfall of people, and we need to stop it consciously. Hanuman killed Simhika effortlessly and continued onward. What we get to learn from this story is that we need to instantly nip any negative thoughts in the bud. We walked on, mythological stories giving us support along with our walking sticks. They helped to keep our energy and enthusiasm up during tough times.

We have to rein in our minds under trying circumstances and train our minds gently. Our inner strength is very much like the arrows in our quiver and the actual skill is in knowing when and how to use them. We have all seen how a mahout can tie up and control a huge elephant with a thin chain, a chain so thin that it can snap with a light tug from the elephant. Why does the elephant choose to remain chained and not break free? That is because it tried to break free in childhood but failed several times and now firmly believes that the chain cannot be broken. There is no one to tell the elephant that the chain is the same but the elephant has grown a hundred times stronger and bigger! It is the same with us humans, but thankfully, we have parents, teachers, our mythological stories and historical tales to build awareness in us and inspire us. That's how the Columbuses, Neil Armstrongs, Vasco Da Gamas and Edmund Hillarys come alive in us.

As I lay thinking on the banks of the Neelganga, my team leader, Hemant, called out, 'Brothers, get up, we have a long way to go; this is just the beginning. *Ye to* trailer *hai;* picture *abhi baaki hai.*' We continued on our journey supporting each other. We were now in the beautiful expanses of the Ali Bugyal meadows. Removing our trekking shoes and walking on the green carpet of grass felt heavenly. Lines by Marathi poet Vinda Karandikar played on my lips: '*Hiravya pivalya malaavarun hiravi pivali shawl ghyaavi…*' (Take shield for the chest from the green and yellow prairie fields, from the ridge of Sahyadris.)

The soft, velvety carpet of green grass seemed endless and I felt like rolling on it like a dog. The peak of Mount Trishul looked so magnificent that I couldn't take my eyes off it. The sight was like a fantasy, one that nudged us to fly high! It was a delight to walk through the colourful vistas of the Himalayas. We had no inkling of the rough and rocky paths that awaited us. The swaying oak trees and the cold breeze indicated the arrival of clouds. As soon as we got into our sleeping bags after a day-long, exhausting climb, lightning began crackling and droplets of rain splashed on our tents. The light drizzle soon turned into a torrent, and water entered our tents. We were drenched and cold as we had not prepared adequately for the deluge. We managed to pass the night with fitful bouts of sleep.

We woke up early in the morning and set out towards Patar Nachauni, but our guide was a novice and led us in the wrong direction. We lost our way and wandered in the forests. An angry Hemant muttered the choicest of Kolhapuri expletives at the guide! That made the guide further nervous, and he began talking about going back with his mules. A few of us tried to cajole him and offered to help him find the way. We were walking fast through a slippery, dark forest. The clouds showed no signs of clearing and we were famished. We had slipped on the forest paths a few times, and our shoes and rucksacks were muddy. We were soaking wet and our feet refused to move further owing to the rain, our hunger and being lost in the forest. We spent the night under the shelter of trees with great difficulty. When we got up in the morning, we realized that the guide had vanished with his mules. It was a double whammy for us. We now had to carry other stuff apart from our own rucksacks on our shoulders. Our return journey too was in peril, thanks to the guide deserting us. All of us cursed Hemant to no end, as he was the one responsible for the guide running away. We were a little relieved when Hemant said he had a compass and that reassured us. We found the right direction and began walking again. Gradually the forests began to thin, and we suddenly found a mud path—the route of our trek. After walking for some distance on the mud path, we met an Australian trekking group on its way back. We confirmed from them whether we were on the right track and got all the necessary details from their guide. We had another two days to go. There would be one halt at Bhagwabasa and then it was the final ascent to Roop Kund. The news energized our tired bodies.

The trek across the jungles behind the Kalu Vinayaka (Black Ganesha) temple was extremely treacherous. The path was uneven and winding. We had to watch our step and tread carefully. Even a small slip could damage our backs. The journey to the Bhagwabasa camp at 14,000 feet above sea level was a divine experience. On one side stands the huge Trishul peak and on the other is Mount Nanda Ghunti of the majestic Himalaya. We reached Bhagwabasa, and we caught a glimpse of the snow-clad paths leading to Roop Kund. We were freezing in the biting cold but the final trek was beckoning us. Dense clouds covered the pristine white peaks around Roop Kund. Chilly winds were blowing and rains looked imminent. I cannot forget the date: 5 October 1998. Hemant said, 'Brothers, this day could very well be our death anniversary!'

We woke up the next morning to see snow falling. The perfectly round Roop Kund was inviting us. Our trekking shoes were dripping wet, and we had blisters on our feet. Had nature been more benevolent and the guide not misled us, we would have completed the trek quite easily. But inadequate preparation, overconfidence and taking nature for granted had worked against us. However, our coordination was better now and we were determined to reach Roop Kund with each other's help and support.

Let's help one another

'When the going gets tough, the tough get going.' We decided to follow this proverb on our journey further. The snow would start melting if it got late, and it could be dangerous. We took one step after another with each other's support. Perhaps, the academy had organized this trek only for us to understand the words of Sant Tukaram, '*Eka meka sahaya karu avaghe dharu supantha*,' which means, 'Let's help each other, just keep going.'

A story I heard during childhood began with a rich industrialist's car getting stuck in the mud while he was travelling to a village to look for land to buy. As he looked around to see if he could seek help from someone, he saw an old farmer walking towards him with a bull. The rich man stopped the old man and requested him for help. The old farmer looked at the wheels of the car carefully and said, 'You will need Tukya's help!' The industrialist was confused and thought that Tukya was a mechanic and said, 'Call Tukya with his toolkit, I will pay him for his services.'

The farmer replied, 'No need to call him, Tukya is right here!' The farmer tied the rope hanging from the bull's neck to the car's fender and shouted aloud, 'Tukya pull … Namya come on … pull Pavalya …' The bull, enthused by the farmer's calls, pulled the car with all its might and got it out of the mud. The industrialist was thrilled but he wondered, there was just one bull, why had the farmer called out three names?

He asked the old man, who replied, 'It's like this with these animals. My Tukya is old and almost blind. He can hardly see. So, he is not aware that he is the only one tied to the car. I took the names of two more bulls so that Tukya feels that there are two more of his group with him. He then uses all his strength and works harder.' The industrialist realized that this was the real 'team spirit' spoken about in the corporate world.

We had made use of the same team spirit while we were scaling the mountain to reach Roop Kund. Though our team was a little weak and we were short of resources, it was still united and strong. We were certain that the entire universe was there to support and help us. We used the combined power of our personal strength and our collective energies while covering the last leg of the Roop Kund trek. We walked up the narrow, uneven path, digging our feet firmly into the hollows and pits with each other's support. By the time we had climbed to 16,499 feet, we were out of breath due to lack of oxygen; there was just the last 4 km left to reach Roop Kund, which was still covered by cloud.

We walked carefully, ensuring not to slip in the melting snow, and finally reached Roop Kund and sat at the banks of the lake for a while resting, getting our breath back. The thrill of victory began throbbing in our bodies. We peeled our shoes off our sore feet and sank them in the cold snow. Suddenly the clouds dispersed and the lake became visible. Human skeletons lay mangled on the banks. According to local legend, many years ago around 300 sadhus had got stuck in a hailstorm on their way to Mount Trishul and it is their skeletons that are still found in the area. We began our return journey before it became hot and made our way back, slipping and sliding, to the base of the mountain.

Our life is not about winning big wars, it is about winning numerous small battles. We, too, felt immense satisfaction after having won a small battle under tough conditions and we learnt a lot from the trek. We realized that anything could be achieved through strong willpower and determination.

Once we returned to the academy from the trek, we underwent debriefing. It involved an analysis of what went wrong and what had worked. Our course director said while addressing us:

> We had deliberately not provided you with everything you needed. The guide misled you as per our plan and also deserted you midway. But other guides were watching you all the time and would have informed you

> at the appropriate time in case you were heading toward deep gorges and steep valleys.

We were quite peeved hearing this and began to raise voices of protest, but the director said, 'The basic purpose of this training is to make you leaders and you will be faced with similar situations while handling epidemics, riots and natural calamities.'

The sixteen-week basic foundation course was passing rapidly. We learnt to use computers as well as the basics of horse riding. There were seminars held on law, administration and organizational abilities. The basic idea was to give us exposure to all these subjects. The real test for us IPS probationers would be the ten-month-long tough training at NPA in Hyderabad. One of the objectives of the foundation training course was to enhance the coordination and communication between the officers of different services. And one part of it was the visit to the villages.

Village visit

We were sent to a small village in Shahjahanpur district of Uttar Pradesh. Our goal was to study the social and economic structure of the village and to see how effective its administrative machinery was. The village head and the registrar came to meet us and enquire about our comfort.

When I stepped out for a casual stroll it started to rain and I took shelter under a hut, waiting for the rain to stop.

'Tanik andar aa jao bitva!' [Come in son], the voice of an old woman called out. I turned around startled and looked at her. She was removing wet clothes from the clothesline in the yard and hanging them on the ropes inside.

I replied, '*Rahne do chachi, barish ruk jayegi.*' [It's all right aunty. The rain will stop.]

But she refused to let me go. She said, '*Tum bheeg gaye ho beta! Thodi garam chai peeke jaana, accha lagega.*' [You are drenched, my son. Have a cup of hot tea. You will feel better.]

I tried to refuse once again, not wanting to trouble her, but I was shaken by what she said next. '*Aree beta, tumhare liye nahi, mere liye tanik andar aa jao. Na jane kaun se roop me subah subah bhagwanji aangan me aa sakte hain! Baad me aisa na bole ki unhe pahchaanaa nahi.*' [Son, I am calling you inside not for your sake but mine. Who knows in what form God might visit me in the morning? He shouldn't say later that I didn't recognize him!]

What amazing devotion and a sense of service stemming from it! It is only owing to such a culture that despite not having much to go by on, our villages are still able to survive and flourish. I was reminded of something I had learnt in childhood. 'Eating what is on your plate is normal, snatching food from someone else's plate is abnormal; to starve oneself and yet feed someone is real culture.'

I couldn't refuse the old lady any more. I sat on a broken bed inside her little hut and savoured the tea brewed on a wood fire and sweetened with jaggery. I gave her my address and phone number when I left. Around four years later, when I was posted as the superintendent of police (SP) of Latur, I received a letter from the old lady at my village address. Her grandson was working in Navi Mumbai and had been thrown out of his job without being paid his salary for two years. I got all the details and found that his complaint was valid. I asked him to file a complaint at the nearest police station, and after a lot of negotiations and discussions, he received his arrears and was given his job back. He remained in touch with me and came to meet me with his grandmother when I was posted in Mumbai.

She said, '*Maine kaha tha na beta, bhagwan kaun se roop me aa jayenge, kya pata? Tum mere liye bhagwan ban ke aaye aur mere budhape ka sahara bane.*' [Didn't I tell you, who knows in what form God might visit me? You came to me like a godsend and became my support in my old age.]

From then on, I pledged that every person who walks into my office is my god. Working became really easy after that. There remained no difference between my professional duties and service to God. I don't recall what else I learnt from my village visit, but I certainly took away the valuable lesson of an optimistic outlook towards life and a foundation in compassion from the old grandma in the village.

Just recently, when I was posted as police commissioner in Nashik, the video of an old woman making her ends meet as a beggar on the railway station had gone viral. Her complaint was that despite her two sons being in the administrative service, they weren't taking care of her. She mentioned in the video that one of her sons was a police sub-inspector (SI) in Nashik. I was curious. I investigated the matter and was able to locate the old lady. We found that her son was not in the police but was a superintendent, a class 1 officer in the Goods and Services Tax (GST) department. The other son was working in the State Transport Division in Nandurbar. There had been an argument between the mother and sons over trivial issues, and unable to take the insults and disrespect, the poor old woman had walked out of the house. She was a self-respecting woman and was now refusing to return at any cost.

I tried to explain the matter to the class 1 officer and his wife in the best manner I could. I also threatened them, saying that the officer could lose his job if there was a legal enquiry. Both agreed to take care of the mother. Even the grandchildren had come to my office, and they were shaken seeing her condition.

The old lady burst into tears, and everybody in the family became emotional and cried inconsolably.[10] The sons and the daughters-in-law fell at the mother's feet, pleaded and asked for forgiveness. The walls of misunderstanding and hatred collapsed, and the mother went and lived happily with them. When I went to their house to enquire about her, she served me food with her own hands. One such morsel of that food was far more satisfying than any medal or promotion.

The sixteen-week foundation course at LBSNAA was coming to its end and the director of the academy invited every group to his house for tea, welcoming each one of us personally, shaking hands. He addressed each of us by our names. While talking to us, he gave detailed information about the personal backgrounds of many of us. I was stunned to see how the director managed to have such detailed information of about 350 trainees on his fingertips. Amazed, I asked him how he did that. He answered my question beautifully and also explained his life philosophy in those forty-five minutes.

He said:

> I always remember a simple principle of Confucius: 'I hear and I forget/ I see and I remember/ I do and I understand'. I went through all your resumes in detail before you all came here. I looked at your photographs carefully. I looked for commonalities and used some

---

10 'Top cop unites estranged mother with her son', *The Times of India*, 2019, https://timesofindia.indiatimes.com/city/nashik/top-cop-unites-estranged-mother-with-her-son/articleshow/68699915.cms

ruses. I have developed this into a habit, and it has been very useful for me in my workplace. I can remember the names of all my colleagues effortlessly. I have gathered a lot of information about different aspects of their personalities and their personal lives. Whenever I enquire about their families, especially about their children with utmost sincerity, I find in their eyes a different level of respect and affection for me. They perform their duties at work with loyalty and honesty.

You need to be aware of the welfare and professional problems and challenges of your co-workers. You need to hold on to your good habits. Like they say, if you focus on your thoughts, they decide your diction and words. Focus on your words and they decide your actions. Focus on your actions and your habits get formed; and your habits shape your character. Your future depends on your character.

His eloquent talk was inspiring. It guided us on good and bad and how to fulfil our duties wisely. He recited a beautiful poem as we were leaving. It was an inspirational poem thought to be written by Spanish poet Pablo Neruda in 1972.

You start dying slowly
If you do not travel,
If you do not read,
If you do not listen to the sounds of life,
If you do not appreciate yourself—

You start dying slowly
When you kill your self-esteem;
When you do not let others help you.

You start dying slowly
If you become a slave of your habits,
Walking everyday on the same paths—
If you do not change your routine,
If you do not wear different colours
Or you do not speak to those you don't know.

You start dying slowly
If you avoid to feel passion
And their turbulent emotions;
Those which make your eyes glisten
And your heart beats fast.

You start dying slowly
If you do not change your life when you are not satisfied
with your job, or with your love,
If you do not risk what is safe for the uncertain,
If you do not go after a dream,
If you do not allow yourself,
At least once in your lifetime,
To run away from sensible advice—

The words 'you are dying slowly' continued to echo in my ears even after I came to my room and got into bed. The words took root in my mind and throbbed in my heart. Life is so beautiful and meaningful and reveals itself through a variety of dimensions. We need to really toil hard to make the most of life. I was determined to create a firm, meaningful, and workable framework for my life. I wanted the canvas of my life to be colourful, filled with the green of progress and nature, saffron of spirituality, pink of love, white of peace, red of power, blue of inspiration, yellow of free-flowing happiness and shades of the seven colours of the rainbow. This was a turning point in my life. The course my life takes is to be determined by the decisions I take now. For that I need to gain mastery over my thoughts, control over my emotions, because it is my thoughts and my feelings that decide my words.

Words should always be chosen correctly, and they shouldn't be verbalized unless the thoughts have been formulated properly. It's my words that will decide the direction of my actions and activities. I need to perform actions with wisdom and discretion. Finally, my actions will become my habits and they in turn will shape my character. My future depends on my character and that is why I will evaluate my thoughts, words, actions, habits and my character on the basis of integrity and wisdom, while drawing the blueprint of my life.

The synopsis of my life will be founded on foresight, resoluteness and strength, I decided. I will not compromise on my self-respect at any cost, because I am someone and my existence means something. My being, my words and my presence matter. I am not any Tom, Dick and Harry. My life has a purpose, meaning, and my self-respect is paramount. I will embrace excellence and climb the steps of progress every single day with conviction. I will resolve to be at the top of any field I choose to be in. I will do whatever it takes to achieve that. I will toil day and night and put my body and soul into my work to reach the top.

I will decide how every second, hour and day of my life will be spent. No rest, no stops! I will be unafraid of stumbling blocks. There will be clouds and storms but I won't stop. I won't rest. I am going to guide my progress to the highest point! I will do my work, my duties with the best within me at all times, with sincerity and passion. Even if I don't become a banyan tree, I will be a plant. If I am not the sun, I'll be a firefly. I may not be a highway, I will be a path. I will try hard to protect nature as a plant, shine like a firefly and show the way by being a path!

Victory or failure is decided not by our external, physical attributes but by our inner strength. I possess the resilience to fight, to persist. The fight and struggle will be for three important principles—eternal truth, justice and peace. My actions will be founded on these three values, though I am aware that it won't be easy given practical circumstances. It will be a rough ride for sure, but isn't that what life is all about? Life isn't fun if it is a smooth ride; it has to be a roller-coaster ride with its jumps, steep drops and thrilling twists! I may not be able to fly but I will still crawl, walk and somehow push forward consistently and keep pace. I will not slow down because of the hurdles that I come across in life. I will be focused on my goal at all times.

The days at the academy were drawing to a close and at the fag end of the course were a lot of cultural programmes, with a display of the traditional attire and food from each state. We got to eat pooran poli, paav bhaji and shrikhand. After all, Indian culture is an invaluable mixture of all the states, their languages, religions, castes and creeds. Unity in diversity is seen all the way from Kashmir to Kanyakumari and Gujarat to Arunachal Pradesh. Peaceful coexistence is based solely on the principles of tolerance and unity in diversity. I left LBSNAA, my beautiful alma mater, with the memories of batchmates from different states and the message of national integration.

In 2006, a young African boy had written a powerful poem on racial discrimination:

When I born, I black
When I grow up, I black
When I go in Sun, I black
When I scared, I black

When I sick, I black
And when I die, I still black

And you white fellow
When you born, you pink
When you grow up, you white
When you go in sun, you red
When you cold, you blue
When you scared, you yellow
When you sick, you green
And when you die, you gray
And you calling me coloured?

This is the portrait of western countries, but similar walls of caste discrimination have been erected in India for generations. Dr Babasaheb Ambedkar's mantra of 'educate, agitate and organize' shook the very foundations of those walls and the scheduled castes and oppressed classes have been growing and progressing rapidly. However, what can one do with the mouldy, backward mindsets of people? While the walls outside are being razed to the ground, what about the toxic mental and internal barriers that raise their ugly heads like worms. The only way to crush them is through ideological battles.

Many of my mental walls and fortresses had fallen following the training at Mussoorie. These were the walls of prejudice, fortresses of age-old beliefs and mindsets. North and south Indians looked like friends and the chasm between the haves and have-nots had all but disappeared. I had developed an affection and interest for my new friends from other states.

I decided to begin my career in the police service armed with these ethics and principles. That is why I have always tried to form a good team with every officer and co-worker I got a chance to work with in my twenty-three-year long career. Not one, officer or worker, became my 'favourite' and I never once transferred anyone along with me. Chhatrapati Shivaji recognized and identified the skills, talent and class among the simplest and most ordinary people, made them his think tanks, and used their skills and talents for the creation of swarajya.

We too should get inspired by the ideologies of our great maharaj and work as a trustee of the people. This was the foundation of my resolutions. The circumstances and environment for their flowering and blooming were waiting for me.

2

Break

The training in Mussoorie ended on 20 December, and our professional training at the Sardar Vallabhbhai Patel National Police Academy was to begin after twelve days. I had to fulfil a lot of responsibilities within that short period and so I went home, buying a lot of warm clothes on my way to give to the elders in the family, who suffered during winters. Giving my parents the gifts that I had specially bought for them with my own earnings made me tearful.

I had ten days to prepare myself mentally for the upcoming brutal training. I was busy thinking about how I could use my 'break' to fill myself with positive energy and ensure a sense of balance in all aspects of my life. This life that we are blessed with is a golden opportunity for us. I had to create the blueprint for how I was going to be healthy, how to manage my emotions and my mental health.

'Not' by Erin Hanson is a beautiful poem that I read years later:

> You are not your age, nor the size of clothes you wear,
> You are not a weight, or the colour of your hair.

You are not your name, or the dimples in your cheeks.
You are all the books you read, and all the words you speak.
You are your croaky morning voice, and the smiles you try to hide.
You're the sweetness in your laughter, and every tear you've cried.
You're the songs you sing so loudly when you know you're all alone.
You're the places that you've been to, and the one that you call home.
You're the things that you believe in, and the people whom you love.
You're the photos in your bedroom, and the future you dream of.
You're made of so much beauty, but it seems that you forgot
When you decided that you were defined by all the things you're not.

This poem reminded me of the resolve that I had taken before my training. I had decided that my life journey would not be directed by physical and external aspects. I would introspect and deep-dive into the innermost recesses of my mind and my inner being. Gavaloba Hill and the huge boulder on top helped me in my introspection. I went up and sat there every morning for ten days and contemplated the balance sheet of my life. I thought about every entry in detail. I was twenty-four years old then.

There is a shloka or couplet in Sanskrit in Kalidasa's Raghuvamsam: *shaishave-abhyasta vidyanam yauvane vishayayashinaam/ vaardhakenivrittinaam yogenantetanutyajaamu* [They studied well in their childhood; they enjoyed the luxuries and pleasures of life in their youth. They took to the hermitage in their advanced age; and they spent their final days in undisturbed solitude meditating upon the Supreme Being.]

We spend our entire childhood studying. Is our youth really for enjoying the pleasures of life? If we fall prey to sensual pleasures, what will become of our goals, our hopes and dreams? We will be able to see nothing new in the balance sheet of our life. Why shouldn't we follow the same mental frame we had in our growing years? Why should we put a full stop to the learning we did in childhood? Learning should be constant in life. Once we ensure that our thoughts and actions, our beliefs and behaviour are in sync, our body, mind and attitude will be pure and positive. Yoga plays an important role in achieving a balance at all these three levels. Affirmative thoughts fill us with positive energy, but the mind does as it pleases. Just as good thoughts make us constructive, negative thoughts and bad company push us towards destructive behaviour. At times frivolous fun is fine, as long as we take care not to cross the lines of decency.

The oath that I had taken in Narsobawadi, of not consuming non-vegetarian food till I succeed in becoming an IAS or an IPS officer, had been fulfilled. I had managed to keep my body in top condition with simple, wholesome vegetarian food for those three years. I now resumed consuming meat with gusto. I had invitations every night for mutton delicacies at some friend's place or the other. A few relatives had sacrificed a whole goat to feed our entire gang. We had mutton gravy, delicious dry mutton, bheja fry, paya soup and pan-fried kaleji fry to name a few. I used to feel lazy and lethargic with all that overeating and indulgence. It was a time when I felt suffocated. On the one hand my mind was trying to be mature and progressive, while on the other, twenty-three years of conditioning, regressive beliefs and my archaic mentality raised their ugly head from time to time. It was then that my family raised the issue of looking for a prospective bride for me.

Wedding bells

Discussions regarding my marriage had begun as soon as I got selected for the services. Alliances began pouring in from rich and well-to-do industrialist families. Tempting dowry offers were being made. Naturally, village elders began advising my family elders saying, 'Grab the chance now, otherwise, your son will not listen to you.' But I had announced my decision firmly—*I will not accept dowry under any condition.* Moreover, being in the police service, I had to fight such regressive traditions. My parents had full faith in me, and they too remained unfazed by external influences. Knowing that I was coming home for a brief period, my father had gathered details of four or five prospective alliances. The plan was to meet about four girls within ten days and decide on one of them.

My aunt's son Tanaji Jadhav was the one who had collected details about all the prospective alliances. Tanaji Anna was a reputed contractor in our area and his Commander Jeep was ready for me at my doorstep. According to plan, we were to go to Kolhapur and see the daughter of a sugar-mill owner in the morning and meet the daughter of an executive engineer in the evening. I had a few friends tagging along with me. Since I had become a police officer, I had grown a long moustache that could be twisted and sharpened at the ends. I twisted the ends of my moustache with ghee to ensure that it remained stiff and didn't sag. I decided to wear a Pathani suit that was in vogue those days. I bought a pair of typical Rayban glasses. My mother made me wear a thick gold chain. With my gold chain, ramrod moustache, Rayban police glasses, squeaking new Kolhapuri footwear and my slender body, I looked like a village roughneck. But my friends convinced me that this was the way to create an impression on the Kolhapuri folk. They pumped me up saying that their Sahib should look no less than a macho Maratha strongman! We reached Kolhapur chatting and sharing stories all the way.

We had a grand welcome at the sugar baron's house. We chatted for some time over plates of delicious poha, with the elders of the family singing my praises and me twirling my moustache with élan! It was now the turn of the real business—meeting the prospective bride! A girl draped in a nauvari, a nine-yard Marathi style sari, came out holding a tray of teacups. She was covered in gold jewellery from head to toe. Her head was draped with her sari pallu. Her biodata said that she was a graduate, but she looked much younger. The elders asked a few questions, and after that, we were to spend some time together in privacy. I was a little uneasy because I had a strange feeling that there was something amiss. I asked, 'Have you really completed your graduation?' She shook her head, saying, 'No, I am in my first year of BA, and I am nineteen years old. I don't want to get married at the moment.' I was stunned.

She began crying softly and said, 'I don't want to leave my parents. And everyone says you could get posted anywhere!' Her imploring words made me realize that the poor girl had been made a sacrificial lamb by her family. 'Don't worry,' I reassured her, 'I will reject the alliance,' and I walked away. When I came back, my friends were looking at me mischievously. I gestured to them that we would leave and we made our way out. This was how my tryst of looking for a bride ended. It was an unexpected encounter, and I was in a foul mood. Only after a hearty mutton meal at the Opal hotel did my spirits rise.

We decided not to wait till evening, but to go to the executive engineer's place that afternoon itself. There were no mobile phones then. Anna tried the engineer's landline number but got no response. We had the address, so we decided to knock on their door without prior notice. Our Jeep stopped in front of a sprawling bungalow. We heard the barking of dogs from within. We walked into the compound gate cautiously. We were feeling lethargic after the heavy mutton lunch and our faces were sullen after the morning fiasco. We looked like tired refugees standing at the door.

Anna had spoken only with the girl's father, and we had arrived earlier than expected. There was utter confusion. No one in the house had a clue that we were coming. The housemaid who opened the door informed us, 'We are not expecting any guests.' Anna persisted, 'We have come here for an alliance for our Sahib.' The maid asked sarcastically, 'Which one of them is your Sahib?' I felt embarrassed at that question because I didn't look like a Sahib in any way. She continued, 'A collector is coming to see our Taisahib this evening! Everyone at home is asleep. Now, get going. Sahib also is not at home. You come back once he is home, OKAY!'

We were quite irritated. At that moment, a luxurious black car entered the compound. The executive engineer got down from the car and smiled seeing Anna. 'Oh Anna Sahib, namaskar!' he said, surprised. 'You were supposed to come in the evening, right? Sorry, I had to go to my farmhouse for some work.' He reprimanded the maid, 'Hey, why have you kept them waiting at the door? Call madam quickly. The guests from Kokrud are here.'

Maushi, the maid, nervously ran inside. Maushi had managed to drain my confidence completely, and I sat down with a long face. Coming face to face with the girl's father all of a sudden had thrown me off-guard. He sent the driver to the market to get cold drinks. He asked one of his relatives, a member of the Legislative Assembly (MLA), to come over. A conversation began similar to the one we had in the morning. Once the family members realized that I was the 'collector sahib' who was supposed to visit that evening, the entire household went into a tizzy. The girl's mother personally came out and asked me what I would like to eat.

As expected, the girl came in carrying cups of tea, but to my surprise she was dressed in modern style. She wore a sari but had left her long hair loose. She was slim, tall, fair and her body language exuded confidence. She answered all the questions from the elders with assurance. Though her style of speaking was Kolhapuri, her language was clear and pure. A sense of satisfaction reflected on everyone's face. I felt a little complex creeping in. The girl and I were called to the first floor to have a private chat. The girl's father led us to an air-conditioned room and closed the door. Despite the air conditioning, I broke into a sweat. I pulled out my crumpled handkerchief from my pocket and wiped my face. I tried to give my moustache a twirl on the sly. I took a deep breath and asked her,

'What are your hobbies?'

My question was clichéd and old fashioned, but her answer was astonishing to say the least. 'I love horse riding and love to go for rides on the Bullet motorcycle.' I was expecting answers like knitting, gardening, singing or reading, but this was a dashing woman indeed!

'I won the first prize in the tent-pegging event at the Rajaram Rifles' equestrian competition. By the way, I can control horses naturally and easily.' I had not understood the drift of her answer. Her voice had unconsciously expressed her arrogance.

What she meant was, 'If I can control a horse so easily, can't I control a husband?'

'If you don't mind, shall I tell you a joke?' she said, taking over the reins of the conversation.

'Why not, please go ahead.' My heart was beating a little faster in anticipation of the bombshell.

'This has nothing to do with you so please don't take it seriously. A couple was celebrating their twenty-fifth wedding anniversary. The couple had never once fought during the twenty-five years of their marriage. They had the reputation of being an ideal couple. The media was present to interview the ideal couple and to spread the secret of their happy marriage. The reporter asked the husband, "Sir, it is difficult to believe that you managed to spend twenty-five years with your wife without fighting with her. How did you succeed in doing that?" The husband answered, "The credit for our happy marriage goes to our honeymoon in Matheran. We decided to go horse riding. The horse that I was riding was a disciplined one. But the horse my wife was riding was a wild one and would jump suddenly. At one point the horse jumped and my wife fell down. She got a little bruised but she got up, patted the horse and said, "This is your first mistake, understand!"

'My wife took hold of the reins and mounted the horse again, and we began riding again. But soon enough, the horse jumped about until my wife fell down. This time, my wife got up without a word, pulled out a pistol from her handbag and shot the horse a couple of times. The horse died instantly. I was shocked and I shouted, "You cruel, heartless woman, what have you done? You are a psycho! You have just killed a voiceless animal. How are you going to atone for this sin?" My wife turned towards me and said coldly, "This is your first mistake!" Since then, our life has automatically been happy and conflict-free.'

Was that a joke or an open threat?

She summed up clearly saying, 'Don't you think some men unnecessarily twirl their moustaches and walk in creaking Kolhapuri slippers to display their masculinity and bravery? We women may look soft and delicate from the outside but can be physically strong and firm mentally. My father has brought me up like a son, and I felt that it is important you know how I am as a person. I have grown up in Shahu Maharaj's place and we are descendants of Maharani Tarabai. I don't want to be trapped by children and household responsibilities. I want to build my own identity. You have become an IPS officer, and my father says that children from modest families like yours who have risen to such heights are ideal children. That is the reason I agreed to go through with these traditions. In fact, I want to complete my post-graduation and go to England for horse riding training. You may go ahead and say yes if you agree to marry a girl like me. My father is a very stubborn man and will not let go of your alliance easily. Do you want to ask me anything?'

My limbs had gone numb. I had realized that I was not the right match for this courageous young woman. I shook my head indicating 'no' and walked out drowned in thought. When I reached the living room, everyone was relaxed and smiling. I asked Anna to tell them that we would let them know in a day or two. Our Jeep crossed the Panchaganga Bridge and raced towards Kokrud. There were dense trees on both sides, backed by vast expanses of sugarcane fields. We would see flashes of the blazing red river from time to time.

'Hey, Brother! It seems you have liked the girl! It's time for the bands to play! Let's get ready for the wedding!' My friends were convinced all had gone well and were pulling my leg. I sat quietly. My mind was racing and irritated and filled with negative thoughts at the unpleasant experience at both places. However,

I soon calmed down and was able to assess the day's events with mature objectivity. On one side was a teenage girl brought up in a restricted environment, and on the other, a woman brought up in a progressive environment, who was confident, independent and capable purely because of her education! My brief meetings with the two women had changed my outlook towards the institution of marriage and the family structure in India. I could understand an Indian woman's life and her suffocation in the family hierarchy.

Mahatma Jyotiba Phule had a dream in the nineteenth century. He said:

> *Vidye vinamati geli, mati vina neetee geli*
> *Neetee vina gatee gekli, gatee vina vitta gele*
> *Vittaa vina shudra khachale, itake anartha eka avidyene kelo*
>
> [Lack of education leads to lack of wisdom, which leads to lack of morals, which leads to lack of progress, which leads to lack of money, which leads to the oppression of the lower classes. See what state of society just the lack of education can cause!]

I, too, am a Shudra, considered as a low-born. I, born in a farmer's family, got the benefit of the right to equality under our democracy with the doors of education being opened for me. I reached where I am owing to that privilege. The political and administrative system has been striving to provide women with education and social standing, but is our regressive mindset depriving our women of their rights? Is it preventing them from dreaming and making their dreams come true? Has it restricted their world to their kitchen and bedroom? Despite all the efforts from different levels to dispel the darkness, why isn't light spreading as rapidly as expected?

Have those women who have succeeded in breaking the barriers and achieved their dreams worked with the same zeal for the upliftment of their less fortunate sisters?

It is important to go to the root of this. We may make tall claims about gender equality, but when it comes to the point of making a choice between a son and a daughter, don't we involuntarily prefer a son a little more? When it comes to the question of who deserves higher education, we comfortably use the labels of the son being the heir apparent, the person who will support the parents in their old age and so on, and give him priority. Even today, it is a common belief in rural India that once a girl attains puberty at the age of twelve or thirteen, she is mature enough to get married and bear children. It is common for parents to think that when a girl has to anyway get married and run her household, why spend on her education?

Boys of the same age enjoy their childhood, wandering around like young bulls. Girls, on the other hand, are deprived of their fundamental rights at home and in society, burdened with inhuman restrictions and often denied even basic health facilities. Movies such as *Toilet Ek Prem Katha* (2017) and *Padman* (2018) have realistically depicted the pathetic and stifled mental and physical state of women, and have shown the sexual harassment women and girls go through when they go to the fields early in the morning for defecation.

It is said: *Jichya haathi paalnyaachi dore, tee jagat uddhaaree/ Jagaateel sagalyat sundar nirmiti mhanje stree.* [The hand that rocks the cradle, rules the world. A woman is the world's most beautiful creation.]

But unfortunately, she has to face dangers in the form of foeticide and infanticide. Yet, she has the ability to change the world because she is a manifestation of the goddess of power, Aadishakti. Despite all the progress we have made, she still has to cross a million hurdles to set foot in a school. Around 1.5 crore girls in India still don't get the basic opportunity to learn to read and write. The state of women and girls who fall victim to child marriage, prostitution and sexual exploitation is heartrendingly pitiful. We have to take this up on a war footing, to find a solution to this serious social problem and bring about a revolutionary change in our society. And to achieve this, we need to change the attitude and outlook at every level of society—the family, school, and the administration. This effort needs to be fuelled continuously from all quarters: it is then that the dream of social reformer Savitribai Phule—of daughters being able to breathe freely and openly in an India free of bias and inequality—will be fulfilled.

According to an African proverb, 'If you educate a man, you educate an individual. But if you educate a woman, you educate a nation.' When you educate a girl child, you educate an entire family. Women's education empowers not only the family but also society and the economy of a nation. It is our individual responsibility to give voice to the voiceless. My mind was racing as our vehicle cruised along the banks of the Panchaganga and Warana rivers.

I thought about the delusive ideas I had about my looks and behaviour! My deep-rooted male ego and my failed attempts at assimilating and defeating it! The second young woman clearly made me realize it, and her blunt words had destroyed me inside out. Why had my male ego not dissolved despite all my education and training? Was I still at the lowest level of Maslow's hierarchy of needs? Was I thinking of marriage purely for satisfying my physical needs? Several such questions began plaguing my mind.

Urbanization increases our social awareness and makes us more refined and mature. Our education and reading, too, make us wise. Introspection helps us understand the difference between love and lust. We learn when to say what, when to keep quiet and what not to speak. We begin seeing God in beggars and the poor. We see helping the needy as a way of getting close to God. We realize that finding the reason a sinner commits sin is more important than punishing the sinner. We understand that words are sharper than knives and swords. We develop an attitude of forgiving people for their mistakes. We make it a rule to respect all elders and be kind towards animals and birds. We realize that our lives on social media, the LOLs and smileys are all fake, and we lose interest in the virtual world.

We learn to deal with serious issues and challenges such as heartbreak, divorce and death of loved ones and accept the shock with equanimity. We understand that these are part of life and are not in any way the end of our lives. We derive immense satisfaction from encouraging others and their success. Loss of any kind doesn't affect us. We learn and formulate new rules for living and these give us hope and optimism. Life begins to look beautiful and complete, and it gets embellished with new feelings and experiences. Soon enough, life becomes a positive and creative celebration.

But, what should we do to achieve such a transformation? Will we become cultured and refined just by wearing fashionable clothes, stylish goggles, thick gold chains and creaky Kolhapuri footwear? Is everything dependent on outer appearance? No, not at all! We need to inculcate the best of what the British taught us and our own Indian traditions, to imbibe manners and etiquette and make it a habit to use them in our daily lives. We can't earn respectability only by dressing up in suits. As Abraham Lincoln said, 'You can fool some of the people all of the time, and all of the people some of the time, but you cannot fool all of the people all of the time.'

Even the best of clothes cannot hide your real self. Coincidentally, there were two auspicious occasions in the family during my break. I had to attend my cousin Vijay Kumar's wedding in Shirala and another cousin Major Parag's wedding in Pune. I resolved to follow all the courtesy and etiquette on both occasions. I decided to wear smart and classy clothes, speak in a civilized and polished manner and create a fantastic impression.

Vijay Kumar's wedding in Shirala was to be held at the multipurpose hall of the Panchayat Samiti. Since it was cold in Mussoorie, I used to wear blazers to class every day, with either a tie or a scarf tied as a cravat, with my shirt. I had worn a tie for the first time for my UPSC interview. As for the cravat, I had never tied a scarf as a cravat before. Hemant Nimbalkar, with great difficulty, tried to teach me to tie the samosa knot, but I still struggled. If the knot was right, the length would be uneven and if I got the length right, the knot would be out of place. Wearing the cravat was complicated, and both my neck and my shirt went through a lot of torture while tying it. Hence, I had bought ready to wear ones with velcro at the ends to tape together.

The cravat under the shirt looked extremely dashing. It not only kept the neck warm but also enhanced my confidence. Vijay Kumar and I had been classmates in Shirala. I was excited about meeting my female classmates at the wedding. Moreover, I had become an IPS officer now and would be the cynosure of all eyes, and I was brimming with anticipation. I dressed up in my favourite light blue shirt with navy blue trousers, a cravat (with velcro) and a smart pair of new shoes, and reached the wedding venue in our Jeep. The wedding ceremony was just about to begin. The moment the compere saw me entering the venue, he made an announcement and invited me to the stage. While walking proudly towards him, my new shoes slipped on the polished floor of the stage. I barely managed not to fall thanks to timely support from a friend, but my left foot had got twisted badly. Fortunately, no one noticed my humiliation in that crowded hall. I limped across to the centre of the stage.

Every guest on stage was being introduced by the compere, and the moment I reached him he announced, 'Our SP Sahib has just arrived post his training. He must have been delayed because of pain in his neck. I request Mayor Sir to kindly welcome our esteemed guest.' As I waited for him to clarify equally wittily—'he has worn the scarf for style, not because of any pain; and he is limping because of a slight sprain in the foot'—the mayor walked on to the stage and garlanded me. He had been requested to speak a few words to bless the couple and to congratulate me on my selection. He began speaking:

> Our own Nangre Sahib seems to have left his training in three months itself because of his neck pain. He is limping and has tied a bandage around his neck. It appears to be a serious injury. But, Sahib, don't worry at all. You seem to be handicapped because of your neck injury. I will talk to the chief minister or even the Prime Minister if needed and ensure that your training doesn't go to waste. I will not allow an officer from our district to suffer any loss. You please take care of yourself. We will get the best of the doctors for your treatment.

I tried my best to interject, 'I am all right! Nothing has happened to me! I am fine and have come home on a break,' but the loud music and beating drums drowned out my voice. Unable to hear a word of what I was saying, he continued to console me. I got irritated and pulled my scarf away. Everyone was looking at me with sympathy. I had been made to look like a fool! At that moment, the wedding ceremony ended and the loud sound of crackers took over. I decided it would be better to leave rather than answer all the questions. All the way back home, my friends wouldn't stop teasing me.

Two days later, I had yet another interesting experience. It was Parag dada's wedding in Pune. Since I knew there would be a lot of people from the army, I decided to wear the new Jodhpuri suit I got stitched at the Academy. The wedding was being held at a fancy venue in an upmarket locality of Pune. Guests and relatives had already arrived. My mother called out to me and pointed towards a tall, smart and beautiful girl, 'She is from my native town. She is very educated and if you like her, I can talk to her parents.' I lowered my head shyly like a bride. My mother realized I liked the girl. A little later, I saw my mother standing and chatting with the girl and another lady. I was sure she was talking about me, when my mother gestured at me. I hurried towards her and she introduced me saying, 'This is my son, Vishwas. He has become a big police officer, and we are now looking for a bride for him.' But the girl refused to acknowledge my presence and ignored me altogether.

I was a little careful after what had happened in Shirala. I followed her to the dining hall when I suddenly realized that the waiters serving the food were wearing black Jodhpuri suits that looked exactly like mine. Even their turbans were similar to the pink one I was wearing. A shiver ran through my body. I was in for humiliation yet again! As I stood wondering, I heard my niece Dolly's voice. She was a mischievous girl always looking for a chance to pull my leg. I was shocked to see her right next to the girl I had followed. Dolly shouted loudly gesturing towards me, 'Mama, here! Please get me some masale bhaat, you look exactly like one of the waiters here!' The girl began to giggle with her head lowered. Flustered, I picked up the rice container and served Dolly a plateful of rice. Then the girl said to me, 'Hey Mama, could you get me some salad and potato curry?' That was it! All my dreams had come crashing down. I had become a waiter, which was fine with me, but a girl who was just three or four years younger to me and the one whom I had liked at first sight had just called me 'Mama'! All this was because of the Jodhpuri suit and the pink turban … or was it because of my misplaced criteria regarding etiquette and gentlemanly appearance? I began thinking deeply about it.

In reality, etiquette and manners should be a natural part of our personality. They certainly prove useful in maintaining relationships, in becoming and staying successful, and in maintaining harmony in these modern times and lifestyles. The transformation that I consciously brought about in myself during my training and service changed my definitions and understanding of personality inside out. To achieve transformation, it is important to introspect honestly and follow healthy and good habits in life!

Etiquette and manners

There are some simple rules to etiquette. Just ask yourself these questions: Do I stand up while talking to elders and people senior to me? Do I get up to welcome anyone who comes to my house? Do I complete my tasks without fuss or complaints? Am I aware that my words and actions could be hurtful to others? Do I interfere in other peoples' personal matters? Do I listen to others while having a conversation? Am I capable of introducing myself and interacting with strangers without being self-conscious? Do I behave responsibly, and in case a situation goes out of hand, do I sulk and complain? Do I try sincerely to bring about positive changes in myself? Am I sensitive towards others' problems and eager to offer help? Do I praise and recognize my family and friends for their good deeds and success? Am I aware of social norms and codes and do I follow them? Do I take good behaviour in the family for granted? Do I leave things lying all around? Do I create a scene or throw a tantrum if I don't like the taste of the food at home? Do I dress and behave according to the place and the occasion? Am I antisocial in any way? Do I introduce new guests properly? Do I maintain a sense of discretion in my language while sending WhatsApp messages?

And if my answer is 'no' to any of the questions in that long list, do I have any plans on how I am going to improve myself and am I willing to make the effort to do so?

It is said that even those opportunities and the doors to progress that cannot be opened with education, can be easily opened with good behaviour and manners. Hence, first learn to listen. It takes sixty-four muscles to frown, get annoyed and angry, but only eighteen muscles to smile! Why should we unnecessarily torture those muscles?

The good manners of a person reflect his or her upbringing. By following proper etiquette, our personal relationships improve and mutual cooperation increases. Our positive and pleasant behaviour can be infectious and affect others positively. Good manners enhance a person's social standing and credibility for sure. Such a person is able to make friends easily. They are capable of diffusing any conflict and are successful at family, social and professional levels. Good manners and etiquette are founded on kindness, courtesy, congruity and mutual respect. These need to be fostered in children from childhood. Good and bad things happen in every generation and that is what forms the foundation of our family culture. There will certainly be differences of opinion and a 'generation gap' between us and our elders, but the future takes shape from the lessons learnt from the past. I once read an interesting story regarding this. A boy asks his grandfather, 'Grandpa, how did you live in your time? Mobile phones, internet and Netflix didn't exist; only the rich could afford to travel by flight, own computers and have air-conditioning in their homes. How did you live in the absence of any comforts? All you had were slow, rickety cars, mud roads, boring music and dull five-day cricket matches! How did you manage to survive in that old, snail-paced world with hardly any technology?'

The old man had a wonderful answer to his grandson's question. He replied, 'My dear, how do you manage to live in this artificial, machine-like, selfish world? No prayer, no devotion, no consideration for animals, no respect for anyone! How do you live lost in your phone all day? There is no cordiality, modesty or regard. You feel no awkwardness while watching adult web series in the presence of your parents. You don't go to the playgrounds to play, all you ever play are video games that are full of mindless violence! Of course, there is no yoga or pranayama, all you have is life-sucking competition and rat race! There is no place for healthy and bias-free friendship or intensive reading. The only things you get to read are perverse texts and silly emojis. Everything is so superficial! So child, there was a lack of technology in our times and there is a shortage of philosophy in your world. I feel we were blessed because we didn't have an overdose of technology. We didn't wear helmets while cycling and we played with our friends freely after school. We didn't lose ourselves in the artificial, illusive and false world of the internet.'

He continued, 'We could drink water from wells, ponds or from taps when we were thirsty and had no need for bottled water. We had wholesome home-cooked meals of bhakhri, vegetables, rice, curd, milk and buttermilk. We didn't become obese consuming fast foods like pizzas, burgers, Chinese noodles and fries. We would come home tired and relax with our family members. We never felt the need for alcohol or other intoxicants. We would wake up early, watch the sun rise and perform suryanamaskars early in the morning! Our day passed with a smile on our faces, our bodies infused with energy. We had no dark circles under our eyes due to excess screen time or hangovers from excessive drinking! We had parties called mehfils every day. We didn't have to go to pubs to party, all that we needed were a few friends, their jokes and humour!'

Grandpa's words ring true and make us introspect, but it is not as if everything about today is hopeless and negative. The current generation is genius with exceptional IQs. It has speed, but needs some speed-breakers. What this generation needs is constructive and creative direction. I used to get up early, at 3 a.m. to study when I was in class ten. Mornings have limitless power—they are magical! The crack of dawn with the gently rising sun and its changing hues is enchanting and allows us to sit in peace and contemplate. To use a technical analogy, this is the best time to format our mental and physical computer and make it free from all viruses. This is the perfect time to drive away selfishness, worries and stress from our lives. We can etch our daily, weekly, monthly and yearly goals on our minds. As they say, 'Be positive and you will be successful. Start the day with positive thoughts and you will be able to make them come true during the day. There is immense power in visualization. We need to visualize that we have already achieved what we aspire for and use our power of visualization to internalize our success. While I was preparing for the civil services, I always visualized myself as having been selected. I would visualize people in the village giving me a grand welcome and reception, and my parents' eyes filled with tears of pride and happiness seeing my success. And yes, our dreams come true based on hard work and well chalked-out plans. As Azim Premji said, 'Success is achieved twice. Once in the mind and the second time in the real world.'

It is widely believed that those who sleep late and wake up late feel lazy and listless. Their lethargy and laziness leads them to carnal pleasures, they lose their vivacity, become lonely and fall prey to bad habits. They lose their concentration and an unnamed fear grips the mind. The best way to break this vicious cycle is to go to bed early and wake up at dawn. If that is not possible, at least get up early. Go for a workout in the gym, go for treks in the mountains, exercise, practise yoga. If you find these boring, do Zumba, learn dancing, but somehow sweat it out! Fill your body with positive energy.

If you read and write early in the morning, the morning becomes all the more precious. Sant Ramdas said, 'Write something daily!' Jot down everything you plan to do during the day. If some question or problem challenges you, find the answer and note it down. Writing clears our mind and makes it light. Read inspiring books and write letters to your near and dear ones. These powerful and magical habits will help you develop a strong mind and a strong body.

I was in my early twenties, and my mind and body was fertile and ready to be cultivated. My mind was abloom and ready, my body fertile, to welcome the new chapter in my life in uniform along with its culture and etiquette. I ran up the Gavaloba hill every morning during my break, just as I used to do earlier. There I would sit on the boulder contemplating, and prepare myself mentally for the forthcoming training at NPA in Hyderabad. Back home, the Ninai Devi Yatra—the annual procession of Goddess Ninai Devi—was coming around. It took place during the last week of December, around the same time that the Urs of Alisha Baba of Kokrud took place. But in rural societies, religious harmony is so strong that both Ninai and Pirbaba are revered equally by both the Hindu and Muslim communities.

Right from childhood, I had dreamt of getting into the wrestling ring (bouts were held during the festivities) and knocking out my opponents, but this dream remained unfulfilled owing to my studies. However, this time, I was invited respectfully to the wrestling competition. The Sarpanch tied a gold-bordered turban or pheta around my head, and I was felicitated in public. It was a moment of pride for my village, because a wrestler's son had become a big police officer! My father's eyes filled with tears of pride. Relieved after my selection, he however looked weak. It was as if his body had decided to relax and take rest now that the load had come off his shoulders.

I took my parents' blessings, boarded the bus to Hyderabad and spent the night dreaming about the police academy.

3

Sardar Vallabhbhai Patel National Police Academy

I alighted at the bus depot in Hyderabad, stuffed my luggage into an autorickshaw and headed towards Shivaramapalli. The entrance of Sardar Vallabhbhai Patel National Police Academy (NPA) appeared before my eyes after a ride of about 14 km. The sentry welcomed me with an energetic, 'Jai hind Sahib'. He noted the autorickshaw number and gave the driver the directions to the IPS mess. We drove on through the wide main entrance. The broad, clean, black tar roads were lined with dense, green trees. After covering a distance of 500 metres, we jerked to a stop at a turning. There stood a massive statue of Sardar Vallabhbhai Patel on a huge rock. I asked the rickshaw driver to stop for a moment. The greatness of the leader responsible for integrating India was reflected in the befitting firm posture, sharp eyes and strong, well-built body of the remarkable statue sculpted in black stone. Sardar Patel was at the forefront of the civil disobedience movement against the British. Once he became the home minister, he integrated 562 princely states into India and helped create this strong Republic of India.

The IPS has the responsibility of keeping India undivided and together for eternity. 'To do anything great, power and dedication are important. Satyagrah is fought at two levels: one against injustice and the second against personal weaknesses.' The statue of the Ironman of India looked alive and was communicating with every probationary officer arriving at the academy. I tried to engrain the image of Sardar's statue into every cell of my body.

Someone had once asked Michelangelo, 'How do you manage to create such life-like statues filled with so much feeling and expression?' He replied, 'Every block of stone has a statue inside it, and it is the task of the sculptor to discover it. I saw the angel in the marble and carved it until I set him free.' As I set foot in the academy, my conscience was reminding me, 'There is a fearless, capable officer hiding inside you and this alma mater is going to bring him out by measuring, hammering, chiselling and moulding him. Both your mind and body are going to undergo training here. The awareness and values needed for public service are going to be instilled into you. A police officer, who is tough but sensitive, strict but humane, physically strong but has a strong knowledge base, and one who is a conscious human being will be carved out of you here. You will learn lessons of courage and business acumen. The motto of the academy is, "*Satya Seva Surakshnam*" or "Truth Service Security" and these golden words are going to seep into your body and mind in the next fifty-four weeks.'

The main objective of the NPA is to prepare leaders for the IPS. The training has been formulated to produce officers with courage, righteousness, benevolence and a dedication towards public service. The central aim of the academy is to develop the trainees' physical and mental capabilities in a balanced manner; to provide them with knowledge of human rights, legal and professional ethics keeping in mind the changing social and economic situations. Law-abiding state, secularism, equality and such national values are ingrained into everyone along with qualities of loyalty, sensitivity and empathy.

The anthem of the academy reflects all these qualities:

Lohe jaisi himmat hain, Lohe sa jasba apna
Aankhon mein liye chalte hain hum, Lohpurush ka sapna
Hum chalte haath liye, Aman prem ki roshni
Desh hi dil desh hi jaan, Is desh ke hi hain hum
Sardar Vallabhbhai Patel Raashtriya Police Academy
Yeh desh mera main desh ka, Har disha se chunkar aaye
Kuch aisa hum kar jaayen, Vyaktitv taraashein aisa
Jo mulk ke kaam aa jaaye
Netritv ki amar kahani, Har saans mein hum dohraayen
Mehnat kar himmat se hum, Desh ki aan bachaayen
Hum chalte haath liye, Aman prem ki roshni
Desh hi dil desh hi jaan, Is desh ke hi hain hum
Sardar Vallabhbhai Patel Raashtriya Police Academy

The All-India Services Act, 1951 was passed to create a law-abiding state and provide equal security to every citizen. The All-India Services, namely, the IAS, IPS and IFS, were created as per the articles 312, 313 and 314 of the Constitution of India. The strong, iron grip of the Indian administration was made possible through these three services. This state of the art, spacious academy with all modern amenities was built to provide training for the officers of the IPS.

My mind was filled with anticipation and excitement as I entered the academy. I felt determination, yearning, perseverance and energy grip me. Along with my body, my mind and soul, too, were going to be exposed to new dimensions. As they say, 'The how becomes easy, when the why is clear.' I would be taught how to do policing and learn why policing was necessary. Not only would my skills develop but I would also get to know the basics and ethics of this great service. Most importantly, I would be able to develop a clear viewpoint about my society and my police department. The fifty-four-week course was going to strengthen and sensitize my body and mind. The tough journey began on 7 January 1999.

Since there had been over 300 trainees in Mussoorie, we had been given twin-sharing rooms, but at NPA we had single rooms in the luxurious police mess. I dumped my luggage and plonked on the bed. A 'welcome and instruction' session was scheduled at 10 a.m. the next day. I stepped into the auditorium of the academy dressed neatly and smartly. It didn't take much time to get introduced because all of us were batchmates from LBSNAA. Within a few minutes, the director, deputy directors and assistant director arrived. All of us gave our introductions and then the director gave us an overview of the training and police service in brief and in an impressive manner.

> My dear officer trainees, I welcome you to a new phase in your lives. In the forthcoming ten months, you will receive training to develop officer-like qualities and skills at this academy. From today onwards, you will have to set aside the attitude of 'me, my rest and my self-interest'. It has to be, 'me, my society and my country'! You will grow every day in order to face extensive and massive challenges. The poor, the downtrodden, the scheduled castes, minorities, senior citizens, women and children will be an inseparable part of your families.

Their pain will be yours and your eyes should well up even if a thorn pierces a farmer's foot. The 'S' in your glistening IPS badge stands for 'Service'! You have now dedicated yourself to the service of the common people, not yourself. Their problems are yours now.

You need to nurture and protect these relationships with empathy. Sensitivity and morality are inseparable parts of the power you will possess. Society is constantly changing and the academy will prepare to face these changes competently. We have moved from the era of colonial police service of the British towards the welfare police of independent India, and the security of the people, protecting their rights, democracy, secularism, fundamental rights and loyalty towards our duty is what is expected of us on this journey.

Even in the face of the biggest temptation, your confidence in yourself and your belief in your uniform shouldn't be shaken even for a moment. You cannot afford to lose your balance and control under the most severe provocation. A person who has no self-control is not a leader. Even in the most challenging situations, you should not lose your poise.

You will undergo an integrated training that will prepare you to solve the smallest of the problems faced by ordinary people and to handle natural calamities, law and order problems and terrorism. All that is needed is your firm determination and a preparedness to undergo physical transformation. Are you ready for this change?

'Yes, Sir!' the unanimous voice of everyone reverberated in the auditorium.

Upbeat morale

I went to the store and gave measurements for my uniform in the afternoon. I got different types of shoes, a belt and a cap. The uniform would be ready in four days. We had been instructed to wake up at 5 a.m. and assemble in front of the mess by 5.30 a.m. It was important to brush, shave, shower and be present at the mess on time in our physical training (PT) dress and shoes. And yes, before that we had to make our beds and organize our clothes for the day. In a couple of days, we would be expected to be on the parade ground in our uniforms soon after PT. We were going to learn to be disciplined and organized.

I remember a speech given by an admiral to his navy SEALs. He mentioned four principles that were important to change the world, and I quote some excerpts below:[11]

> Every morning we were required to make our bed to perfection. If you make your bed every morning you will have accomplished the first task of the day. It will give you a small sense of pride, and it will encourage you to do another task and another and another. By the end of the day, that one task completed will have turned into many tasks completed. Making your bed will also reinforce the fact that little things in life matter. If you can't do the little things right, you will never do the big things right. And, if by chance you have a miserable day, you will come home to a bed that is made—that you made—and a made bed gives you encouragement that tomorrow will be better.

---

11 These are excerpts from the 2014 Commencement Address given to University of Texas graduates by Admiral William H. Mcraven.

If you want to change the world, start off by making your bed.

To pass SEAL training there are a series of long swims that must be completed. One is the night swim. Before the swim the instructors joyfully brief the trainees on all the species of sharks that inhabit the waters off San Clemente. They assure you, however, that no student has ever been eaten by a shark—at least not recently. But, you are also taught that if a shark begins to circle your position—stand your ground. Do not swim away. Do not act afraid. And if the shark, hungry for a midnight snack, darts towards you—then summon up all your strength and punch him in the snout and he will turn and swim away. There are a lot of sharks in the world. If you hope to complete the swim you will have to deal with them. 'Don't mess with me!' This message should be loud and clear.

So, if you want to change the world, don't back down from the sharks.

The Admiral then gave a beautiful example of teamwork:

Over a few weeks of difficult training my SEAL class, which started with 150 men, was down to just thirty-five. There were now six boat crews of seven men each. I was in a boat with tall guys, but the best boat crew was made up of the little guys—the 'munchkin crew' we called them—no one was over about five-foot-five.

The munchkin boat crew had one American Indian, one African American, one Polish American, one Greek American, one Italian American, and two tough kids from the Midwest. They out-paddled, out-ran and out-swam all the other boat crews. The big men in the other boat crews would always make good-natured fun of the tiny little flippers they put on their tiny little feet prior to every swim. But somehow these little guys, from every corner of the nation and the world, always had the last laugh—swimming faster than everyone and reaching the shore long before the rest of us. SEAL training was a great equalizer. Nothing mattered but your will to succeed. Not your colour, ethnic background, education or your social status.

If you want to change the world, measure a person by the size of their heart, not the size of their flippers.

He continued:

The ninth week of training is referred to as 'Hell Week'. It is six days of no sleep, constant physical and mental harassment, and one special day at the mud flats. The mud flats are an area between San Diego and Tijuana where the water runs off and creates the Tijuana slues, a swampy patch of terrain where the mud will engulf you.

It is on Wednesday of Hell Week that you paddle down to the mud flats and spend the next fifteen hours trying to survive the freezing cold mud, the howling wind and the incessant pressure to quit from the instructors. As the sun began to set that Wednesday evening, my training class, having committed some 'egregious infraction of the rules', was ordered into the mud.

The mud consumed each man till there was nothing visible but our heads. The instructors told us we could leave the mud if only five men would quit—just five men—and we could get out of the oppressive cold. Looking around the mud flat, it was apparent that some students were about to give up. It was still over eight hours till the sun came up—eight more hours of bone-chilling cold.

The chattering teeth and shivering moans of the trainees were so loud it was hard to hear anything. And then, one voice began to echo through the night, one voice raised in song. The song was terribly out of tune, but sung with great enthusiasm. One voice became two and two became three and before long everyone in the class was singing. We knew that if one man could rise above misery then others could as well.

The instructors threatened us with more time in the mud if we kept up the singing but the singing persisted. And somehow the mud seemed a little warmer, the wind a little tamer and the dawn not so far away.

If I have learned anything in my time travelling the world, it is the power of hope. The power of one person—Washington, Lincoln, Martin Luther King, Gandhi, Mandela and even the young girl from Pakistan, Malala—can change the world by giving people hope.

So, if you want to change the world, start singing when you're up to your neck in mud.

For a boat to make it to its destination, everyone must paddle. You can't change the world alone—you will need some help—and to truly get from your starting point to your destination takes friends, colleagues, and the good will of strangers to guide them.

If you want to change the world, find someone to help you paddle.

He concluded by saying:

> Start each day with a task completed. Find someone to help you through life. Respect everyone.
>
> Know that life is not fair and that you will fail often. So take some risks, step up when the times are toughest, face down the bullies, lift up the downtrodden and never, ever give up—if you do these things, then the next generation and the generations that follow will live in a world far better than the one we have today.
>
> And what started here will indeed have changed the world—for the better.

Such inspiring speeches and thoughts have been training and transforming both my body and mind.

I have an obsession—to sit with pen and paper and write down all my resolutions. I revise my previous resolutions and pledge to fulfil them. Now I pledged to do every task in a disciplined manner and resolved to do everything with immaculateness. Our training had two parts—indoor and outdoor. Indoor training focused on administration, law and systems, forensic science, jurisprudence, cyber-crime and investigation. Outdoor training included drills, PT, arms training, self-defence, yoga, horse riding, field sports, route marches and tactical training. Apart from this, there were excellent seminars organized on a variety of topics. We had training sessions on how to behave like officers, how to communicate and talk, dining etiquette, and so on. Every day was an opportunity to learn something new and give shape to different aspects of our personality.

The first four days consisted of the introductory sessions of the training course. We were not only going to learn different subjects at the academy, but also, and more importantly, going to absorb and assimilate the spirit of the IPS. I was going to learn self-confident body language. My ethical and moral spirit was going to be strengthened and my commitment towards my service would take shape. Several graduates and highly educated young men and women from different fields had entered the uniformed service and all of them had to be sculpted and perfected in the same mould. This was the biggest challenge faced by the faculty members here. I was going to gain knowledge, skills and build a positive attitude and this foundation was going to stand in good stead at every turn in my career and personal life.

The parade taught me how to be in sync and cooperate with others and sports taught me how to strategize, resist and improve my reflexes. Drill practice taught me how to give commands and accept leadership. I was being taught to follow the spirit of the squad, to be an obedient, disciplined and humble follower while at the same time being taught to become a firm and virtuous leader.

I had to be my own guru, philosopher and guide while leaving NPA. There was only one principle that I needed to adopt at the end of the training: to continuously keep training my body and mind. This would help me reach newer heights every single day in my life. Once I went to the field after my training, I could not become complacent. I would have to keep this training going in order to face the challenges that I was going to face tirelessly.

As police officers there are a variety of challenges we face, such as controlling small-time offenders, handling terrorism, internal security, espionage, cyber and financial crime, managing natural and man-made calamities, protecting human rights, and ensuring the security of women and children. I have been blessed with the opportunity to work on such social issues. This training equipped me with the capability to fight and face all these challenges by utilizing and combining the manpower, facilities, modern technology available and coordinating with the various other governmental agencies. Sardar Vallabhbhai Patel set up the IPS for the integration of independent India. This training was to prepare me to serve my motherland through this great police service.

4

Outdoor Training

The tall and handsome assistant director (AD), Atul Karwal, welcomed us with a fluent speech in impeccable English. This is the same Karwal Sir who scaled Mount Everest. He has also criss-crossed India on his bicycle and is a fourth dan black belt in taekwondo, a form of martial arts. Karwal Sir was the AD for our outdoor training. The AD's inaugural speech set the direction for our outdoor training:

> My dear officer trainees, you all have to improve not only your physical strength, but also enhance your guts, willpower and your indomitable spirit. All of you are going to set clear goals for yourselves from today onwards. You are going to challenge your inner strength and climb a step higher every day. If you don't set goals, you will not be able to move in the direction of your desires and reach them. Hence, it is important that you decide on what you want to achieve when you leave this academy and then mark small milestones. As it is said, it is important to win the war, but we need to first win

small battles. This will make you think about *why* you are doing something. The why has to be crystal clear; there should be no ambiguity. Once that is clear, your path becomes easy and you will derive immense strength.

And yes, if you want to be successful in your career ahead, learn to take responsibility—for both success and failure. You should neither whine nor blow your own trumpet. In case something goes wrong, don't blame others. Learn your lesson and move on. You will face a lot of obstacles in the field here, and we will try to teach you the necessary skills and knowledge to overcome them. But it is you who will decide whether you want to win or lose, fight or to face it, or hide! What you choose in life will shape your future. There are some people who are whiners or complainers, while some others are winners or conquerors. While the winners find a path, take the initiative, accept their mistakes and change themselves, the whiners constantly complain, find fault with others, give excuses, keep procrastinating and shirk responsibility. They certainly end up unsuccessful. You have to decide which side you want to be on. Every time you learn something new, you must continuously think about how you would do it yourself and how you can use the learning in your life and how it can benefit you. Despite falling and failing repeatedly you should strategize on how you can propel yourself forward and leap ahead. As they say, *a bad workman blames his tools.* If you blame your circumstances and your co-workers for your failures, your downfall is certain.

Self-discipline is most important during outdoor training and you need to work hard to develop it. Your final result will depend on whether you relax and have a good time in your room after fourteen hours of training, or whether you contemplate on how to make yourself even better. Make full use of the course material, gym, audiobook, computer and the faculty members. Once you complete your training and go to the field, your colleagues will be able to gauge your potential and capabilities instantly from what you say, how you say it and the questions you ask. Read a lot and listen to good stuff for the betterment of your future, your mind and your personality. Develop new hobbies, listen to inspiring words that enthuse and energize you.

Plan your day to fit all this into the twenty-four hours you have at hand. You will need to be more organized and better planned than you were while preparing for your UPSC exams, because henceforth, your decisions will not be restricted to you alone but could affect and endanger the lives of lakhs of people. The workload is so much that if you don't manage time effectively, you could get extremely stressed and unsettled! Here you are going to be involved in various activities like sports, PT, firing, tactics and drill. You will have to coordinate between various subjects like law and order, crime, traffic, terrorism, human resource, management and social welfare. You will have to face multiple challenges and problems at the same time, and you will have to instantly choose which of those is most important, fight it effectively and resolve it. You will then take up other issues on your list and complete them.

While 10 per cent of your challenges will be unexpected, the remaining 90 per cent will be those that were anticipated or expected. Therefore, if you can have a weekly, monthly and sometimes yearly plan for those 90 per cent of the challenges, you will be able to handle them with determination and confidence. The proficiency in performing tasks comes only through planning. Planning means deciding how, when and who will do a particular task, and most importantly to make a time-table and complete the tasks according to a PERT Chart.[12]

All I want to say is, you can't climb the ladder of success with your hands in your pockets. Take your hands out, challenge them and make them strong. Then you see how effortlessly you will be able to pick up new skills and become competent. However big your dreams may be, they will remain so if you don't strive hard to fulfil them. So, don't indulge in simple posturing, take action. Prove yourself and in the next fifty-four weeks, work hard every single day and learn new lessons, shape yourself and ensure that you play an important role in creating a good society in future. All the best!

Karwal Sir's rousing words pierced through my mind as I tingled with anticipation. Yes, the coming year was going to lay the foundation for my life, and I was going to get the best out of myself. I swore to myself that I would do everything possible to the best of my physical and mental abilities and learn everything I could with sincerity. Every single class and demonstration was important during training. I knew that if I didn't realize their importance on the very first day, it would certainly lead to repentance and failure.

I had read a story about JRD Tata, how a friend of his used to misplace his pen so often that he only used cheap pens to avoid

---

12 Programme Evaluation and Review Technique Chart.

worrying about losing them. However, the friend wasn't happy about his own carelessness. JRD suggested he buy the costliest pen he could afford and see what happens. The friend did so, purchasing a 22-carat gold Cross pen. After nearly six months JRD met him and asked him if he was still misplacing his pen. The friend said he was very careful about his costly pen and was surprised how he had changed! JRD explained to him that it was the value of the pen that made the difference; there was nothing wrong with him as a person!

This is what happens in our life. We are careful about the things that we value the most. If we value our health, we will be careful about what and how we eat. If we value our friends, we will treat them with respect. If we value money, we will be careful while spending. If we value our time, we will not waste it. If we value relationships, we will not break them. Carefulness is a basic trait all of us have; we know when to be careful! Carelessness only shows what we don't value. Hence, I decided to value every opportunity, every lesson and every moment of the outdoor training and to learn every lesson carefully and honestly.

Drills, parades and marches

We were a total of seventy-two trainees who had come to NPA from different parts of India. We were divided into six squads of twelve trainees each. There was a drill master and an assistant assigned to each squad and a commandant-level officer to oversee our field training. All these officers came from the central paramilitary forces and all the outdoor training personnel were of SP rank and reported to the assistant director, who is of SP rank IPS officer.

All of us assembled in front of the mess at 5 a.m., dressed in our clean PT uniforms on the first day. I was in squad six.

There were three Maratha friends in my squad—Ilme, Vhatkar and Kamble. Drill Inspector Sharma greeted us and introduced himself calmly in his firm, assertive voice. He and his assistant Rawat Ustad were going to test us to our limits in the coming fifty-four weeks. Our bodies had become stiff with all the studies at LBSNAA and though the stiffness had reduced a little bit thanks to the mild exercise we had done in Mussoorie, it was time now to shed all the lethargy and make our bodies powerful!

The day was to start with PT. The theoretical principles behind the activity had been given to us the previous day, to prepare ourselves mentally for it. There is a scientific basis to everything, and we were made aware of them. We were given a brief of the 'what' and 'why' of our field-training activities. The inaugural drill practice was to be conducted in a spacious concrete field. As we were supposed to assemble on this field in uniform after the hour-long morning PT exercises, we would quickly get out of our sweaty PT clothes and into our stiffly-starched khaki uniforms. Every lesson and activity had an aim, and we had to change from one uniform into another within seven minutes. Such practices prepared our minds and bodies to be battle-ready and face unexpected challenges, whether man-made or natural disasters, effectively. Our quick reflexes and responses could prove life-saving for several people in future—it is the 'golden hour' following a crime that provides direction to the investigation. Horse riding training helped us build physical and mental resilience and boldness. Swimming was another complete exercise and diving into the pool from a height was a thrilling experience.

It is such activities that teach us to take risks, make courageous decisions and help us to build our administrative capabilities. Martial arts and sports make our physical reflexes sharp and swift and also build camaraderie and team spirit. Yoga is taught, as it is the key to developing mastery and proficiency in all aspects of life. Marksmanship training is not only to get us battle-ready, but also about concentration, steadiness, and steely resolve. Such outdoor training activities ensure all-round personality development.

Getting out of our sweaty, dripping PT uniforms and into clean, starched, stiff khakis was a challenge, and we would wear the ankle boots first (lest the pants lose their crisp folds) and then the rest of the uniform. Then, dressed as per protocol, we would arrive at the ceremonial ground for fall-in with our rifles at 8 a.m. We would stand for the drill in three rows, according to height and build. Then, either the drill instructor or Ustad Rawat would inspect our uniforms very minutely. A lot of care was taken to ensure that there were not even small deficiencies. The drill would begin with commands of 'attention' and 'stand at ease'. The main aim of the parade was to improve camaraderie and team spirit. A sense of pride in our team and uniform was constantly instilled in us through the marches and parades.

In reality, it was a little difficult for our highly educated batchmates to digest all this easily. The average age of our batch was twenty-seven, and it wasn't easy for the minds and bodies to bend. We had a topper, Atul Singh, in our batch. He was tall, hefty and had the memory of an elephant! He began protesting on the very first day. He insisted that he would stamp his feet lightly during the drills because stamping them hard repeatedly might damage the brain. Most of us read a book word-by-word, or by sentences, but Atul Singh read the book in paragraphs. He had a photographic memory and could finish a book within a few hours. We presumed he skimmed through them, but he could recall each page. Atul had scored 250 on 300 in the UPSC interview. No doubt, this intellectual found these drill practices too arduous.

'I will not participate in this group activity,' he protested. 'I object to such forms of training, and I will not follow instructions blindly. I will become a mule because of such training methods.' Karwal Sir took on the challenge of preparing a topper like Atul to accept and undergo our British-era drills. He told us the importance of physical training, and his words continue to inspire me to this day:

> The foundation training is ten months long. Your daily routine involves running miles without a stop, horse riding, swimming, unending physical exercises and sleepless nights. Added to this are the uncomfortable and oppressive weather conditions! Expert trainers are here to make your life tough! The only purpose is to find the raw, weak and timid parts in you and make those strong and tough with constant pounding and hammering. The basic purpose of this training is to bring out the real leader in you—one who faces the constant stress with courage, handles chaos and challenging situations in a professional manner, one who doesn't get devastated by defeat and is unafraid of adversity. In these ten months, you will be fed the most potent medicine that will give you all the skills and techniques you will need to handle the challenges you come across in your life. Every single person and unit of this academy is constantly striving to make that happen.
>
> You may have to perform seemingly superficial tasks every day, but there is a purpose behind everything that you do here. We will be checking if you are keeping your room clean and making your bed. If you do the small things perfectly, the bigger tasks will automatically be perfect because of your inherent habits. Moreover,

you have to do things together, with teamwork. You cannot possibly change the world alone; you will feel the need for help at every juncture. Make friends from the beginning, take your colleagues into confidence and let even strangers be beacons in your journey. Drills and marches are the means for that. When you follow the drill commands, you are making the foundations of equality and unity strong. Your colour, attire, race, education, and social status will gradually melt away. You have to become strong inside out to perform miracles and achieve the unimaginable.

Your uniform will be scrutinized minutely to check whether it is starched properly, whether your shoes and belt are polished perfectly, whether your cap and buttons are in the right position; every aspect will be checked ten times. And most of the time, faults will be found, however perfect you may try to be. Your shortcomings will be pointed out for sure. The purpose of the drill is basically different. Even after taking all the care while facing challenges in life and being prepared well, you sometimes fail. Then you either curse yourself or your bad luck. All these efforts are aimed at getting rid of such mindsets. Life is never fair and doesn't always award merit. Destiny tests us from time to time and tries to break us and pull us down. That is when you will realize the importance of this drill. You will fight and combat any circumstance with your optimism and positivity and emerge victorious.

You will be given new challenges during the outdoor training like long-distance running, route marches and horse riding from trotting to galloping. You will have to come down hills rappelling and climb up tall buildings using ropes. You will have to take hits while learning self-defence. Your body will be tested to its limits daily while doing push-ups, pull-ups and other exercises. All these activities are aimed at testing your mental capabilities and resilience. You will have to achieve certain targets and standards, and you cannot qualify otherwise. In case you fall short, you will be made to practise more. More daily practice will mean added fatigue and increased agony, but this will build your inner strength. You will become stronger and more competent by the day and come out with flying colours in the final test! But all this is possible only on one condition: you have to accept the daily practice wholeheartedly, learn with full commitment and hone your skills and overcome every weakness with determination. This commitment and resolve will make your journey over the next ten months easy. This is the time for you to take this oath, my brave young people!

Drills, parades and the uniform are going to turn you 'khaki'. Just take one pledge—my colour is khaki, my character is khaki, my dharma is khaki. I am khaki at all times, be it Diwali, Ramzaan, sun or rain, storm or calm. I am the khaki that is ready to sacrifice for the honour of my country. No obstacle or danger can dishearten me. Khaki is my honour, my pride! Jai Hind!

The stirring and illuminating words from Karwal Sir melted Atul's self-importance and ego, and he began excelling in all the physical activities. The ground seemed to be inadequate for him! He would swim without a break and refused to look back while running. He began racing horses at lightning speed and would work out in the gym non-stop! All this endless exercise made him ravenously hungry. He began going to everyone in the mess requesting for extra chicken and mutton at mealtimes. But this was the fun part; Atul had become extraordinary! Coincidentally, Karwal Sir's first name was also Atul, hence the guru and disciple pair had become the talk of the academy. Atul Singh's life philosophy and beliefs about himself may have been different, but as a result of Atul Karwal Sir's rousing words and tough role, he was forced to take a U-turn. Atul Karwal had won the first round in the academy and had got every trainee under his influence.

Atul Singh got posted to Nagaland after training. It was a time when Nagaland was infested with rebels on a rampage, and insurgency was on the rise. Atul's thought processes and ideas were modern and revolutionary. His seniors were stumped and couldn't handle working with him. In response, Atul Singh wrote a curt resignation letter that said, 'This service is not fit for me,' and went away to America. He is unmarried and is enjoying life to the hilt reading, writing, travelling around the world and living a life of his choice. He visits India once in a while and makes it a point to call me or meet me at least once. Talking to him opens up new vistas and ways of living. His thoughts and viewpoints on life are very different and unique.

It is almost impossible to understand the meaning and goals of one's life and most people wander through life aimlessly. The most important mantra to live long and happy lives is to be delightfully and meaningfully engrossed in life. Once you are able to identify your innermost passion, it gives your life a purpose, and your eyes begin to sparkle with joy! Your heart races and your life becomes a beautiful melody. We must find what interests us and live our lives involved in it. This is what is called 'deewangi' in Hindi. Atul had found his deewangi and had embarked in search of his God, his Khuda. Everyone's deewangi or passion is hidden deep inside their own selves and to find it is the main purpose of one's life. Each one of us has our unique and independent passions, and we have to pursue them extremely diligently. We will then find new meanings and new colours each day. We need to be active in life, rest a while, walk a little, eat healthy, be fit, have good friends, have a good laugh and be with nature. We must live in the present moment and keep our minds exuberant and agile. These must be the simple mantras of our lives. But we invite complications into our lives ourselves, and stress is the first one!

Constant stress can make us fatigued, sick and age faster. At such times, we are bound to do only what we have been appointed to or what is thrust upon us. We are forced to disregard our inner voice, and we are unable to express our innermost feelings. That is when everything goes haywire. Both our minds and bodies become mechanical and gradually begin to degenerate. Our awareness begins to get blunted and emotions get numbed. Once we put off doing what we are passionate about, the enjoyment, enthusiasm and joy of living get eroded and we feel like slaves. That is why it is important to continue this quest and keep the thirst for our desires alive.

I have always tried to connect my occupation with my passions. It was a challenge and I did face a lot of criticism as well, but things become easy once our goals are clear and the intentions are for social good. When we ensure that our goals don't cause any harm to anyone, we can progress on our journey following our passion with freedom and confidence. Once we are done with our day at work, we need to find spare time to follow our passion. We must bring happiness to people's lives with our service and affection.

Being with youth gave me the energy to move forward in my journey. I grabbed every chance to be with them. I conversed with them, shared their sorrows and laughed with them. I pranced and danced with them, but was also strict with them at times. I did not allow myself to lose my sense of balance or lose my patience while handling students' agitations and revolts. The one time I was tough and ordered a lathi-charge was when a group of agitating youth attacked the Mumbai Municipal Corporation with fireballs and resorted to violence. Several policemen had been seriously injured in the attack. Hundreds of youngsters had broken limbs, and one person died in that incident. I wasn't stressed when facing the adjournment motion or the enquiry, but I was shaken seeing the injured youth and the dead body of the young man who lost his life to anarchy.

We often have to arrest alcoholic young men who are at each other's throats, and handcuff drug addicts. These are duties that we have to perform within the boundaries of law. These acts may be appropriate and pertinent, but sometimes unacceptable to our conscience. Hence, we need to take time out and guide the misled youth and help them channel their energies in the right direction.

We use innovative ways of communicating with the youth in collaboration with NGOs and academic institutions. It is satisfying work and reduces stress. Even the adventure sport activities, such as horse riding, that I learnt during my training at the academy help raise my morale. It also taught me how to love animals and reduce my stress of being around them.

Horse riding

All of us were most scared and curious about horse riding. When the time to mount the horses came, our hearts were racing and we had knots in our stomachs. Our only exposure to horse riding was watching Bollywood heroes riding horses on screen. I had tried to ride the donkeys belonging to my neighbour in the village and had to pay quite a price for it! I lost half my tooth in the attempt and the moral of the story was 'don't play around with donkeys and any species resembling them!' I did try to sit on a horse once during my sister's wedding, but the moment it pawed the ground with its hooves, my courage deserted me and I changed my mind.

Since then, I had not had the opportunity to sit on a horse. There was a lot of preparation to do before we could mount a horse at the academy. We bought the riding uniform from the canteen and got ready, wearing our helmet, riding boots, tight-fitting pants and gloves. That gave us some confidence. We were taken by bus to the special ground for horse riding, which was in the other camp across the highway. All of us assembled for the introductory briefing by our instructor:

> My dear officers, you have assembled here for an exciting and courageous experience today. You are going to ride one of the most handsome and regal animals. To control a horse is not everyone's cup of tea and to ride a horse without fear of falling is an art. You must be thinking, 'Why do we need to ride a horse in this era?' Friends, there is a lot of similarity between horses and the administrative services. You can't sit on a horse and immediately start riding freely. You need to build rapport with the horse and earn its confidence. You have to pet it and pamper it. You have to be extremely patient, and that is when it will allow you a smooth ride. This is exactly how the administrative service or the police department functions.

> Getting a grip on the administration is as difficult as controlling the reins of a horse. You are all here to learn the art. When you ride a horse, you are completely unaware of the language of this silent partner. You will have to use a language and signals that are very different from your regular language. When you are astride a horse, apart from the language, you also have to maintain your balance. You need to coordinate with the horse and remember that the horse will do exactly what it wants, irrespective of what commands or signals you give. When you are on the field, you will have to tame a lot of such wild and brazen horses. This training will help you improve your communication skills in order to handle such challenges.
>
> You will have to overcome new challenges and face new problems the moment you mount a horse. Being alert and agile is the only answer. And yes, you need to focus a 100 per cent while riding a horse, and no other thought should cross your mind once you are saddled. You have to be in the present moment, and it is a kind of dynamic meditation. It takes you away from your day-to-day stresses, and the horse becomes your best friend, just like your pet dog. While riding a horse, the world around you seems to be beautiful and peaceful.

These words of our instructor were very reassuring, and we all nodded in agreement. But our minds were still nervous.

The conversation in the academy was all about how many people had broken bones and got injured while riding. According to one story, a probationer had lost his life when he fell, because his legs had got caught in the stirrups. A lot of my batchmates were in a state of shock thanks to these stories and rumours.

Some of them carried chickpeas in the hope of befriending their horses.

We had been told that a horse measures the confidence of its rider from the rider's body language. We were trying hard to mask our nervousness. We were not scared of sitting on the horse per se, but to make it trot, canter or gallop was no less than a nightmare. On top of that, we had to pass an exam! We were also constantly worried about the consequences of the horse going out of control and what would happen to the rest of our training if we fell down and broke our backs. We had heard that falling from the horse could cause a fracture of the tail bone, and we would have to sit on tyres and tubes in the classroom till it healed. It would be extremely embarrassing to come to class carrying a tyre-tube and sit on it.

When we recall negative and humiliating experiences, we start finding ways of getting rid of them or learn how to fight them, but when pleasant memories are etched in our minds, we attract positivity and try to attain them with effort. So, I tried to learn this challenging sport sincerely. I learnt from the trainer that we need to be careful, to understand the drill, take all the safety precautions and wear the right gear. Horses are brilliant animals, and they can measure your confidence, fear and state of mind instantly.

The first thing to do is the 'horseman's handshake'. It's a simple gesture that allows you to introduce yourself to a horse. With an extended arm, offer the back of your hand to your horse's nose. If the horse touches your palm with its nose, your friendship is sealed! Once you have the reins in your hands, you need to focus on the path. You need to be slow and steady and confident. If you trust your horse, he too will not let you down. I kept all these instructions in mind, and gradually, I was able to make the horse trot, canter and gallop. Soon enough, I was enjoying riding a lot.

Horse riding is a skill related to the battlefield. We were also trained in other equestrian events such as dressage, show jumping and tent pegging—all of which require a competitive spirit. In tent pegging, you need to hit a peg fixed to the ground, while riding a horse. In this, more than competition, it is superior skills that matter. All decisions are taken mentally, and the body follows accordingly.

The ultimate skill is to identify the signals from the horse and pass on the right signals to it. To be keen to bring out the best in oneself is the real endeavour. There is a beautiful Sanskrit verse that describes the effort, commitment and dedication needed for it.

> *Prarabhyate khalu vighna bhayena neechaihi*
> *Prarabhya vighnavihit, viramanti madhyaha*
> *Vighnaih punah punarapi pratihanyamaanaaha*
> *Prarabdhamuttama janaanaparityajyanti*
>
> [Weak-minded people do not begin anything at all through fear of difficulties; mediocre begin a task but abandon it no sooner than an obstacle comes in their way. But strong-minded persons, though repeatedly hindered by difficulties, do not give up what they have once begun.]

This is the true secret to achieving excellence, and the faculty members at the academy had taken upon themselves the task of creating the best police officers in the country.

Sport and sportsmanship

The academy gave more importance to team sports, rather than individual ones. The only team sport that had become immensely popular all over our area in my childhood days was cricket. That was because of India winning the cricket world cup in 1983. Each one of us wanted to be Kapil Dev or Gavaskar. There is hardly any awareness of or interest in any other team sport in rural areas. I remember having played a game like volleyball with a rubber or plastic ball. In those days, our regular attire consisted of striped shorts, sleeved vests and slippers. We had never played basketball, hockey or football ever in our lives. We had watched a few football and hockey matches on TV, but we didn't know the rules for any game other than cricket. Even with cricket that we played on the fields or on our terraces, we only knew about batting, bowling, fielding and wicket-keeping. It was only in the academy that we spent money buying uniforms for various sports.

The last hour of our outdoor training was reserved for team sports. Sometimes, there would be scuffles and fistfights during these games. During the initial days, I could hardly make contact with the ball. Even if I did, I was unable to hit it or pass it. My squad members had a good time teasing me for my lack of skill. I never scored a goal in either hockey or football. I could never basket the ball while playing basketball. I used to practise playing basketball alone after everyone had left and felt very happy if I managed to shoot the ball into the basket. I would have shown my skill had they allowed us to play games like kho-kho or kabaddi. Though I never became good at playing any team sport, I did learn sportsmanship and team spirit while playing them.

Teamwork

A shloka in the *Kathopanishad* can be translated thus: 'O God accept our unity/ Give us strength/ Keep our capabilities and intelligence sharp/ Keep us away from malice, hatred and envy.' This is what team spirit means. Teamwork is how we are able to handle both natural and man-made disasters efficiently, with the cooperation of the different governmental agencies and optimum utilization of the inadequate resources at hand. We all have heard the story of the rabbit and the tortoise, but I recently read a modern version of the story.

In the original version, the rabbit challenges the tortoise. They race against each other, and the rabbit runs fast and goes far, far ahead until he suddenly spots a green patch with fresh green grass. He stops to eat to his heart's content and dozes off. In the meantime, the tortoise catches up, overtakes the rabbit, reaches the finishing line first and wins the race. The moral of the story is '*slow and steady wins the race*'.

In the new version, the rabbit wakes up and realizes his mistake. He challenges the tortoise to a new race. This time, he decides that he will not stop or rest on the way. The results are as expected, and the rabbit wins the race easily. The moral of this version is: '*Those who work fast and consistently prove to be better than the slow and steady.*'

Now the tortoise challenges the rabbit for yet another race, but changes the course. The rabbit runs fast and non-stop on the new route, but finds a river on the way. He stands there stumped, while the slow and steady tortoise catches up with him, and swims across effortlessly, steadily moving forward, and reaches the finish line. The moral of this version is: '*Even if you are slow, select your route carefully. Identify your core competency and then change your playing field.*'

The new version of the story continues. The tortoise and the rabbit have become close friends after the three races. They decide to complete the race together. So, the rabbit carries the tortoise while they are on land, and once they reach the river, the tortoise carries the rabbit on its back and swims across. They reach the finishing line together in record time! This is called a 'win-win' situation. Both win and have the satisfaction of having completed the race! What this means is: *It is good to be individually motivated and personally capable, but until you learn to work in a team and make full use of your team members' capabilities and talents, you will not achieve team goals.*

All team sports require your physical and mental strengths, your decision-making abilities and your strategic abilities to be in sync. Do you remember that inspiring (Kabir Khan) Shahrukh Khan scene from the movie *Chak de India* (2007)? He gives this rousing talk to his players during the break of the women's hockey world cup final match.

> Seventy minutes ... You have seventy minutes ... Perhaps the most important seventy minutes of your life—
>
> Whether you play well or not, you will remember these seventy minutes for the rest of your life ... Because in the years to come, no matter how you play, whether you win or lose, nobody can take these seventy minutes away from you—
>
> Today, I am not going to tell you how to play. All I will say is go and play the game from your heart. In the coming years, no matter what happens, whether you win or lose ... nobody can take these seventy minutes away from you. I am not going to tell you how to play this game. Instead, you will tell me—by playing the game. Because I am confident that if every player in this

> team plays the best hockey of her life ... then even God himself cannot take these seventy minutes away from you. So, go forth—and from yourself, from your life and from every person who ever doubted you, grab these seventy minutes.

In all these team sports, you need to strategize your game plan every single minute, with coordination and according to the situation. Intensive practice and deep knowledge of the game are extremely important. While playing a competitive match, you have to be aware of both personal skills and collective responsibilities. For that to happen, there must be mutual cooperation, trust and coordination within the team. The same principles apply in our family life and profession as well. Even if there are eleven players who play on the field and win, there are so many other people who have worked hard on the side lines to ensure success. People outside the field play an active role in management, deciding tactics and game plans, despite being invisible. Our family members, too, play a major role in our success on the field. It is the game and the circumstances that decide the value of one's role and contribution. Hence, it is important for the team to come together, decide what should be done and what should not. They must have a vision for the team.

One has to constantly hone one's skills to be on top of one's game, while playing any field sport. Situations change every moment, and the tide can turn at any time. It is important that your focus remains in the present moment. For example, in football and hockey, the constantly moving ball decides your position and focus. You must be aware of your opponent's movements at all times, and work towards defeating them. Every decision you make should be ultimately for the team's benefit. You cannot think about individual glory and success at the cost of the team. That will prove disastrous. Success is guaranteed only when everyone is together and works with team spirit.

The rules for team sports are fixed and every player is always bound to follow them. However, these rules may be changed by the organizations from time to time and ignorance of the rules can never be an excuse. Even in society, we need to follow constitutional laws and regulations. If you say that you did something out of ignorance of the law, you will end up in prison. Even the Constitution is amended when necessary and laws change with the times.

Playing sports helps us maintain a balance in life. It is the same with our position and contribution in a game. Every sportsperson should give more importance to the team than to his or her individual aspirations. We need to consider the team leader's decision as final and perform the duty assigned to us with sincerity and commitment. We should not complain or hold any grudges and bitterness.

When we don't enjoy the role given to us, we become unhappy and our mood gets spoilt. And once that happens, our performance suffers—once this becomes consistent, we lose our place in the team. That is why it is vital to change ourselves at the right time and, through hard work, make ourselves worthy of the role we are seeking. We *will* face such challenges in our personal and professional lives too. We will receive both brickbats and bouquets during our postings and promotions throughout our careers—this is the most important lesson that team sports can teach us. Competitive sports also teach us when to move forward and when to step back. Only the team that plays with cooperation, coordination and mutual encouragement finally wins.

When competition within any team (whether sports or work) becomes very high, distrust and disrespect increase and ego problems crop up. Rewards, recognition and money are the root causes of such conflicts and rivalries. It is the team leader's responsibility to maintain harmony and balance within his team. It is important for the leader not to allow one member's mistakes to ruin the careers of others or make the entire team suffer. If this happens, dislike for that member will follow. The leader must ensure that such things are not repeated and to see that such issues are diffused as soon as possible.

Competition between sportspersons or work-team members should be healthy and professional. The moment jealousy creeps in, there will be discord and team performance will suffer due to mutual blame games. The players become emotional, losing control and concentration. All plans collapse like a house of cards, while the opponent succeeds in scoring a goal against us.

That is why every team member's role, responsibility and remuneration should be transparent and just. This is the real challenge faced by the coach and the team leader. Once this is sorted, success is inevitable. We have seen how a player celebrates when he takes a wicket or scores a goal. He jumps up and down, jumps over his teammates, and gives high-fives to his teammates. All this keeps the team spirit high. It is important for each team member to be aware of the role of other team members so that roles can be exchanged and strategies quickly decided in critical situations.

Just as we use our breaks during our exams for revisions, we need to use the intervals between a match to revisit our skills and strategies and plan ahead. We should not have any negative thoughts in our minds during the break and we should visualize victory and keep our energy high. We must be exuberant and respond to every attack from the opposition with well-planned strategies and use our mastery to achieve victory. We need to give ourselves positive and motivating auto-suggestions like, 'Come on! Yes, you can do it! You are a champion! You are the architect of your victory! *Jo jeeta wohi sikandar*! Har Har Mahadev!'

There are a lot of similarities between leadership needed in our work environment and team sports. Let's take the example of the super hit movie *Lagaan* (2001). This movie shows strategy on the cricket field and management skills off the field. Every scene in the movie gives us valuable life lessons and practical tips. Whenever you want to make your dreams come true or to take a big leap forward in life, you must ensure that your past experiences don't come in the way of your aspirations. Bhuvan (Amir Khan) wants the lagaan tax levied on his village to be removed, and fights the tyrannical British rulers. They issue an almost impossible challenge to remove the tax, that the villagers defeat them in a cricket match. Bhuvan accepts the challenge, without bothering to get the villagers' consent first.

An English proverb says 'Look before you leap', but if you sit staring at the ditch, you will never be able to accept the challenge and overcome it—neither will you leap, nor will your leap transform into flight! While chasing something big in life, instead of whining and complaining, you need to give it your all and go for it like a pole-vaulter. Bhuvan looks at the challenge as an opportunity in favour of the villagers and accepts it courageously. He not only accepts the challenge but prepares to face it squarely. He takes all the stakeholders into confidence and plans his moves.

We have an attitude where we want others to fight our battles, while we sit around doing nothing, accepting our fate and whatever comes our way. But Bhuvan is different. He does not have illusions about others helping him to win the match and takes up the initiative himself. He creates his own crude bat and ball, and plays trial matches with the kids. This draws the villagers' attention. Only when we close all doors to the past do doors to the future begin to open. Bhuvan takes a lot of revolutionary decisions and admits an 'untouchable' player in the team, going against the social norms of the time. We, too, will have to challenge a lot of social ills while working in our profession. We may have to fight well-heeled and powerful people.

The biggest lesson *Lagaan* teaches us is that despite having the weakest team, the village team is able to win because of the commitment, passion and determination of each member! Each member of this village team is unique and special. Even Chhatrapati Shivaji chose the right people for the right roles and achieved miraculous results and victories.

Whenever the English batsman hits the ball, all the fielders in Bhuvan's team chase it. Even in our profession, whenever we are faced with a crisis, everyone drops whatever they are doing and gets together to solve the crisis. But this creates new problems for us. That is why the leader should be aware of the strengths and weaknesses of each and every team member. For example, Kachra, in Bhuvan's team, was handicapped but he could spin the ball. Bhuvan was able to spot these special talents accurately. Similarly, Bhura was an expert at catching hens and had very sharp reflexes, which is why Bhuvan placed him in key fielding positions.

Once the team is finalized, all the team members must be clearly told about their goals and everyone's role should be clearly defined. The team leader should answer their questions and clear their apprehensions. Then the team leader brings all five fingers together to make a solid, tight fist that is ready to face the world! Hard work, right training and practice can make champions out of anyone. As they say, 'Necessity is the mother of invention.' You can make up for any shortcomings with sincere and creative efforts and ideas.

Bhuvan proved to us that even the most ordinary players can beat a strong and trained opponent, with team spirit. What is most important is to fight and give it your all till the very last second. Bhuvan was a leader who led from the front and never gave up hope till the end. He had complete trust in his team, and he helped those simple villagers achieve the impossible. Similarly, each one of us has immense courage and marvellous strength hidden within. To bring that power out with determination is the key to outdoor training.

Ashtanga yoga

Two sessions per week were allotted for yoga practice. The energetic yoga guru, in his sixties, explained to us in simple terms the importance of yoga in our daily lives. If done in the correct, traditional manner, yoga can prove to be something that will ensure your mental and physical well-being throughout your life. Yoga benefits every part, joint and organ of your body, mind and brain. When you do a task with full involvement and are into it with complete focus, it brings positive changes in you. Our personality takes shape based on our experiences, words, thoughts, relationships, emotions and feelings. This personality gets stuck within a frame and our bonds peg us down. Everything in the world is cyclic and keeps coming back.

For instance, at just a year old, it is an achievement even to stand up without support and walk without falling. At four, not wetting the pants is something great. At eight, coming home without losing our way is considered wonderful. At twelve, the definition of success changes even more and acceptance by our peers is the biggest achievement; at eighteen, getting to drive a vehicle seems ultimate.

In the early twenties, achievement means to become a graduate; at twenty-five, it is getting a good job and at thirty it is to raising a family. In the mid-thirties, we aspire to be in a stable job and earn well. At forty-five, hiding our real age and looking young becomes important. At fifty, educating our children well—their higher education—means success. By fifty-five, having fulfilled all our duties sincerely is considered successful. At sixty, being able to drive well and ensuring that our licence doesn't get revoked is a big thing. At sixty-five, all that matters is being free from illness; while at seventy, not being a burden on anyone is a mark of success. At seventy-five, keeping in touch with our old friends means success; while at eighty, we win if we can come home without forgetting our address. At eighty-six, not wetting our pants is an achievement; at ninety, being able to walk without support feels great. So, we see that life is a circle, a water wheel.

Sometimes we feel suffocated, trapped in this cycle and struggle to free ourselves from it, to express ourselves freely and allow our personalities to flower. Yoga is the bridge that helps us break the barriers, express ourselves spontaneously, be creative and develop a personality free from the ego. Yoga helps to free us from the confines of our personality and enables us to live in the present.

Sport is indeed a form of dynamic meditation, but if you want to make your mind sharp and as strong as your body, yoga is the path. Yoga is the most valuable contribution Indian culture has made to the world. The word yoga comes from the root word 'yuj', which means to join. Yoga brings the mind and body together. It does not involve just asanas, postures and meditation. According to Maharshi Patanjali, yoga means '*chitta vritti nirodhah*', which means 'removing the fluctuations of the mind'. Our minds are constantly bombarded by our senses—taste, smell, touch, sound and sight. Along with these, we also feel the associated emotions of anger, greed, jealousy, love and malice. These emotions, coupled with the sensory stimuli, are called 'vritti'. Yoga is the calming of this 'unsettled and wandering' mind. Yoga has eight (asht) arms (anga), hence 'ashtanga'—yama, niyama, asana, pranayama, pratyahara, dharana, dhyana and samadhi.

Yama includes truth (satya), non-violence (ahimsa), non-stealing (asteya), non-hoarding (aparigraha) and celibacy (brahmacharya). Niyama includes the rules and regulations of life such as cleanliness (shaucha), contentment (santosh), dutifulness (tapa), study (swadhya) and complete surrender to God (Ishwar prapti).

These two arms (yama and niyama) are important for the purification of the mind, and it is important to follow these before practising the third, i.e., asana. Asanas are the most visible and popular part of yoga. 'Sthira sukham asanam' means every asana should be 'steady' and 'comfortable'. Normally, we perform asanas for physical health, but if we follow yama and niyama, the benefits of the asanas will be far greater.

The fourth arm of yoga is 'pranayama', which means controlling breathing with awareness. Omkar, bhastrika, kapalabhati, anulom-vilom, bhraamari are types of pranayama that, when done for half an hour with focus, can improve both our inner strength and oxygen production in the body. All the pores get cleared, and the body gets energized. We feel energetic the whole day and always feel fresh.

The fifth arm of yoga is 'pratyahara', which enables us to control our sensory organs—the biggest challenge in our youth. There is a constant conflict between what the body wants and our restraint. To learn pratyahara, we need a trained master, and the best teachers in the world are our scriptures. These encourage us, show us the right path and prevent us from slipping away. We need to take the path of knowledge and contemplation while testing ourselves.

> *Yesham na vidya na tapo na danam, gyanam na sheelam nag una dharmah*
> *Te martyaloke bhuvibhaarabhoota, manushya roopena mrigascharanti*
>
> [Those who do not have learning, have no austerity, do not give to charity, have neither knowledge nor character, have no good qualities, no righteousness. They are nothing but a burden on this earth in the form of people and are animals that simply graze.]

When we fall for the demands of the senses, what is the difference between us and animals? This is the question that pratyahara allows us to answer.

The sixth arm is 'dharana', which means concentrating our minds on a single point. When you are able to do this over a prolonged period, it becomes 'dhyana'. In the state of dhyana, only the point of focus and concentration remains. Everything else melts away. The highest level of dhyana is samadhi, which is the eighth arm of yoga. In this state, the yogi forgets himself and his existence and becomes concentration personified.

The practical importance of yoga is described beautifully in the Bhagwad Gita as '*Yogah karmasu kaushalam*'. When a person accepts happiness and sorrow or loss and gain with the same calmness, that state is called yoga. In simple terms, skill in our karma or actions, or proficiency in actions, is called yoga. Our yogacharya at NPA made all the concepts of yoga clear to us. The yoga that I learnt in the academy is an integral part of my daily routine even today.

You can do yoga in the morning or in the evening, and both timings have their own benefits. You should take care not to eat anything at least half an hour before doing yoga. You shouldn't do asanas immediately after any other form of exercise. It is best to do yoga in an airy and open place, and if it is quiet, nothing like it! The mind and body should be peaceful and calm.

There are eighty-four asanas, but one need not know all of them. Sitting and working for hours together makes the back and neck stiff. It is said that our youth and fitness depend on the flexibility of our spine and back. That is why we should do asanas that are focused on the stomach and back. The rest of the organs will be taken care of automatically. Perform each asana for three to four minutes. Don't be in a particular pose for too long unnecessarily.

I do a few asanas daily. Always start yoga practice with chanting the Omkara and the Gayatri mantra. Then perform twelve Suryanamaskar while chanting the twelve names of the Sun god and prepare your body for the asanas. Suryanamaskar helps to stretch the whole body and loosens all the joints. You need to rest and take at least five deep breaths before every asana. All the muscles of the stomach and the back get energized by doing Pavanamuktasana. It helps in reducing indigestion and constipation. It aids in improving appetite. Sarvangasana makes the spinal column flexible and strong. It is very useful in the treatment of thyroid problems. Matsyasana stimulates all the glands and strengthens the neck, waist and spine. Bhujangasana is also called the cobra pose, and it stretches every muscle in the back and the spine. It helps in removing tiredness.

Shalabhasana benefits the liver, kidneys and pancreas. It exercises the body parts below the waist. Dhanurasana stretches the stomach and prevents visceral problems and spinal issues. Chakrasana reduces the girth of our waist while Mayurasana strengthens our arms and prevents diabetes and piles. Yoga Mudra helps strengthen the hands, legs, spine, hips and lungs. Abdominal fat is reduced. Doing Padmasana regularly builds concentration and strengthens the legs and hips. Sheersasana improves blood flow to the brain and helps cure problems related to the eyes, nose and throat. You should begin and end yoga practice with Shavasana. It regulates our blood circulation and relaxes the mind and body.

Yoganidra

Yoganidra is an effective way to reduce stress. We can perform yoganidra whenever we are tired and have slept very little. Whenever I work late at night and don't get enough time to rest, I perform yoganidra. I get immense energy by doing this after heavy exercise. You will remain fresh the whole day. There are fifteen-minutes to two-hour-long videos of yoganidra on YouTube in different languages.

Yoganidra is a kind of spiritual sleep, where we are asleep, yet aware and conscious. According to the Puranas, the gods rest in this way. Our yoga guru taught us this magical method. In this method, suggestions are given for stress relief. This is a creative conversation that hypnotizes the person in a positive way. It improves our personality; helps rid us of our bad habits; and controls blood pressure, diabetes, headaches, asthma, insomnia, joint pains, and neck and spine problems. The auto-suggestions and resolutions made during yoganidra are extremely useful during sports and winning tough campaigns.

Yoganidra should be performed in a peaceful place. You should be dressed in comfortable and loose-fitting clothes. You should lie on a mat in Shavasana, with your feet about a foot and a half apart. Your hands should be six inches away from your body. Keep your body still. Try to still your mind but don't block your thoughts. Relax your mind and body. Inhale and exhale deeply. Listen to the instructions of the yoga instructor carefully. If you are not listening to outside instructions and doing yoganidra on your own, then give auto-suggestions to yourself. Move towards hypnosis through your auto-suggestions. Focus on one body part at a time and relax it.

Once the whole body is relaxed and ready for yoganidra, mentally state your resolutions. These could be for reducing your worries, getting rid of bad habits and addictions, or improving your attitude and personality. In this hypnotic and aware state, we can mentally visit the most beautiful and sacred places on earth and enjoy them. We can invoke our favourite deities and have a conversation with them. This is a visualization technique that activates the chakras in our bodies. In the final stage of yoganidra, the mind is focused on the mid-brows, and the resolutions are repeated. It is ended with deep breaths and Omkara chanting. You will feel that all your negativity has been drained, and the body and mind are purified, cleansed and energized—inside-out, as if your batteries have been charged.

Such healthy habits were inculcated in us at the academy. We assimilated them into our lives and implemented them in the police force for their well-being.

Swimming

I used to splash around with my friends in the river, lakes and ponds a lot in my childhood. We enjoyed diving into deep wells. Our weekends and vacations during summer and Diwali were spent in the fields, rivers, hills and pastures. When the water from the dam would be released, jumping from the bridge into the cascading waters was nothing less than nirvana! The ego would melt and flow away with the gurgling, rustling and gushing waters. The water level would shrink in summer, and the dam gates would be closed. The farmers would dig deep into the dry riverbed until the pits they dug filled up with slushy water. Then they would use engines to pump this water out and to their fields. We were so crazy about swimming that we wouldn't hesitate to jump into those muddy pits with reddish mud. Our bodies would be red with the mud. I do not remember falling ill because of ingesting the muddy water or catching a cold after roaming around dripping wet. That was our swimming!

Our gang of friends would assemble at the riverbank, and we would hang from the overhanging branches of trees and jump into the water. The pleasure of floating along with the current is indescribable! I was extremely fond of water and swimming. Real swimming means doing it in a disciplined way in a swimming pool, and I was eagerly looking forward to swimming in the blue waters of a swimming pool.

Till I reached the academy I only knew how to jump into water like a frog and would thereafter just manage to keep my head above water and reach the banks kicking my legs. Now we were going to undergo formal swimming coaching in the academy. Back home, we swam in the river in our underwear or khaki shorts. In our college days, we would don underwear with elastic waistbands for swimming. When we went swimming in the river in childhood, many of our friends had holes in their underwear! The village women would come to the river to wash clothes, and it would be a tough task for us to avoid being seen in our tattered underwear. Sometimes, we would scrub ourselves clean in the soapy froth from the clothes they were washing. This is how our swimming and water sport is till date.

We had to buy a list of swimwear items for our swimming lessons—special trunks for swimming, goggles, swimming cap and sunscreen lotion to prevent getting tanned. We couldn't just jump into the pool as we had in childhood. We had to take a shower in the changing room and be in proper swimming gear before getting into the pool. The Olympic size, 50 metre pool in the academy was excellent. The names of the annual swimming champions shone on the board at the entrance to the aquatic centre. Our hearts filled with pride seeing Ashok Kamte Sir's name for the 1988 batch. My excitement knew no bounds. Swimming was child's play for me. I wasn't very good at other games, but I was determined to be the swimming champion.

It was the first day, and I was keen to show my rustic talent. I got into the pool, splashed about vigorously and began swimming but soon realized that I was really slow compared to the others. Also, my random hand movements were coming in the way of the other swimmers. I was splashing so hard that water was spilling out of the pool. Rawat Ustad walked over to the edge and said, 'Sahib, if you swim like this it will take you an hour to cover 50 metres, and you will surely send a few of your friends to the hospital with the movement of your hands!' I was a little embarrassed and came out of the pool to understand what mistakes I was making.

Rawat Ustad started telling me the basics. 'Sahib, swimming is a disciplined sport where you have to learn different strokes. You must rotate your hands from the shoulder joint, push the water behind and move forward. In freestyle and backstroke, you should use each hand alternately while in breaststroke both the hands are used simultaneously. The hands and feet must move in coordination. There is a particular way in which you take your head out of water to breathe. The breathing technique must be rhythmic. You are not competing with others but with water. Thinking about others will unnecessarily tense you and you spend more energy. You will be tired, your speed will reduce, and you will lose your form and rhythm. One should use all the energy while keeping the wrists loose as you pull the water back, thus propelling your body forward. It's an important moment when your body's stance changes from pulling to moving forward. So, *dum lagaake haisha*!'

I tried swimming keeping in mind the tips that Rawat Ustad had given, but the moment my face went under water, I felt suffocated. I was not able to get the rhythm between my arms and neck. In the next lane, a lady trainee was swimming ahead fast. She was an expert at all the strokes and swam effortlessly like a dolphin, and was able to cover the 50 metre distance easily. My inferiority complex increased further. I had to win at least in swimming. I dreamt of seeing a Marathi name again on the champions board after Kamte Sir.

The term was about to end. The coach called out, 'Do any of you know how to dive?' He was looking for volunteers to demonstrate diving from sixteen feet and twenty-five feet diving boards. Atul and Amitabh stepped forward eagerly. I, too, was itching to show my skills at the academy. I had jumped into the river from the trees and dived into deep wells in childhood. I had to take the risk and prove my worth. I went ahead. The coach asked me, 'You know how to dive, don't you?' My heart skipped a beat, but I nodded. Atul and Amitabh went right up to the twenty-five feet diving board and dived into the pool gracefully. Diving from sixteen feet didn't seem difficult for me. But since the other two had dived from twenty-five feet, it had become a prestige issue for me. I climbed up the steps gingerly. My legs were wobbly, and my stomach was knotted. I reached the board and my legs began to tremble. I was breathless and my heart was racing. My batchmates were egging me on from below, but I did hear a few voices that said, 'He won't be able to do it!' I shut my eyes tight and dived off the board with all my might. But my body let me down. Instead of entering the water gracefully, I fell flat on my stomach with a loud noise and the water went splashing out.

My stomach and groin were hurting badly as were my thighs. My stomach and chest were red as though they had been painted. I had come up for air, but was unable to move my hands. The coach realized that I had dived wrong and chucked an inflated tube at me, which I held on to and managed to come out. I tried my best to act nonchalant, but my red chest was telling the story. I couldn't walk properly for a week. I learnt that day that a champion is not made in a day—it needs years of effort to become one.

Recently, I heard about the inspiring life of the winner of twenty-three gold medals in Olympic swimming—Michael Phelps. Our entire country hasn't won these many medals till date. Six feet tall, handsome and with a chiselled body, Michael Phelps swims one lakh yards in a week. During his preparations for the Olympics, he would be seen either in the pool or in bed. He would write down his goals clearly and follow them to the last word. Though he had written down his goals for the next five, ten and twenty years, his focus would be on the next race and his practice. He says:

> I focus only on my lane. I have nothing to do with what others are doing. I only do what is important for me and think only for myself. I have removed the word' impossible' from my dictionary. And hence my possibilities have expanded, and I have achieved even seemingly impossible goals with ease.

For this strikingly good-looking Olympic gold medal winner, to keep himself fit and swim seven days a week must have meant giving up on so many luxuries and temptations. Life becomes a penance, and sacrifice becomes the main mantra of life. Phelps never got affected by people who trolled him out of jealousy and malice. He used those words as fuel to propel him forward.

If you want to achieve the heights of success in sports, like Phelps did, you need to have patience and resilience. If you have the guts, tell the world your dreams and achieve them with the snap of a finger. Measure your strengths and weaknesses accurately, and strive to become the best in what you are good at. You must be able to assemble the dream team that can take you to your goals. Start with baby steps, then take long steps, jump, leap and pole vault … take calculated and assured steps towards your milestones. Be disciplined to the core, forget disillusionment and disappointments; focus only on success. You must be steadfast about your goal and not allow anything or anyone to come in the way. You should not let go of the reins till you achieve what you have set out to achieve.

I had to work hard to master swimming. It was difficult for me to achieve it within ten months along with the other courses at the academy and our packed schedules. I decided to do as much as I could under the circumstances. I learnt all the strokes properly and have been practising them sincerely till today to keep myself fit and healthy. I want to add that swimming is a complete exercise and makes you strong inside out. If you can swim for an hour a day, you will be able to breathe as deeply as a snake and run as fast as a cheetah. The cold water helps rid your body of your lethargy, and all your aches and pains. Swimming improves your clarity and thinking power by leaps and bounds.

The new generation and health

I have faced a lot of challenges in my twenty-two years of service in the police force. I have experienced several ups and downs and faced intense physical and mental stress. I have gone for days without sleep and rest. I have faced a lot of casualties and adversities. I have fallen ill, but this strong body gave me the power to face all these challenges with poise. The foundations for building this strong and healthy body were laid at the academy. As we know, 'A healthy mind resides in a healthy body.' The inputs I received at the academy for developing a strong body and sound mind transformed into habits, and they have played an important role in my life.

Exercise is important to develop all-round health. Absence of disease doesn't mean health. Holistic health means providing the body and mind with the best physical, mental, ethical, and spiritual inputs. With increasing progress in the medical field and all its various specialities, the identification of illnesses and disorders, too, has increased. In this fast-paced life, we have completely neglected our health. Neck and back problems and digestive disorders have become chronic. Diabetes, cancer, and other such diseases are destroying our youth. Till one suffers a major disease and gets bedridden, they do not appreciate the importance of health. The main reason for all this is stress and an undisciplined lifestyle. A little bit of age-appropriate, regular exercise is the simplest way to keep healthy. As they say in Marathi, *jo hitabhook, mitabhook ani ritabhook asto, to nirogi asto*. One who eats healthy food, eats in limited quantities and has earned the money to buy food by ethical means is healthy. Health is something that cannot be bought from a medical store or from reputed hospitals. It must be earned through hard work and cannot be stored for the future. It is a work in progress.

I had neglected physical exercise till my early twenties due to my studies, but it didn't affect me much because of my youth. I received the key to health at the academy at the age of twenty-four. I have kept it safe and have been using it to open new locks of energy and capabilities every single day. That is the reason my life has been full of energy, youthful and disease free. It is said that you should use the '21/90' formula for changing your lifestyle and habits. Once you do something new consistently for twenty-one days, it becomes a habit and transforms into your lifestyle in ninety days!

I had ten months at the academy!

Once you invest time and energy in improving your mind and body in your youth, it will ensure a perfect life in the future. Some people become excited about exercise after seeing their favourite film stars and TV stars and their six-pack abs. The message that girls fall for men with six-pack abs is constantly reinforced in movies and on TV. The young men get influenced and burn themselves out in the gym doing strenuous workouts for six-pack abs. Some consume steroids and poor-quality proteins in the race to exhibit their rippling muscles! These artificial supplements are said to cause brittle bones, invite kidney problems and other serious health hazards. A few even fall prey to the waves of new fad diets and may get addicted to them. Not following the scientific and traditionally proven methods lead to diseases. For example, running long-distance marathons causes knee problems leading to surgery.

So, what should one do?

I am forty-seven years old now but can run 42 km non-stop because I have built my mind and body constructively over the past twenty-three years. If one tries to run a marathon without any proper preparation, they are bound to develop chronic knee and other problems. However, if one practises regularly and diligently, they can run even the Ultraman, or the Ironman challenge. My batchmate Krishna Prakash has completed these in record time. The Ultraman challenge lasts for three days and involves running 84 km, cycling 450 km and swimming 10 km in the Pacific Ocean. Believe me, it is possible! But only with regular, unstinted practice and organized training. To succeed in such torturous challenges, every muscle, ligament, tendon and joint of the body must be trained. One must consume healthy and nutritious food and keep away from any bad habits and addictions. It is no less than a penance! Do you know how much time Usain Bolt has spent on the Olympic track? Just two and a half minutes! And these two and half minutes have earned him crores of dollars. But there is a lifetime of hard work, sweat and blood behind these couple of minutes. There is no point in digging a well after you are thirsty. Similarly, if you want to keep yourself away from disease you need to exercise. You need to understand your mind and body prepare a proper plan for its upkeep and follow it with discipline.

We were taught anatomy and physiology in detail, along with practicals at the academy. Our time at the academy, sweating it out during our physical training has stood like a rock and shown us the path to a healthy and disease-free life.

A healthy body and its care

We were taught exercises in a systematic manner at the academy. There are two types of exercises—aerobic and anaerobic. Aerobic exercises are also called 'cardio exercises' and include walking, running, swimming, mountain climbing, dancing and marathons. These exercises need resilience and patience. Aerobic exercises are those that use oxygen in the muscles. Anaerobic exercises include weightlifting, sprints, push-ups; you will feel breathless within a few minutes. Your body should get warmed up properly before doing exercises of the joints and the muscles. The body should also be cooled down after a workout. If this is not done, there will be more damage than good. Exercises should be performed for our fitness and well-being at all levels—mental, physical and spiritual.

These days we see a lot of our youth suffering from conditions such as cervical spondylitis, indigestion, breathing problems, obesity, high cholesterol, insomnia, diabetes and joint pains. All this is caused by cortisol. Extreme stress, unhealthy competition, addiction to mobiles and internet, lack of discipline and planning in life is causing an elevation in cortisol levels. By the time we realize the importance of health and a healthy lifestyle, it is too late. That is why it is important to change our diet, do exercise and make necessary changes in our lifestyle right now. Nutritious food, exercise and adequate sleep are the three cornerstones of health.

The human body is a magnificent creation. Our veins and blood vessels are sixty miles long. Our heart pumps about sixty lakh litres of blood in an average lifespan of seventy-five years. During the same period, it beats over 350 crore times. Each of our kidneys has about ten lakh filters. Our ears can pick up over 1,600 frequencies of sounds. Close to 12,600 white blood corpuscles travel to every corner of our body and protect us from infectious organisms. If we spread out the alveoli or air sacs of the lungs, they can cover an entire tennis court. Our body is such a complex and brilliant creation! In short, health can be achieved only with our own hard work and efforts and not from hospitals or medical stores. This is not a one-time activity whose results stay for a lifetime; it has to be worked on every single day.

These days, doctors have boards with lines of degrees and specializations of all kinds. They offer all kinds of tests and surgeries in hospitals. I am not saying that all this is useless, but it is important to see if some of the tests and surgeries can be avoided. Let me give you a personal example. I was thirty years old and posted as SP at Latur. I was fit and healthy. Our family had gone to Essel World in Mumbai for an outing. The water park there has a slide named 'Black Demon'. It is a ride in which you have to slide through a 40 metre-long dark pipe really fast. My brother, Vikas, and I went for the ride with great excitement. Before one person reaches the bottom, the guard does not send the next person, but he did.

I went up first and was sliding down, controlling my speed, when the guard allowed Vikas to ride when I was only halfway down. Vikas is about 15 kg heavier than me and he came down at a rapid speed towards me. Before I could understand what was happening, I had fallen into the water. And when Vikas came and fell hard into the water, his leg hit my neck. My head reeled but I maintained my balance and came up. My shoulders and right hand were paining severely. I came back to Latur with excruciating pain and got an MRI scan of my vertebral column. The cartilage between the fourth and fifth vertebrae had got damaged and was impinging on the nerves. That is why my shoulder and hands were hurting so badly.

The doctor put me on traction and put weights on my shoulder and legs. I remained on the bed for a month, but the pain remained. Finally, I was referred to a reputed hospital in Pune where three or four neurosurgeons and orthopaedics conducted different tests and decided that they needed to do an operation on my spinal column. Coincidentally, a friend of my father-in-law, Dr Dayanand Dongavkar came to see me. He objected to the surgery and asked me to get admitted to a naturopathy clinic for rest. I went to the ashram and got some massages done, ate simple, wholesome meals and rested well. The rest and simple living reduced my stress. My acidity came down and the inflammation of my nerves reduced on its own. The pain and the numbness in my hands slowly disappeared. Once the pain receded, I began gentle exercises for the spine and started picking up light weights. I still follow some of the habits I picked up there. For example, I don't use a pillow; I stretch myself every two hours while travelling and don't bend down and keep looking at my mobile constantly. I wear a neck supporting collar while travelling so that I don't jerk my neck when I doze off.

I have not had the cervical spondylitis problem in the last sixteen years. Moreover, I am able to lift heavy weights and run marathons, play six sets of tennis at a stretch and cycle for miles. What if I had listened to those specialists and undergone spinal surgery at the age of thirty? What if the surgery had failed? They had told me that my voice box could have been affected by the surgery. They had warned me that I wouldn't be able to lift weights or run too much, which meant that I would have invited handicaps! I strongly believe in nature. Human body is called 'prakriti' or nature in Sanskrit. If there is some problem with the body, it produces the systems to fight it. But to keep this army within the body fit, we need to exercise, eat well and take good care of our bodies.

In today's hybrid times, our bodies and minds are trapped in the mire of pollution and bad habits. We are moving away from our fundamental nature and falling into ill health and instability. Our grains, fruits and vegetables are being poisoned by chemicals, fertilizers, insecticides and pesticide sprays. Adulterated milk is causing heart problems in children. The worst danger is from antibiotics that people take for every small health problem such as a sore throat, a cough, cold, flu and fever. This has damaged our body's immunity and resistance.

The World Health Organization (WHO) has named this health risk of pandemic proportions the 'antibiotics resistance crisis'. Due to the excessive and indiscriminate use of antibiotics, the treatment of diseases such as pneumonia, tuberculosis, venereal diseases and poisoning has become increasingly difficult. Antibiotics are used to prevent infection from bacteria, but once these bacteria mutate or change form, the antibiotics become ineffective. Once the bacteria become resistant to the antibiotic, the risk of infection increases and treatment becomes extremely difficult. This causes an increase in incidences of hospitalization, medical expenses and death.[13]

In his final days, when my father was unwell, twenty-three out of twenty-four antibiotics were ineffective. He was not able to fight his pneumonia. The doctors explained it this way—his body was being attacked with AK 47 rifles but was fighting back with sticks. We lost the battle eventually. My father suffered for four months in hospital before he breathed his last. We were all just mute spectators. Antibiotic pills and injections are taken like chocolates and peppermints by people in small towns and villages. We look for instant remedies, and it is believed that a doctor who doesn't give tablets and injections is worthless.

In the West, antibiotics are given as a last resort, while for us it is the first option. We must stop this indiscriminate use of antibiotics at the earliest. Along with this, we have to alter our lifestyle. We need to get vaccinated, wash our hands, build our immunity, do regular exercise, have safe sex and eat a healthy and nutritious diet to prevent infections.

The book *New Dimensions of Healing* says that there is a close relationship between virtues and positive intentions, and our mental health.[14] Empathy heals our heart and improves our digestion power. Courage keeps our kidneys and urinary bladder strong. Chastity keeps our spleen healthy. The spleen is

---

13 Antibiotic resistance, WHO, 2020, https://tinyurl.com/4ru3jabz

14 T. Saraydarian (1992), *New Dimensions of Healing*, Cave Creek, AZ: TSG Publishing Inc.

strengthened by the satisfaction we get from art and beautiful things. Service and a helpful nature detoxify our muscles and keep our lymphatic system strong and capable of fighting diseases. Love and generosity keep the electric impulses in our nervous system active. Naturally, our life span improves. Forgiveness heals our mental and physical wounds, while patience removes all problems related to our reproductive system. An optimistic attitude toughens our pancreas and every hopeful thought sends a positive electric impulse to the pancreas. Empathy and sympathy improve our eyesight, while silence and polite speech work as a tonic for the thyroid gland. I am not aware of the scientific logic behind this, but I agree with it a 100 per cent.

Like Samarth Ramdas has said: *Mana sajjana bhakti panthechi jaave, tari shreehari pavije to swabhave. Janeen nidhyate sarvasoduni dyaave. Janeen vandyate sarvabhave karaavo.* [Let us follow the path of honesty and devotion. This path will lead us to Shri Hari. Let us shun everything that is condemned and do everything that is commendable with the full devotion of mind.] At NPA, we received positive inputs and words throughout the day. We developed good habits and performed good deeds by assimilating those inputs. These were shaping the effective virtuous character of the IPS officers and laying the foundations of a bright future.

5

Indoor Training

The academy was determined to make all the trainees not only physically fit but also well-versed in law, skilled in crime investigation and able administrators. Tests were conducted regularly, and the marks we got in these internal assessments were included in our final academic evaluation. We had weekly holidays only on Sunday and the entire day would be spent preparing for the tests. Our director, Mr Rajagopal, had started this system from our batch and we were quite upset about it. Our indoor training was under Mahendra Reddy Sir from the Andhra Pradesh cadre. He had a quiet and serious personality, and he explained the importance of indoor training:

> We are going to give you the skills and knowledge required to be excellent police officers at the academy. You will develop new facets of your personality every single day. You will learn new subjects and gather new information daily. For that, you need to keep your eyes and ears open, your brain sharp and alert. You are in this academy to develop the necessary skills, gain knowledge

and inculcate good habits. Once you complete your training, you will hold senior posts in the service. Apart from the force, people, media, political leaders and senior officers will have their eyes on you. Every moment is going to be a challenge and we are going to prepare you to face them. We will guide you on appropriate social behaviour and attitudes. Your organizational abilities and decision-making skills will be honed here.

Our responsibilities change with societal changes. Hence you and your staff need to keep your knowledge and skills updated. Change can happen suddenly and take you by surprise. If you are not trained properly and prepared well, you won't be able to handle these situations effectively. If we gather all the information and take administrative steps before a man-made or natural emergency strikes, we will be less affected. We will show you situation-specific examples of creative, inventive and novel ways of handling them. The police force is an inseparable and important part of the criminal justice system. You will be given high-class professional and technical inputs, but people-oriented policing is as important as knowing scientific investigative techniques. Moreover, you will also be responsible for maintaining law and order. At the academy, you will be trained to be scholarly but sensitive police leaders.

Reddy Sir clearly spelt out his role. After field training till 8.30 a.m., we would go for breakfast and, thereafter, change into our civil dress and tie and be in class by 9.30 a.m. Grilling physical training earlier in the morning followed by a sumptuous breakfast made it difficult to sit through the boring theory classes with our eyes open in the air-conditioned classrooms. Many of my classmates would be snoring with their eyes open. Some took advantage of the darkness during the PowerPoint presentations and slept on the back benches. Realizing this, the administration removed the ACs and got us used to sitting under the hot breeze from the fans in the oppressive heat of Hyderabad!

Investigation skills and regimentation

A model police station has been erected within the academy premises. We were given detailed information about the various duties and responsibilities and explained the ideal organization and management of a police station. We were able to see up close, the way in which a crime, including the witness testimony or 'panchnama', was recorded and how a crime scene was investigated. We were shown demonstrations of the investigation procedure, procedure for arrest, recording statements and first information reports (FIRs). We were given in-depth training on how to investigate various types of crime such as dowry harassment, thefts, robberies, accidents, murders and small-time quarrels. We were taught how to handle crowds and maintain law and order through rehearsals on the field. We were taught counselling and its role in crime control and investigation. We got to know the difficulties faced by the constables while on night patrol only after we experienced them first-hand. We learnt new ways and ideas for making our police stations more modern and active.

We have seen in movies, how the police arrive at the crime spot only after the crime is done. If they are lucky, they might be able to pursue the offender and capture him. Once the offender is caught, he/she is arrested, a case is registered, and a chargesheet filed in court. At NPA, we were taught the basics of how to solve a crime when the criminal had not yet been caught and when there was no clue available. This was taught to us through simulation experiments.

There are several stages in the process from the time the crime is committed till the final report is submitted in court. Once the police officer visits the crime scene, she/he collects all the physical, forensic and scientific evidence. The crime scene is cordoned off with tape to prevent the destruction of evidence. Proper assessments are made, and the witness testimonies are recorded in the presence of Panch witnesses. Photographs of the crime scene are taken and the measurements are taken. All the eyewitnesses, people related to the crime and onlookers are questioned in detail.

All eyewitnesses are interrogated in person, separately, because each one might have a different version of the crime. If any of them is found to have seen something related to the crime or heard something or has been in contact with the accused in any way, they are questioned very carefully because their statements are very important. All these details are recorded by the investigating officer, along with his own observations in a formulated manner, and this case diary is sent to the other investigating officers, senior police officers and the public prosecutor, so that they get a complete understanding of the case. Based on the evidence and information available, the crime is reconstructed and the next steps are determined. If the accused is hiding somewhere, raids are conducted to nab him. More evidence is collected based on the search and seizure, for which an official and legal order must be received from the court.

Investigative abilities, experience and professional execution, are all very important while cracking a case. During training we were taught how to investigate in depth, how to note the minutest of details and prepare a logical and watertight case. The position of the killer, bloodstains, clothes, the condition of the light (how bright or dark), temperature and many such factors are noted accurately. Fingerprints and biological evidence for the DNA test are submitted to laboratories for testing without any waste of time. Every link in the chain, from the time of evidence collection to its testing and producing in court, is recorded meticulously.

Interrogating the accused carefully and catching any inconsistency in the statement is an important skill. Getting a forensic report is an expensive and time-consuming exercise. It is faster to get the accused to confess to the crime by interrogating in a professional manner. Interrogation is not a skill but a science. At the academy, we were given basic training on how to gain the trust of the accused, understand their body language and make them talk.

Behavioural science and the study of body language are very helpful in untying the various knots in the crime. We are strictly instructed to avoid using third-degree methods to get a confession, because these go against human rights, but have heard of several police officers using them as shortcuts to extract a confession. Good investigating officers should use their interrogating skills and other tricks to make the accused talk. We need to be alert and ensure that no innocent person ends up behind bars due to our selfishness or negligence.

There will be a lot of cases in your career that will test your brain and challenge you. Criminals use their skills and brains to ensure that they don't leave behind any clues or evidence while committing the crime. There is often a contest between the police and the criminal, like the story of the monkeys and the cap seller. The story goes like this: there was a cap seller who went from village to village selling caps. He had to cross a jungle on the way. Whenever he was hungry, he would put his box of caps down, eat his packed lunch and take a nap under the shade of a tree. One day, when he awakened from his nap, he saw that his box of caps was open. Monkeys sitting on a tree had picked up all the caps and were playing with them and trying them on.

The cap seller noticed that the monkeys copied everything he did. When he threw a stone at them, they hit him with the fruits on the trees. He sat, his hand on his head not knowing what to do next. The monkeys imitated that too. Seeing this, the cap seller stood up and threw his cap into the empty box. Seeing him throw the cap into the box, the monkeys pulled off the caps from their heads and threw them into the box. The cap seller shut the box and walked away from there. The moral of the story is that you need to inspect well. *You should not get nervous in times of adversity; you should work cleverly and wisely.*

I read the second part of this story recently.

The cap seller's grandson too was walking through a jungle with a box of caps on his head. The cap seller had taught him the trade and told him about the incident with the monkeys. Coincidentally, the grandson too sat under the same tree, ate his lunch and went to sleep. When he got up, he saw that the box was open, and the monkeys had taken away his caps. He remembered his grandfather's experience and the trick he had told him. He confidently pulled off his cap and flung it into the empty box and waited for the monkeys to do the same, but none of them did. As he looked up in annoyance, the big leader of the monkeys came down from the tree, gave the boy a tight slap and said, 'Are you the only one who has a grandfather? Like your grandfather told you about us, our grandfather too told us about you. Now, get lost from here!'

What do we learn from the second version?

Never underestimate anyone. Like we have gurus, they too will have their own advisors. A 'one size fits all' approach doesn't always work. The same key cannot open all doors. We need to change not only the keys, but also locks. We need to move from regular lockers to digital lockers, or someone can rob us of our valuables. Like the police undergo training, thieves have their own drills. Even prisons are places where such training is imparted. Plots are hatched and foolproof plans are made to ensure success.

The Muthoot robbery case was one such incident in my career. It took place in Nashik. A software engineer was killed during a daring robbery in the commercial district in broad daylight. The robber escaped and the media trashed the police force. Editorials were written against me. A reputed TV channel ran a prime-time debate titled, 'What's happening in Nangre Patil's Nashik?'

Being the police commissioner, the responsibility lay with me. Rumours of my transfer began flying, but I kept my cool, took my team into confidence and got to work patiently. I opened the bag of tricks I had learnt at the academy and managed to crack this extremely challenging and tough robbery case. It was like finding a needle in a haystack, but we arrested the robbers and put them in prison under the Maharashtra Control of Organized Crime Act, 1999 (MCOCA) with stiff punishment. The newspapers that had thrashed us were now patting the back of the Nashik police and wrote columns after columns singing our praises. The channel that had run a negative series in my name was now doing positive stories saying, 'Nangre Patil saved the day'. All this was possible only due to a combination of three factors—hard work, patience and knowledge. This was a case study of how to find the whereabouts of the criminals without any clues whatsoever, and how the evidence was linked and the case solved.

It occurred on the morning of 14 June 2019, when six men armed with pistols stormed into the 'Muthoot Gold Finance' bank at 11.30 a.m. They knew that the bank lockers had mortgaged gold worth Rs 16 crore. As per their plan of action, the six men barged in and held all the employees and customers hostage at gunpoint. But one of the employees, twenty-nine-year-old Keralite Saji Samuel, rang the alarm. The brave young man fought the robbers single-handedly, but his efforts proved inadequate. The robbers fired five bullets into his abdomen and the brave heart breathed his last before medical help could arrive. The robbers were taken by surprise by the alarm, and in the ensuing confusion, they ran away without taking even a gram of gold.

We began our investigation and checked all the highways and travel routes. We put up barricades and checked residential locations. We obtained CCTV footage and interrogated individuals with criminal records. We spread our net of informers but got no clues. The robbers had planned their crime very meticulously. The six robbers in the gang didn't even know each other's real names, and none of them used mobile phones. They had conducted a detailed survey of the crime scene eight months earlier. Three separate teams had checked Google Maps and verified escape routes. Each one had a specific role. Pappu had convinced the guard to unlock the shutter saying that he had to mortgage a gold chain. For such a large establishment, there was only a single guard on duty, and he weighed just 47 kg.

The robbers easily overpowered the guard and walked into the bank and took over the place. Unfortunately for them, Saji Samuel was working in the same office. The moment he came to know of the attack, he sounded the alarm bell. Confusion and chaos spread the moment the alarm bell rang. The robbers panicked, caught Saji Samuel and beat him up. Saji tried to fight back but he couldn't cope for too long. Three of the robbers opened fire and shot Saji dead. The whole drama lasted six minutes, and because of Saji's presence of mind and bravery, the robbers could not loot anything and had to run away empty-handed. The planning and execution of this crime was the brainchild of dangerous criminal Subodh Singh, who hatched this plot sitting in the Behur jail in Patna. Under his leadership, the gang had attacked several such gold finance offices in several parts of the country and looted quintals of gold. As per the information gathered by Subodh, the Nashik office had gold worth Rs 16 crore. The plan was that if they succeeded, each one would get a crore worth of gold. Subodh selected his team from across the country and did a recce of the Nashik office three times. When two of the gang members were shot dead by the Bihar police in an encounter, the plan had to be put on hold.

The plan took off again in May. The robbers observed the movements and activities of the Nashik office employees carefully and noted the routes they took to come and go. They procured the motorcycle and the tempo needed for the crime, and changed their number plates and chassis numbers to Nashik number plates. They bought six pistols and bullets. They did not come in contact with anyone other than a local security guard in Nashik, named Subhash Goud. They also planned their escape meticulously. Their robbery failed, but they were able to escape on their three bikes. They changed their clothes and partners before they fled on their bikes.

We received information about the robbery attempt within ten minutes of the incident. We matched the description of the robbers and their number plates with the CCTV footage. We sent information about the robbery to police stations all over the state. We created ten teams to investigate the crime. We got our first link when we received information that the robbers had abandoned their bikes 25 km away from Nashik. Our forensic team reached the spot and checked the bikes carefully. But all the three numbers were false, and the chassis numbers had been pressed and destroyed. But the law catches up sooner or later!

We got our trail from the forensic tests. We checked records of lakhs of bikes manufactured at the Chakan Bajaj motor factory. From the information we dug out, we reached a dealer in Surat and then to the owners of the bikes. We were able to reach the second level of connections who gave us all the details. Our team, disguised as Bihari locals, sat in wait in a village close to Patna, and one by one we had all the pawns in our net.

Through this episode, I want to bring out the importance of patience and common sense during investigations. We need to use the information gathered, analyse it thoroughly and once sure that the target is in range, nab him. Usually, the police officer becomes lax once the criminal is caught, but the real task is to produce the accused in court and all the evidence collected should stand during the cross-examination. The effectiveness of an investigation is tested by whether the crime is proven. The police officer's skill is in collecting the evidence diligently, preparing the case papers professionally and presenting them in court. As a result, the culprit should get the appropriate punishment and learn his lesson.

Such police officers receive praise from the courts too. What is needed to achieve this level of professionalism is an in-depth knowledge of the law, understanding of how the courts function, awareness of scientific methods of investigation and skilful compilation of reports. It is also important to study and update oneself with the judgements made by the high courts and the Supreme Court and the changes in the various laws.

Etiquette and formal dinners

The academy had taken painstaking efforts to instil grace and etiquette in us. We had to salute our seniors. All of us had to stand up in attention whenever the officials entered the classroom. We had to take appointments from our seniors in case we had to register a complaint. We were expected to apologize immediately if we made a mistake. The penalty for falsehood was most severe. We could not argue or fight with anyone. Disciplinary action was taken if any of us created unnecessary hassles. We were expected to behave very respectfully and politely with women. In case we fell ill we could go to the dispensary only after getting the requisite permissions. It was impossible for us to bunk classes or take leave without permission. It was very difficult to get leave unless it was an emergency. The academy worked towards making all this a part of our lives.

We were sent for a four-day jungle camp to the rocky areas near Hyderabad. We were exhausted after the day-long route march and field tactics practice. The camp was supposed to end on Saturday. We were looking forward to a day's rest on Sunday but were informed that the camp would continue on to Sunday as well. We had to trek up a hill in the blazing summer heat. All of us were very annoyed because we didn't want to give up our Sunday. We decided to rebel and refused to have breakfast on Sunday, did the bare minimum and returned to the camp. We had come back famished and found that there was no lunch cooked for us. So we completed the day's training and returned to the academy. The director was waiting to welcome us. He expressed his displeasure at our behaviour. He spoke to us, beginning with the four lines that his havildar had said during their training:

> There is no single treatment for every illness. '*Laaton ke bhoot, baaton se nahi maante*,' which can be loosely translated as 'at times, a hard kick works better than soft words'. You will be trained in the language that you understand best. Once you leave the academy, you will be faced with law and order problems, serious man-made and natural disasters. Under such circumstances,

> will you sit on a hunger strike in protest saying you won't work on a holiday? Or will you go out and face the challenge? It is for you to decide. Your life mission is to save lives and the peoples' belongings. Remember, you have no option of running away from your duty. You must work on a war footing day in and day out! Those of you who don't accept this or can't understand it can resign immediately and leave the academy.

Sense was knocked into our heads by keeping us hungry and giving us a rap on the knuckles. We learnt our lesson the hard way. We must inculcate obedience and respectful behaviour first. We must follow the orders we receive during a crisis, without thinking about our own comfort and leisure. This message was loud and clear to us.

Just as we had rules for behaviour, there were rules for conversation and dining. We were taught table manners. We were taught that we should sit only after the seniors and ladies were seated. We should not eat fast and lick our fingers. We shouldn't gulp down water but sip it slowly. We shouldn't mix everything on the plate, and we should eat small portions. We shouldn't waste food and take only the quantity we can finish. We shouldn't look for good chicken or mutton pieces during a buffet. We must not burp and if we do, we must ask to be excused. We must not make sounds with our spoon and mouth while eating. We must avoid making comments about the food after dining. We must not share our food with others, nor speak on the phone or read the newspaper while eating. We must not get up to leave till everyone has finished eating. We should speak politely about positive things with the person sitting next to us. We must avoid rude language and swear words.

In sum, do not stuff your mouth with food. Take small morsels of food and avoid speaking with food in your mouth. Learn how and when to use the knife, fork and spoon. Don't play around with them. You must first start with the spoon placed farthest from you. Don't keep your used spoon on the table; place it on the plate. Once you have picked up a bite of food with your fork or spoon, eat it in one go. Bring the spoon close to your mouth and don't allow it to touch your teeth. Avoid onions, garlic and other strong-smelling foods during social dinners. Don't pick your teeth in front of others. Don't create a scene if you find a small stone or strand of hair in the food. Call the waiter and change the plate discreetly.

Wear formal attire for social dinners. Don't stumble or trip around. Don't heap your plate with food, and adjust your speed with others while eating. Check if the food or drink is too hot before consuming it. Don't allow your tongue to be scalded and either blow on the food or spread it on the plate to cool it. Wait patiently for the food to cool. Sit erect on the chair; neither move back too much nor hunch forward. Sit close to the table. Learn the usage and order of all the bowls and cutlery, like the dinner fork, dessert fork, soup spoon, teaspoon, knife, salad plate, bread plate and water glass placed next to your plate.

It was difficult for a person like me, from a rural background, to learn and get used to such formal etiquette. I used to get confused in the beginning and once drank the water with the lemon in the finger bowl! To eat with a spoon used to be a literal battle. The courses used to be served but removed so fast that even after eating seven courses, I used to be hungry. I was not alone; it was the same case with most of the others as well.

Once, my friend and I had gone to a senior officer's house for a social call. My friend saluted so hard that his peak cap flew off his head! He was so nervous that he ate the dog biscuit kept on the table with the tea.

But gradually we learnt etiquette, and our habits and behaviour began to suit our service.

6

Management: Personal and Professional

Dr Saxena was going to teach us management science, but seeing his impassive and vapid face, we didn't feel that he would be able to make an impact. But once he started speaking in his bookish and serious manner, we started getting simple concepts about management skills. He spoke confidently:

> I am going to make fundamental changes in your personality. In the next ten months, you will learn all the management principles needed to become extraordinary managers. But for that to happen, you must make up your mind today. Changes begin to take place in you the moment you decide to do something or set a goal. If you want to change yourself, you have to assess your strengths and weaknesses. We have to earn self-respect and happiness from whatever we do. The more you read, gain knowledge, speak well and maintain yourself, your self-confidence will grow. Self-confidence and happiness

> have a direct correlation. When you love yourself, keep yourself calm and peaceful, and are content, your happiness will flow like a river. And remember, no one is perfect. Everyone has weaknesses and flaws, but don't allow them to become permanent obstacles in your path.

I have followed Dr Saxena's mantras all my life. I decided not to live life with a single perspective. I divided my life into three parts. One-third for me and my family, a third for my profession and a third for society. I made specific plans for my own physical, mental and spiritual progress. I linked it to my family. I made yoga and exercise a family activity. I go running, swimming, cycling, trekking and to the gym with my wife and children. I have fixed an hour for each activity per day. I make a point to climb one hill every week. We spend two days a month with nature. I expose my children to village life, traditions and values. I ensure that the children are in contact with their grandparents, despite being far away. I love running the marathon, and I spend entire Sundays doing that. Initially, this left me very little time with my family. My wife was naturally angry, but I found a way out. I got her to run marathons with me. I trained her properly, and now she is able to run the 21 km half-marathon with ease, and at a good pace.

Life is a tough race, which is a marathon at times and a lemon-and-spoon race at other times. It is no use crossing the finishing line first, if the lemon has fallen on the way. You have lost the race! That is how life is too. Your relationships, friends and health are like the lemon. You cannot let them fall off the spoon of life. Professional success alone means nothing. If you are ill and suffer from insomnia even the coolest AC and the softest mattress cannot make you sleep. If you have committed sins, your conscience will prick you. Even with full pockets, your mind is empty and your conscience burdened. If you get a promotion by playing tricks and lobbying, you will not receive genuine respect. There will be a lot of pressure in your professional life. Your integrity will be tested by your family, society, media, and the political administration. You need to have the moral and physical strength to withstand this pressure.

We were shown excellent videos on personality development and forensic science at the academy. Dr Saxena had shown us an inspiring speech by Field Marshal Maneckshaw. I watch it on YouTube every time I am uncertain or faced with conflicting situations. I derive a lot of strength, energy and courage from it.

Moral and physical courage

Field Marshal Manekshaw has spoken about the stress factors in our lives and the two types of courage—moral and physical:

> Moral courage is the ability to distinguish right from wrong and, having done so, to say so when asked, irrespective of what your superiors might think or what your colleagues or your subordinates might want. A 'yes man' is a dangerous man. He may rise very high; he might even become a minister or a Field Marshal, but he will never be a leader. He may do anything but he can never make a leader because he will be used by his superiors, disliked by his colleagues and despised by his subordinates.

To illustrate moral courage, he gave the example of his disagreement with the then Prime Minister Indira Gandhi.

In 1971, when Pakistan clamped down on its province, East Pakistan, hundreds and thousands of refugees started pouring into India. The Prime Minister, Mrs Gandhi had a cabinet meeting at ten o'clock in the morning. She asked,

'General Manekshaw, what are you doing?'

'Nothing.'

She said, 'I want you to enter East Pakistan.'

I said, 'Do you know that that means war?'

She said, 'I do not mind if it is war.'

'But we are not ready for war. This is not the right time to go to war. The monsoons will start soon, and the rivers will become like oceans. The whole countryside is flooded. I cannot take any action under these circumstances. I will require every road, railway train, truck, wagon to move them. We are harvesting in Punjab and Haryana; we are also harvesting in Uttar Pradesh. And you will not be able to move your harvest. If there is a famine in the country afterwards, it will be you to blame, not me.

'The ice has started melting on the Himalayas, and the Himalayan passes are opening now, and if the Chinese gave us an ultimatum, I will have to fight on two fronts. If you still force me to go to war, I guarantee you a 100 per cent defeat.'

After the meeting, Mrs Gandhi asked [then] Gen. Manekshaw to stay behind. He looked at her and said, 'Prime Minister, before you open your mouth, may I send in my resignation on the grounds of health, mental or physical?'

She replied, 'No, sit down, Sam. Was everything you told me the truth?'

He said calmly, 'Yes, it is my job to tell you the truth. It is my job to fight and win, not to lose.'

The Field Marshal also spoke on physical courage:

> Fear, like hunger and sex, is a natural phenomenon. Any man who says he is not frightened is a liar. It is one thing to be frightened. It is quite another to show fear. If you once show fear in front of your men, you will never be able to command. It is when your teeth are chattering, your knees are knocking and you are about to make your own geography—that is when the true leader comes out!

He illustrated this with another example from his life. In 1942, he was a major and commanding a Sikh regiment in Burma.

> A sepoy named Sohan Singh who was most undisciplined and a 'badmash' was annoyed with the colonel because he had stopped his promotion from lance naik to naik because of his poor track record. Sohan Singh had picked up his rifle and declared that he would shoot the major and kill him. The subedar of the company arrested Sohan Singh. The moment colonel Manekshaw got to know about the incident, he asked Sohan Singh to be presented before him. He gave the soldier a loaded pistol and said, 'You wish to kill me? Come on, shoot me.' Sohan Singh cooled down and said, 'Sorry Sahib, I made a mistake.'
>
> Manekshaw ordered Sohan Singh to be released, but everyone in the company was a little nervous. The subedar told Manekshaw, 'Sahib, don't trust him; he

will kill you tonight.' Manekshaw got angry and said, 'Where is Sohan Singh? He will be posted as the sentry at my tent tonight.' Manekshaw called Sohan Singh and told him, 'You will be my security guard tonight and you will wake me up at 5 a.m. with a hot cup of tea!'

That is exactly what happened. Sohan Singh stood in front of Manekshaw with a hot cup of tea at five the next morning. He had followed all the orders perfectly. Manekshaw said, 'If I had shown fear in front of my men, I would never have been able to command. I was frightened, terribly frightened, but I dared not show fear in front of them. You must never show fear.'

If Manekshaw had posted Sohan Singh elsewhere, the message to his company would have been, 'Sahib is afraid.' And that one action would have made him lose his credibility and respect as a leader. When a sergeant is fighting on the war front or managing a riot, he is filled with physical courage and resilience. A true leader should also have the same courage.

I, too, have been faced with such situations several times in my career. Every time I had to step forward knowing very well that the situation was life threatening or when death stared me in the face, Field Marshal Manekshaw's words would ring in my ears. They would empower me and motivate me. Training is nothing but preparing the body and mind to face challenges depending on the circumstance and situation. Once we are clear about our goal and purpose, decision-making becomes easy. We become firm, maintain our balance and the journey becomes thrilling. Such situations polish our personality and our self-confidence, and our strength gets enhanced. We automatically become more professionally skilled. That is why I love Manekshaw's mantra of shaping habits and character. Focus on your thoughts, because your words originate from them. Your actions follow from your words and gradually become your habits. Habits form character, and our character determines our future. This is such a simple formula for deciding our future path!

When I entered the Taj Hotel with my guards at night on 26/11, I was welcomed by the sight of dead bodies lying in puddles of blood and the bloodcurdling sounds of AK47s and grenades. The frightened screams of common people compelled us to enter the hotel. My bodyguard and I could have waited for our bulletproof vests and automatic rifles to arrive for our own safety, and no questions would have been raised.

The terrorists had entered the hotel at 9.40 p.m., had already killed several innocent civilians, and hundreds of lives were in danger. Usually, the police arrive at the crime scene after the crime is committed, but here, the crime was taking place as we arrived and people were losing lives. At such a time, my bodyguard and I entered the Taj at 9.51, just eleven minutes after the terrorists, and witnessed the dance of death; but not for a moment was I afraid of death or was shaken. I went ahead confidently and fought the terrorists to the best of my ability. I was determined. My goal was clear: do or die for the country.

I read this beautiful couplet in Hindi:

Duniya me mil jayenge ashiq kai,
magar vatan se khoobsoorat sanam nahi hota.
Sone se simatkar noton se lipatkar mare hain kai,
magar tirange se khoobsoorat kafan nahi hota.

Tukaram Omble fought the armed terrorist Kasab with a stick and, despite being shot five times, did not loosen his grip on the terrorist. Similarly, Date Sahib and Kamte Sir came running to fight the terrorists, even though it was not their territory! It was possible because of their mental, physical and moral courage.

The Chakan riots

Chakan was aflame on the 4 August 2018. The march taken out for reservation had turned violent and several buses had been set on fire. The mob had burnt down a police post, attacked a police station and burnt down three vehicles parked at the police station. The 8,000-strong mob had gone out of control. Many police officers, including the DSP and inspectors, had been seriously wounded. I reached a point 500 metres away from the riot scene with a small unit. I could see flames and clouds of smoke. I could hear screams and announcements.

I felt that it would be dangerous for me and my unit of fifteen constables to try and control the mob. We weren't equipped with adequate safety gear, and I felt it wouldn't be right to put the lives of my colleagues at risk. However, I took a decision. It was a suicidal one and to some extent stupid as well. But I had a gut feeling that it would work. I had worked as the SP of this district and had been working as the IG of this range for the past two years. I had been working with sincerity and integrity. I had been communicating with the youth constantly. I decided to face them unarmed and alone.

Removing my helmet, I drove straight into the riot scene with one of the constables on his scooty. Within a few seconds, some of the rioters recognized me. I had guided a lot of youth with speeches at schools and colleges in my area. The mobsters were stunned to see an officer of IG rank alone, unarmed and without any security. The rioters calmed down; their leaders came forward and appealed to me to address the crowd. I gestured to the crowd with my hands to sit down, and the yelling crowd sat down quietly. I requested them not to resort to violence and not to take the law into their own hands for ten minutes. I spoke to them in a language they could understand. I touched their emotions and the situation changed. The same rioting youth stood by me and several of them touched my feet in respect and saw me as their elder brother. The situation came under control gradually.

The riots had spread across the state on the same day. Chakan had been controlled, but the situation in Rajgurunagar worsened. A throng of 5,000 people marched towards the police station. The inspector and the other staff were trapped inside. They started making panic calls on the wireless system. I asked the SP to handle the situation in Chakan and reached Rajgurunagar. This time, we had a lot more force and all the preparations had been made to overpower the crowd. However, if we used force in one place, there was a danger of the news spreading like wildfire and causing problems across the state. I decided to use the same strategy again. I called the leaders of the crowd and the mob collected on the banks of a river. On one side of the mob was a police station and on the other, a college.

We stopped our police Jeeps on one side of the bridge. A colleague, my bodyguard and I went across the bridge to the river bank on a single Jeep to talk to the crowd. Here, too, the crowd calmed down seeing us. I called the college principal and asked him to talk to the youth. We were able to connect with them emotionally in a positive manner and achieve the desired outcome. The agitated youth cooled down and dispersed calmly. When youth are in a crowd, they are emotionally charged, and sometimes lose their cool. They then begin to attack with whatever they can lay their hands on—stones, sticks, rods, petrol and kerosene bombs, and even swords for no reason. The crowd has a single goal: to hit, burn and hurt. A lot of innocent people lose their lives. A fierce mob like this takes on a beastly face and damages public property. Though a lot of people behind these masks are blameless, once their beastly side comes to the fore, they become party to unlawful and violent activities.

I spoke briefly about industrial development and the reassuring steps taken by the administration. I said, 'The protest will end today, but the police will nab a lot of youth based on the CCTV footage. Then cases will be filed and arrests made. The parents of the accused will get trapped in organizing the bail and running to courts. You will not know how long you will be stuck with lawyers, courts and jail terms. Your names will get into the criminal records, and you will get rejected during passport and visa verification or character certification. You will not be able to get a government job. Moreover, the police will come and take you into preventive custody during every festival or protest. Do you want to get caught up in this vicious cycle? It doesn't mean that you shouldn't fight for your rights and justice. You should—but do it constitutionally, peacefully and patiently.'

The crowd was a little impatient, but once they realized that I was addressing them like a brother and a teacher, and not like an official speaking from a position of authority, things calmed down. Official and legal actions followed, but the protest didn't fester further. Aggression and violence came down, congruence and wisdom had won.

Mental and physical strength is needed to tide over any crisis and overcome any fear. There will be obstacles in life, but we shouldn't stop. Just tell your goal, 'Wait for a little while, I will meet you soon.' If our goals are clear and our vision set, nothing can bind us and we will never stray from our paths. We will progress on the path of victory with sincerity, integrity and confidence. The little pearls of wisdom that we received in the training taught us how to handle the toughest challenges in life.

It taught us that some battles can be fought without actually fighting but with the right communication and messages.

> *Shateshu jaayate shoorah sahasreshucha panditah*
> *Vaktadasha sahasreshu daataa bhavativaanavaa.*
> Among 100 persons only one person happens to be brave, and among a 1,000 such brave persons only one person is also learned and wise. And it is not surprising that among 10,000 such learned persons, hardly one person is also an excellent orator.

The director of the academy used to say, 'If you want to be a good leader, you must communicate well. You should be able to put forth your point convincingly. We should speak simply, in a language that the listener can understand. The police force has to be in contact with the people constantly. Your body language and gestures are as important as your words. You should gauge the problem, mood, and interest of the listener and decide your language and style of speaking. Your words may hurt someone's feelings and disappoint them. We should be aware that our words could humiliate someone. If you use appropriate and effective words, you can enthuse your audience, inspire them and enhance their confidence. Along with the words, the rhythm and clarity are also equally important to make your speech effective. Your facial expressions, hand movements, body language, style and posture reflect your confidence and conviction. You need to make eye contact with your audience and wear clothes suitable for the occasion. Your hairstyle, facial grooming, attire, and even footwear should be appropriate for the occasion. Your uniform is your identity. Your clean, ironed and crisp uniform can automatically change your body language and gestures.'

Being a good orator is a blessing. It has to be gained with a lot of practice and skill. Your fluency, gestures, expressions and bearing gradually make you mature and an effective communicator. Your words create an impression not only about you but also about your organization. An opportunity to give a speech brings out the researcher and the analyst in you. You start to work out how to say what you want to say. For everything to fall in place, practice and evaluation are vital. If you include your observations about a place, the people and your experiences, your speech doesn't sound preachy. If you study the topic of your speech in depth, it sharpens your choice of words and enhances your confidence by leaps and bounds. I implemented this knowledge of the importance of communication learnt at the academy into my own life.

Police officers are often called to address and guide school children and college students. We are invited to sports day celebrations and cultural festivals. We are asked to address peace committees and to attend religious festivals and social occasions. We have to brief our officers and colleagues during security arrangements. We are expected to speak according to the context and the situation. For example, we can't speak about senior citizens' issues in front of students. The police need to talk to them about addiction, social media, cyber-crimes, traffic rules and religious fundamentalism, and guide them. I have developed an excellent habit of having a separate diary for every subject. I note down inspiring events, anecdotes and descriptions of interesting and inspiring people that I meet. I write down interesting quotes, poems, couplets, shlokas and maxims according to the subject.

Security arrangements for festivals and anniversaries are real challenges for the police, especially Ganapati festival and Durga puja, Eid, Dr Ambedkar Jayanti and Shivaratri. A large number of youths come out for processions and during idol immersions. Sometimes petty quarrels and crowd excitement cause serious law-and-order problems. I have always had specific plans on how to maintain social and religious harmony during such festivals, and that includes using these festivals as an opportunity to communicate with the youth. It is possible to guide our youth participating in these festivals in the right direction and ensure that festivals are celebrated in a constructive manner through community efforts.

When I was the IG of West Maharashtra, our police department encouraged the youth and with their active cooperation made the Ganapati festival an opportunity for social change. The effort was spoken about at all levels. Following is a short description of our efforts.

Dolby-free Ganapati festival

Why does Ganapati—the God who protects his worshippers, and swallows all their sins into his belly, and fulfils their wishes—cause so much tension for the police? This question plagued my mind time and again. Maybe our attention was not in the right place, and hence the tension! Just before the advent of the ten-day Ganapati festival, the atmosphere in the police stations becomes like preparing for an annual examination. From the highest officer to the lowest employee, everyone's role and responsibility are decided. Police efforts include those for security and prohibitory arrangements, meetings with the various mandals and organizing committees. We guard and watch the sensitive areas very carefully right from the time of installation of the Ganapati idols. The routes for the processions are planned with extreme care to avoid communal tensions. All the temples and places of worship are thoroughly checked and screened in the morning, noon and night. Since the danger of terror has increased significantly, all the beat constables at the various police stations, the intelligence services are alert and watchful. Once the Ganapati idols are immersed on Ananta Chaturdashi, the tenth day, the police are able to breathe easy. In our childhood, we would be tearful during the immersion of our beloved God and we would be very sad, but now we shed tears of joy when our beloved Lord is immersed without any hitch. It's no less than passing a tough exam with flying colours!

During the festival season, a public interest litigation (PIL) was being heard in the high court about the declaration of a 100 metre perimeter around temples, places of worship, schools, hospitals as a 'silence zone', banning the use of loudspeakers in that area. The courts had reversed the decision of the state government and reinstated the 'silence zones'. Loudspeakers were banned in any of these silence zones. There are temples and schools in almost every small lane, so the Ganapati mandals wondered where they could have any loudspeakers at all. The high court asked why the festival couldn't be celebrated without loudspeakers. Maintaining law and order, or implementing decisions of the court, is a tightrope walk for the police.

To compel the mandals to keep the sound below the restricted limits is a big dilemma for us. These days, having tall loudspeakers with Dolby sound, playing ear-shatteringly loud music and obscene dancing has become a symbol of masculinity and reputation for a lot of mandals. For some these processions are the only opportunity for youngsters to get drunk and dance in front of the police. If the police try to request these mandals to reduce the volume or avoid using Dolby sound, tensions increase. The mandals blackmail the police, threatening to leave the Ganapati idols on the road. Many conflicts between the mandals and the police have arisen out of impatience.

With this background, we decided to ensure the implementation of law. We used every trick in the book to do so. The first step was counselling! We organized talks by ENT doctors to explain the ill effects of the use of Dolby systems to the mandal workers. The doctors made PPT presentations to show how seriously the loud sound affected the sick, the elderly and pregnant women. As they say, it is easy to wake up those who are asleep, not those who pretend to sleep. Some mandal leaders argued with the doctors, saying, 'Why don't you shift your patients to a different place for thirty-six hours?' Some asked, 'Don't you realize that the festival comes once a year?' But the police decided that come what may, the law would be enforced this year. We held meetings with the mandal organizers and made our intentions clear.

There were hunger strikes and protests staged against the police. We stood our ground. We took the help of social organizations and NGOs and got the media on our side. We kept giving out messages about the harmful effects of the use of Dolby sound systems. Decibel level measures not only volume but also vibrations. The Dolby system has three parts—base, mid and top; the base produces vibrations. These vibrations cause walls to vibrate, and give a feeling of an earthquake. In 2009, an old building collapsed in Kolhapur because of the use of a Dolby sound system, and two people died. At this time, the memory of a young bridegroom dying of a heart attack while dancing to the music being blared from a Dolby system was still fresh. The 'tunnel' or 'earthquake' effect of such loud sound causes an increase in the heart rate, especially of the elderly, and they become vulnerable to hearing loss, heart attacks and brain problems.

I am reminded of Lata Mangeshkar's words in this context. She had started singing in the Dagdusheth Ganapati Mandal when she was fourteen. Once while singing, her father, Pandit Deenanath Mangeshkar, had a severe bout of cough. Seeing him indisposed, she completed the song. I remember her mentioning somewhere, 'Place these speakers at different locations and play classical music or Ganesha stotras, which will create melodious sounds and positive vibrations. Lord Ganesha will be pleased.' Recently, there was a cartoon circulating on social media where goddess Parvati is shown advising her young son Ganesha, 'Once you go to earth, shut your ears tight. Last year you came back singing "Shanta bai, Shanta bai," this time you will come back singing some other filmy song.'

We tried our level best to make the mandals understand that their fun was becoming a punishment for others, but they retorted saying, 'Why don't you ban the Dolby systems in pubs, discotheques and at big music programmes?' We had to make them understand the difference between a crowd that wants to listen to loud music voluntarily and those who are forced to.

I have personally raided rave parties three times. RAVE stands for 'Radical Audio-Visual Experience'. Repetitive beats are played at high amplitude on Dolby systems at these parties. The electric lighting that is done during the Ganapati processions is similar to the laser beams used in rave parties. Once someone has consumed liquor and drugs, the music enters the ears and creates an effect as if he or she is walking on those laser beams. Such events entice the youth into the dark pits of addiction and ruin them. Lord Ganesha is the ruler of the fourteen skills and sixty-four forms of art—should we be dancing cheaply to songs with double meaning and obscene lyrics? A philosopher once said, 'Tell me the songs that the youth of your country sing, I will tell you the future of your country.' If we play such vulgar songs and dance suggestively in front of our mothers and sisters, are we not putting their safety and security at risk? We had decided to take recourse to law if counselling didn't work. As per the earlier Mumbai police laws, we used to file cases with minimal punishment on the mandals. But the high court questioned us, asking why we didn't file cases under The Environment (Protection) Act, 1986? We pleaded saying we didn't have decibel metres to measure loudness.

Following the orders passed by the high court, now every single police station has a decibel metre. Hence, we have made the young organizers and workers of the mandals aware that we have no choice but to file cases for cognizable and non-bailable offences against them. We started issuing summons and warrants for cases filed under the Noise Pollution (Regulation and Control) Rules, 2000. We told them that once these cases were filed and the offence proven, there was a five-year prison sentence and a fine of one lakh rupees. We reported through the media that when verifications take place for jobs, passports, visas, people with such cases registered against them will have negative remarks noted against them.

This strategy worked and 5,000 people voluntarily took out a silent procession in support of the police. Several newspapers and social workers openly praised our police department for its initiatives. We had won half the battle. The district magistrates (DMs) of Satara, Sangli, and Kolhapur put restrictions under Section 144 in their respective districts. They banned the use of Dolby sound systems in Ganapati processions. They also confiscated such systems wherever they were found. Usually, trucks are remodelled to accommodate the huge Dolby speakers, but the DMs along with the Regional Transport Offices (RTOs) took stringent actions against such vehicles. Every such vehicle had to pay a fine of four to five lakh rupees. Several mandals that were earlier using Dolby systems, came forward and gave written commitments to the police saying that they wouldn't use Dolby systems and would play only traditional devotional music. The atmosphere, overall, was very positive, enthusiastic and creative. The five districts under Kolhapur division celebrated a Ganapati installation and immersion procession without Dolby systems, instead using traditional musical instruments.

No Dolby means no alcohol and the absence of alcohol means no arguments, quarrels and violence. All these mean no communal tension and riots. The Ganesha festival was thus celebrated in an extremely harmonious and peaceful manner. Owing to the initiatives of the Sangli police, the money saved by the mandals on Dolby rentals was used for the construction of ten aquifers. This time, the mandals organized a series of socially beneficial programmes and took up social issues such as patriotism, history, environment, female foeticide, drug addiction, blood donation camps, and tree plantation drives. With the contributions collected, the mandals of five districts set up over 500 CCTV cameras in public places. In the pre-Independence era, the Ganapati festival was used as a platform for building awareness about Independence. The collective energy of lakhs of youth can be channelized in a positive manner to create a creative and constructive festival. This can certainly lead to a strong nation in the future. Ganapti Bappa Morya!

The question of law and order, agitations and riots, has to be handled with a cool head, sweet words on the lips and weapons in hand. Sometimes the situation goes out of hand despite the best of efforts, and force has to be used. It starts with tear gas, followed by a lathi-charge if the crowd doesn't come under control. The last resort is firing. While the situation may be controlled then, enquiries follow us for days after that. Many times, private offences are filed against us, but as they say in Hindi, *'Satya pareshan ho sakta hai, paraajit nahi'* meaning 'Truth can be troubled, but not defeated.' Like gold purified by melting, when the intentions behind your actions are pure and socially beneficial, you eventually win.

I was posted as the DCP of South Mumbai. A group of 10,000 protesters from a political youth organization came to the Mumbai Municipality head office, raising slogans against the water problem in Mumbai. These organizations are considered to be extremely violent and brash. We had made all the security arrangements, but these proved grossly inadequate. I was keeping an eye on the developments from my office. The procession reached Azad Maidan and the situation got out of hand. A senior police inspector and the ACP were trying their best to control the mob, but soon, the mob started pelting stones. A few youths were carrying bottles of petrol. They tried to barge into the municipality office after lighting the bottles. The guard of the office was injured. I had two platoons of the state reserve police with me. I decided to go to the spot and got into the police Jeep with my helmet on. The mob had become violent. I stood in front of the main office building and appealed to the leader to come forward and speak to me. The stone pelting stopped and my name was called. I, along with two platoons of SRPF officers, entered the crowd to talk to their leader.

The crowd was still sloganeering. The young leader got enthused seeing a DCP coming to negotiate. He started abusing the police. Seeing their leader's bravery, the mob too started shouting nasty swear words. Fist scuffle began and my helmet fell down. The reserve police platoons immediately started lathi-charge, and the mob began to run helter-skelter and disperse. A young political worker fell down in the melee and suffocated in the stampede. He breathed his last on the way to the hospital. Fifty of the young agitators suffered fractures in the lathi-charge. We arrested the leader and put him in lock-up.

We had taken action, quite naturally a reaction was expected. The Legislative Assembly session began and an adjournment motion was passed against the police. Why was a lathi-charge ordered before using the tear gas? A young man lost his life. There was a demand for a human rights violation case to be filed against the police department. There were all kinds of statements made in the Assembly.

It is not always possible to handle situations by the law books and follow what we were taught during our training. It's not that negotiation skills work every time either. Sometimes, we have to use the language the other side understands. Some instant decisions have to be taken according to the situation to prevent loss of life, but they don't always fall under the rules. We have the right to use force, but there are no clear rules on how much to use and why. We get straddled with enquiries. The rule book may say that force has to be used in a controlled manner, or at least in a balanced way, when absolutely necessary and in accordance with the situation.

It's quite an ordeal to face enquiries and answer the enquiry board questions. That is why, when the police experience such situations, they say, *'Dangal se dar nahi lagta saahab, enquiry se lagta hai!'* which means, 'We are not afraid of mobs Sahib, we are afraid of enquiries!'

7

My Organization: My Family

My skills were improving day by day at NPA. I would be famished after the physical and mental efforts throughout the day. I would feel groggy following a hearty meal and go to bed after studying for an hour or so. Eating a heavy meal when you are really hungry and the sleep earned through hard work gives a different kind of satisfaction. In today's lifestyle, we hardly experience true hunger or thirst. We sleep only after tossing and turning for a long time, and our sleep is so light that we wake up at the slightest of sounds. We have nightmares and get up sweating. Going back to sleep becomes next to impossible, and we lie awake the whole night.

Exercise, nutritious food and a good night's sleep are the three pillars of health. We experienced this during the training at the academy. We waited eagerly for Sundays so that we could get rest and go to Hyderabad or Secunderabad to have delicious biryani. We would go for a movie once in a while. We had watched Aamir Khan's *Sarfarosh* (1999) on one such Sunday. It is a film that portrays the story of a young IPS officer, the challenges he faces in his career and his personal life, his determination and struggles. Coincidentally, this film was being shot in the Fort area in Mumbai when I used to go there for my IAS preparations. I remember watching the shoot at night, hoping to see Aamir Khan in person. I had never imagined that I would spend my life working in the same profession shown in the film. The police uniform is not just a garment; it becomes part of us like a second skin. I had promised myself that my sense of duty would not remain restricted to my profession but would be a part of my thoughts, my mind and my dreams.

Once while we were in a market in Hyderabad, a young girl's mother was furiously berating two young men who had eve-teased her daughter. One of the boys slapped the mother right in front of my eyes. I lost my cool and beat up the two boys black and blue. Finally, the police arrived and took the three of us to the police station. The mother intervened and narrated what had happened. Despite that, an offence was registered against the three of us under Section 160 of the IPC for creating a ruckus. I asked permission to make a single phone call but even that was denied to me. Finally, I had no choice but to show my academy ID card. The moment my identity was revealed, their behaviour changed, and the arrogant and brute language turned into salutes.

Wherever I have worked, I have ensured that the rights of the common man are protected at all costs and that they are treated with respect. I allot a large amount of time to meet them on a daily basis. I instruct my officers to address the simplest of complaints. Stress and duty go hand in hand. The atmosphere in the police station and contact with criminals and offenders creates a huge impact on the attitude of the police personnel across the board.

Many institutions are researching this issue. A lot of initiatives such as fixing the working hours, duty allocation, revision courses, and yoga are being taken, but it is the intrinsic nature of the individual that comes to the fore while working in the police department. A service mentality, commitment, integrity, discipline and professionalism are the souls of the department. *'Sadrakshanaaya khala nigrahanaaya'* or (we stand) 'to protect good and to destroy evil' is the motto of Maharashtra Police. Every complainant comes to us with his or her grievance and feels that their side is right. They are troubled and vexed. Some come bleeding and wounded. Some of them cry pitifully while registering their complaint. They are forced to knock on the doors of the police station as a last resort, when all else fails. No one really wants to climb the steps of a court or the police station in their life.

A woman, especially, comes to the police station only when it is absolutely unavoidable. She is forced to come to the station when she faces domestic violence, or is tortured by her husband. We, as police officers, should make efforts to make her feel at home and provide her moral support the way her parents or siblings would. This is empathy in the real sense. The ones who are aggrieved and troubled need empathy and not sympathy. A physically challenged person will be able to better understand the problems and sorrows of another disabled person.

Due to the daily work pressures and stress, even the senior officers lose their inherent sensitivity with time. The police are made to lose their self-respect by the way they are portrayed in films, TV and the print media. Even the courts don't trust the police and any statement given in the presence of the police is not acceptable in court. It is assumed that the statements have been recorded by force or coercion. That is why we have to go by the aphorism 'trust begets trust' and work without any appreciation for our efforts.

August Vollmer, former chief of police, Berkeley, California says, and I quote:

> The policeman is denounced by the public, criticized by preachers, ridiculed in the movies, berated by the newspapers and unsupported by prosecuting officers and judges. He is shunned by the respectable. He is exposed to countless dangers and temptations. Condemned while he enforces the law and dismissed if he doesn't. He is supposed to possess the qualifications of a soldier, doctor, lawyer, diplomat and educator with remunerations less than that of the daily labourer.

I had been accorded the responsibility of leading such a force. I studied the subculture and history of the department deeply. This organization is trapped by British-era laws, influence of the army and expectations of being an administration that is focused on public welfare. The force is still facing the pangs, constraints and confusions of transitioning from a 'police state' to a 'welfare state'. We have to bear the punches quietly.

We are expected to shout out commands even during training. We have no choice but to obey orders. This leads to dryness and vapidity in our behaviour. Once we wear our khaki uniforms, our relationship and exposure to the arts and finer things in life are lost. We get to be anywhere near a movie theatre or an auditorium only when making security arrangements for VIPs. It is almost impossible to go to such events with family. We lose the courage to include music and melody into our world of 'attention' and 'stand-at-ease' commands! The police are entrusted with the task of stopping the vulgar dances of the youth at pubs, bars and parties. So, dancing and singing remains a pipedream for the police themselves.

At one of our police conferences, I asked a havildar on the cusp of retirement, 'Have you ever watched a movie with your wife?' His answer was shocking. He said, 'Sir, my wife is from the village. We hardly got time when we were young, and if we go for movies now in our old age, our children laugh at us! We have lived our lives cloistered in tiny 350–400 square feet, single-bedroom flats. Our children are grown up and where is the question of privacy! We have twelve-hour workdays. We leave home at 5.30 in the morning, and by the time we reach home, it is 11.30 at night. We go home only to sleep, Sir. Our biological clocks are reset every week. We have day shifts and night shifts alternately, and we hardly get good sleep. I now suffer from hypertension and diabetes. We don't get our weekly off for months on end. And even on those holidays, our time is spent going to the hospital, paying our bills and visits to the bank. I don't know when my children grew up, and I hardly remember enjoying family time. My life has got churned in the waterwheel of Mumbai, Sir. I will go back to my village after my retirement and learn how to live! I am honoured that you at least bothered to ask me this!'

The story of the havildar reflects the bitter truth of the life of a policeman. My colleagues go to the beach to patrol every morning, but they never get a chance to enjoy the cool sea breeze or stand with their feet in the cool waves. All they can think about is how soon they will be able to reach their homes in Mira Road, Nala Sopara or Bhiwandi, hanging in crowded trains, sweating and suffocating. Even if they are on duty in beautiful parks, they can be seen sitting and doing the crossword of an evening tabloid. They are troubled by the riddles of life. I have witnessed this subculture and have experienced it since my childhood.

My maternal uncle was a havildar in the Pune Rural Police. We would go to Pune during school vacations in May and during Diwali with my mother. My uncle's small two-room house in the police colony would be overflowing with guests. We would all sleep on the terrace. All the boys in the colony would get together and chat. We would rarely get to hear anything positive in those chats. The youth of that area seemed to be interested in the world of crime, drugs, politics and bad influences. There was fierce competition between every house in the colony—who got a posting ... who bought a fridge or a TV—were hot topics of discussion. No one ever spoke about each other's problems and challenges. It was as if the colony had prohibited things like art, sport, music, culture and literature! A few families were exceptions and focused on their children's education and careers. But these families were made the laughing stock, and unfortunately, I too was a part of this subculture.

Due to my exposure to this in childhood, I constantly thought about ways of changing this subculture. I decided to begin by making a change in myself. I made it a point to absorb every new idea for change that we received at the academy, because the training was an investment for life. I was determined to use this knowledge for the betterment of my police family. We should not be happy but spread happiness around us. You all must have surely watched the movie *Anand* (1971). It had a simple and straightforward philosophy. The movie beautifully and effectively shows building relationships, bringing people together and loving them unconditionally, giving us a philosophy of life. I recently read a wonderful WhatsApp message. I am not sure how true it is scientifically, but it is interesting to read:

> A happy life depends on our attitude. Attitude affects our bodies and our minds. Our body is nothing but a collection of biological chemicals. Whenever we eat junk or unhealthy food, do things that are unavoidable, and undergo stress, an imbalance in our system is unavoidable. There is an increased production of a hormone called

> cortisol in the body, which disturbs our sleep and pushes us towards disease and ill health. Cortisol is released when we have bloated egos, selfishness, instability, lust, excess, and addictions, and messes up our health. Our body gets gripped by serious illnesses. That is why it is important to stay away from stress and bad habits. Does that mean there are only harmful hormones? No, there are a lot of hormones and chemicals in our body that enhance our mood, and improve our mental and physical health. Endorphins, dopamine, serotonin and oxytocin are miraculous hormones that make us happy, content and calm.

When we exercise, the body produces endorphins that reduce the pain caused by exercise and hard work. That is why we start enjoying our workouts once our body is warmed up and we exercise regularly. Our body is a miracle! Just as addictions and bad habits stick to us, good habits stick to us too. I love running and am passionate about marathons. I read somewhere that the veins and nerves at the soles of our feet are extremely sensitive. In fact, apart from the reproductive organs, these form the most stimulable nerve tissue. That is why, once the body is warmed up, we get a kick while running or exercising. If we can get an endorphin kick by exercise, where is the need for us to go looking for kicks and highs from alcohol, drugs or physical relationships in our youth?

Intense exercise, yoga, and sports can give us the same satisfaction and pleasure. It is most important that this pleasure is pure and natural. We should keep away from consuming supplements, steroids, drugs or other harmful alternatives. It is better to not even look in that direction because it can drag us to the pits. A lot of young men are doing harmful experiments with their bodies and consuming dangerous supplements in the race to get six packs. It is best for all sports persons and bodybuilders to strictly say NO to chemicals, processed foods and supplements. This advice should be followed at all times. I have discussed this with actor Akshay Kumar several times. He has managed to keep himself super fit and healthy with discipline and natural methods. And yes, laughter too aids in the release of endorphins. There is nothing wrong with watching comedy films, plays and TV shows repeatedly to get a good laugh. YouTube is full of funny content and stand-up comedies. So, what we need to do is exercise for at least half an hour daily, laugh heartily for half an hour, and earn enough endorphins to keep us going the whole day happily.

The second neurochemical is dopamine, which is also called the 'feel-good hormone'. We perform a number of activities on a daily basis and our successes cause the production of dopamine in our bodies. When we get appreciation for our work at home or office, we feel overwhelmed because dopamine permeates through our body and shows its magical effect. Housewives are often upset and sullen because we do not value their work and contribution. We take them for granted and disregard their work. Just try going home in the evening from the office, sit with your mother or wife, hold her hands and tell her how hard she works for the family. See her face light up and tears well up in her eyes. This is because of the alchemy of dopamine. This neurotransmitter is produced when we learn something new, buy something, answer a question, solve a riddle or learn to play a musical instrument. That is why it is important to constantly learn something new, listen to music, and cultivate hobbies.

The third positive hormone is serotonin. Its secretion gives us internal peace and positivity. When we help others unconditionally or when our deeds benefit others, serotonin is released in our bodies. When we give back to nature and society, pray to God, work for our country, write well, solve other peoples' problems, and post useful stuff on social media, this hormone is released. We get blessed with this hormone when we spend our energy for the benefit of our society. Serotonin enhances our mood, helps us sleep well and improves our appetite. Our digestion improves and our memory gets better. We get encouraged to learn new things.

This is the biggest problem facing the world today. These things have become rare and expensive. We never knew that happiness and health could be achieved by such simple means.

I read a mythological story in my childhood, which said that God had to really work very hard to create human beings; but his problems became worse once they got created. God summoned all the other gods and complained, 'I regret having created these beings. They keep calling out to me with their selfish and greedy wishes day in and day out. They keep complaining about each other, beating their chests at my door, and pouring out their miseries. I have lost my sleep. What can I do? Where can I hide? Please suggest a place where these selfish, scheming and cunning human beings cannot find me easily. Let it be a place where only true devotees who are in search of peace and liberation can find me.'

The gods suggested different places but the intelligent, shrewd and sharp human beings were able to find these places with ease and continued to pester God with their demands and desires. He was fed up. Finally, an old and experienced god suggested a unique place. He said, 'You go and hide inside the human being.' God was pleased with the suggestion and made his place inside the human conscience and lived in peace.

The moral of the story is that God exists within us but we forget that and search for him outside and all over the world. There is a saying in Sanskrit: *apsudeva manushyanamadi videva maneeshinaam. Baalaanaam kaashtaloshtheshthu budhyasyatma nidevata.* [Love is equal to God, for human beings. It is what a seeker sees in his study and his scholarship. The ignorant beings search for it in idols while those who serve others, are kind, forgiving and work towards peace find God within themselves. That God is formless, attribute-less and omnipresent.]

This means that those who dedicate their lives to love, service and helping others automatically turn inward. Serotonin comes to their aid at such times and brings them in contact with God's love, affection and friendship, and they become one with God.

The last hormone is oxytocin, which is a life-giving one. It produces feelings of love and intimacy and is a beneficial hormone. When you hug someone lovingly, shake someone's hand affectionately, pat someone's back appreciatively, or grip someone's shoulder supportively, oxytocin is released in the body. You might remember the 'jadoo ki jhappi' or magical embrace from the movie *Munnabhai MBBS* (2003). Munnabhai gave this potent medicine and managed to bring a patient in coma back to consciousness. Do you realize why when a father returns home tired and irritated after a hard day's work and picks up his infant son, all his exhaustion vanishes and his face lights up with a smile instantly?

We have taken several initiatives for the welfare of our employees who have lost their day-to-day pleasures. A special programme named 'Umang' is organized by artists from the Hindi film industry (Bollywood) for the police department. Top actors and actresses perform and entertain the policemen. The rights for this programme are sold to TV channels and the crores of rupees earned are utilized to set up good schools, hospitals, study centres, canteens and guest houses for the police employees. As the additional commissioner of police (Addl CP) of West Mumbai, I was given the charge of organizing this event for three years.

We made a unique strategy for the first year. We got permission for the programme to run till midnight. Because of that, the programme, which started at seven in the evening, went on for five hours. This made it possible to show it in two parts on TV. The mainstream channels competed with each other in an auction to purchase the rights for the show. This led to a three-fold increase in our welfare fund. But, on the day of the programme, a major incident happened in Mumbai. A religious guru died and a stampede took place as people gathered to pay their last respects. Around twenty-seven men and women died in the melee. There was tremendous pressure to cancel the programme following such a tragedy. The chief minister and the home minister declined to come for the programme. The police commissioner had to take a decision at his own risk. Over a crore of rupees had been spent on the organization of the programme. The stars would not be able to give us dates for another year. I stood my ground and somehow managed to conduct 'Umang'. The police welfare fund managed to collect twelve core rupees. The department set up an air-conditioned study centre for the children of the employees. A placement centre was also set up to help the children get jobs.

When I was IG for Western Maharashtra, we invited over 150 multinational companies to recruit deserving candidates from our police family. The recruitment camp was organized at the Pune Rural Police headquarters, and company representatives interviewed candidates from five districts. Over 300 young men and women received job offers in a single day. When I took charge as the IG of Kolhapur district, the welfare fund there was bone dry. A programme for generating welfare funds that had been organized six years earlier, had ended in a mess. The SP had decided to drop the idea of having a fundraiser programme after that. That is why their funds had dried up and even taking a loan of fifty lakh rupees from Pune to pay for the annual scholarships was becoming difficult. We made a new plan.

We decided to offer the citizens of Kolhapur a programme called 'Marathi Taarka' or 'Marathi Stars'. We decided to hold the same programme in four other districts, so that we could reduce the organizational expenses in collaboration with the organizers. As planned, we were able to organize all four shows spending less than a crore, and we managed to raise ten crore rupees for the welfare fund. We gave all the deserving police wards their pending scholarships. We got sanctions from the police headquarters to set up police public schools in Satara, Pune and Sangli. We set up a beautiful police park in Kolhapur police headquarters in association with a voluntary agency and industry. We installed sculptures displaying Indian history. We erected a 300-feet tall monumental tricolour that would be visible from any corner of Kolhapur. We installed floodlights so that the proud flutter of the flag would be visible at night too. Hordes of children began visiting the park. We also set up a traffic park within the police garden to raise awareness about traffic rules among the next generation.

If you garner the trust of the police force and take care of their needs, they support you wholeheartedly. They never shy away from any social welfare activities, but the police chief has to ensure that they get proper training and guidance for the same. I have always adopted the attitude for empathy and police welfare that was taught at the academy. That is why I have always received the trust of my colleagues and the officers. We have to transfer around 500–600 personnel every year. I circulated the details to everyone about the vacancies through police notices to ensure transparency. I dedicated seven days to listen to the complaints and issues of all the employees who had been given transfer orders. I ensured that the employees got posted to one of the three options they had chosen and that is why I never had to face their disfavour, political interference, or face enquiries or complaints from their seniors, the courts or the Maharashtra Administrative Tribunal (MAT). I was able to implement these things practically because of the foundation in organizational management that was built at the academy.

Don't fear Corona

The COVID-19 pandemic gripped the world in 2019. The virus infects those who are vulnerable, affects their lungs and kills the patients. It spreads through the nose and mouth and infects us. The entire world had been put under lockdown to stop its spread. Why the COVID-19 pandemic happened, how it spread and how it can be treated is not my area of expertise. But I can say for sure that this pandemic has cast fearsome and terrifying shadows across the world and even healthy people are losing their mental balance. For a while, nothing other than COVID-19 was discussed and talked about on social media, on TV and in newspapers. The administration got down in full strength to stop its spread, but it was not coming under control and the situation continued to worsen day by day. Cities became desolate and physical distancing became a norm. All programmes, functions and festivals were banned. The world changed completely.

We slept in one world and woke up in another! Disney had lost its magic; Paris had lost its romance; Mumbai, New York and other major cities went into a deep slumber. The walls of China could not contain the coronavirus. Hugging and caressing became lethal and life threatening. Avoiding meeting grandparents and parents became a sign of caring. This new world suddenly realized that power and wealth were worthless. People got frustrated being cloistered indoors. The police beat up anyone who was found on the streets. Despite all this, the Corona monster could not be stopped. There were no signs of either a treatment or a vaccine for the virus. The responsibility of imposing the curfew and managing the lockdown was handed to the police. The police were also at the risk of contracting the disease while fulfilling their duties. The infection originated in Wuhan in China and soon spread to Italy, Iran, America and other nations, and the world watched the havoc and death it caused. Everyone in India was sure that the disease would reach their city, town or village sooner or later.

So, we created a blueprint on how to handle and fight this epidemic at the local level. We created a 'Corona Emergency Prohibition Plan' to fight the disease at every level. We discussed, in simple terms, all the preventive and responsive measures against the pandemic in detail. The most important factor was to ensure that the morale of officers and personnel at the forefront of the fight against COVID-19 should be high.

The pyramid of health is founded on three elements—adequate rest, nutritious food and exercise. The moment the curfew was imposed, we cut down the twelve-hour duty shifts to eight hours so that the police employees got enough rest. They were able to get a sixteen-hour break following eight hours of duty, which helped them sleep well and get enough rest. We made it a point to tell them that this break was meant for them to rest. We provided them with face masks, shields, sanitizers, and liquid soap for their safety. The mealtimes and hence food habits of police personnel are disturbed, and so we made sure that they get the appropriate vitamins, minerals and proteins. We gave a list of our requirements to the voluntary agencies and people who came forward to help. We included Chyavanprash, vitamin C, calcium and zinc tablets, dry fruit packets, green tea, glucose, juices and other healthy items in the list.

We realized that the habit of having cold water and cold stuff during the hot summer months was difficult to control. Throat infections are said to happen because of consuming cold stuff; throat pain leads to cough and cold, fever and chills. The coronavirus waits to attack weak and tired bodies. It attacks lungs and chokes the airways leading to breathlessness. Patients have to be administered oxygen or kept on a ventilator. Despite trying all the possible treatments, several people joined the list of COVID-19 casualties.

Other than taking all the normal precautions, we also procured 3,500 thermos flasks that would keep water hot for twenty-four hours and provided every police station and branch office with an electric stove to heat water. We did this as drinking or sipping warm water is said to be both beneficial and protective to the system. We checked whether the personnel on night duty had hot water. We gave them Tetley green tea sachets. This helped in restricting the consumption of sweet tea with milk, which causes acidity. The green tea with blood-thinning properties proved very beneficial for their health.

While the disease was spreading, I received a phone call from actor Akshay Kumar. He donated 500 smartwatches that could identify COVID-19 symptoms to the Nashik police. The watches proved extremely useful. We downloaded its app on our smartphone and linked the phones to our control room. There were two dashboards on it—one for COVID-19 and the other for wellness. The first symptom of the COVID-19 infection was high temperature, and this watch measured the body temperature 3,500 times a day. The moment someone's temperature went above 100 degrees Fahrenheit, we would get a signal in our control room. If the wearer placed a finger on the watch dial for ten seconds, it could measure the blood pressure (BP). We could see that information on the dashboard in the control room. We were thus able to provide medical help during the first golden hour of the disease and give them leave.

We could also monitor the wearer's heart rate and sleep patterns and allow the teams to rest whenever needed. Apart from all this, the watches measured a lot of wellness parameters such as the number of steps walked every day, the number of calories burnt, the level of hydration and also whether we got up from our seats every hour or not.

I had made a rule in the control room those days. All personnel below the age of fifty had to walk 10,000 steps compulsorily every day, and those over fifty had to walk a minimum of 5,000 steps daily. I sent the notice to all the constables who lazed around. The environment became healthy and hygienic.

Most importantly, I increased my communication with them, sending them reassuring messages on the wireless to reduce their stress. I explained that they could be protected from COVID-19 if they kept their immunity levels high. We took special care of older personnel with co-morbidities. We also advised them not to fall prey to misinformation on social media and focus on their duty sincerely. Eighty per cent of those who tested positive for COVID-19 showed no symptoms. They didn't even come to know when they got infected and when they recovered. In fact, they were fine and just showed positive and negative test results. We told such staff members not to get worried while listening to news about COVID-19 constantly. This really helped calm people down. They maintained discipline, were cautious and fought hard to keep the public safe from the spread of the virus.

Our mindset should be fearless in order to face crises in life. Fear is a primaeval instinct, and if we want the next generation to overcome it, the foundation has to be laid in childhood. We should not protect our children from small things. We need to give them lessons to be independent, self-sufficient and wise at the appropriate times. We need to tell them that freedom comes with responsibility. Parents need to move away from being guardians, supporters and nurturers at the appropriate stage; we must become outspoken critics and observers. We should not blindly follow the West in this rapidly changing world, otherwise, it will become very difficult to contain a generation that has gone astray. True manliness is in doing our duty fearlessly, proving our mastery.

As the couplet goes: *naabhisheko na sanskaarah sinhasya kriyate vane. Vikramaarjita satvasya swayameva mrigendrata* [Nobody declares a lion as the king of the forest by doing rituals. By sheer might of his own, a lion achieves the status of lord of the animal kingdom.]

The fearless attitude that I developed at the academy and the achievements during my career gave me the authority to guide my subordinates and people at large.

8

Community Policing and Leadership

The rule of law swings up and down on a daily basis in society. When the law-and-order situation worsens, the quality of life suffers. The life of the weak and marginalized becomes difficult. The corrupt, adulterous and antisocial elements have a field day, while the administrative machinery gets rusty. This is when we need leadership that has vision and clarity. Such leaders are needed in political, social sectors and the bureaucracy—especially in the police department. Such leaders have innovativeness, professionalism, skill, discipline, fearlessness and unquestionable integrity. Being able to motivate others is an invaluable quality. Positive thoughts, good words, unbiased actions, positive habits and honest character make exceptional leaders.

Dr Saxena had explained to us lucidly the difference between management and leadership. All IPS officers are selected based on criteria such as fearlessness and trustworthiness. They are responsible for creating a new generation of officers. Like they say in Marathi, '*Bole tasa chaale, tyaachi vandavi paaule*', which means 'I bow down to the one who walks his talk.' The words and actions of our faculty demonstrated ideal leadership skills. They taught us through various on-field experiences and examples the importance of planning, organization, direction and control in the management of the police force. It would be unfair to say that a high-ranking official is a leader if they ensure that orders given in an authoritarian manner are followed by all subordinates out of fear of punishment. There is a vast difference between completing a task under pressure or force and doing it through free will, full commitment and dedication.

We have often seen seniors in uniformed services creating chaos, using physical force, intimidating juniors, and creating an environment of fear to extract superficial obedience from subordinates and calling it 'leadership'. Unfortunately, because of this mindset, an officer who is patient, restrained, calm and earns the trust of his colleagues is considered weak. In times of crisis, we are forced to make extremely tough decisions and implement them with an iron hand, but such actions are restricted to emergency situations only. If we daily use the same criteria and rules, it won't be long before our work ends in a fiasco and we face humiliation. That is why we need to stir up the emotions of camaraderie and cooperation among our co-workers and ensure that we get the best out of them in the long run. This is what true leadership is all about.

If an officer instils the fear of punishment at every step, it will become a case of 'crying wolf' for him or her. Everyone is aware of their own judicial rights and sphere of authority. Maintaining good faith and communication with colleagues, being aware of their training needs, being involved with their problems and challenges, and being committed to solving their problems are all dependent on the dedication and respect of your team towards your leadership qualities. If the intentions of your co-workers are true and they make errors because of the pressures of work, as the leader you should support them; but if someone has underhand dealings or shirks responsibility for selfish reasons, then it is important for the leader to take a firm view and stem the attitude in the bud.

A police officer is not just an employee restricted by his area of authority or a leader of his men. Even those he is appointed to serve—the public—look to him as their saviour and leader. Controlling crime and maintaining public order is his main duty, but his primary responsibility is to create a sense of security in the minds of the people. Once a sense of security and fearlessness is created in society, it truly becomes mature and progressive in the real sense. Art, culture and sports flourish, and life becomes more beautiful. In short, police leadership has an important role to play in making life beautiful and free from fear.

It is said that every policeman is a citizen in uniform and every citizen is a policeman without a uniform, but citizens and the police have spats frequently. Whether it is an anniversary function or a celebration—a procession is taken out. The moment the youth spot policemen, they start dancing with a vengeance. The police stand watching the fun helplessly, and once the procession ends, they fish out these perky troublemakers and set them right in the language they understand. Until proper steps are taken to strengthen out these relationships, the vicious cycle of mutual distrust cannot be contained.

Once the police-public relationship is strong, unlawful acts stop, corruption is controlled and transparent policing begins. People are always interested in fostering a relationship with the police, but they don't know how to go about it. The police should follow the principle of '*dil mile na mile, haath milakar to dekh*', or 'whether hearts meet or not, let's try shaking hands'. The police can connect with the public through various initiatives such as police mitra, peace communities, mohalla samitis, women's safety committees, gram suraksha dal, slum panchayats, special police officers (SPOs), counselling, cyber messengers and so on and so forth. The people have to play the double role of pressure as well as support group. Whenever the police take a wrong approach, there is an increase in unlawful activities and antisocial elements. At times like this, the public should put pressure on the police department. When natural disasters or man-made crises happen, the rôle of the police is appropriate; but when the police are put in trouble, the people should support them firmly and motivate them. Whether it is the media or people in politics, their roles are dependent on the public.

Under normal circumstances, the police can sit in their ivory towers, but when there are emergencies, the police personnel cannot afford to remain detached. That is why police officers should constantly analyse their strengths and weaknesses, and strive to learn new skills and improve on a daily basis. The police should work consciously towards making the police-public relationship more robust. They should show high levels of character, credibility, integrity and morality. To achieve that, maintaining a fine balance between the personnel they lead and the people they work for is paramount.

Experience is the greatest guru. Wisdom means learning lessons from one's own and other people's experiences and making the necessary changes in oneself. Those who are dedicated to their work are able to gain expertise and skill in their work. This is professionalism, but sensitivity and empathy are more important.

We need to have a clear goal in life. This quote by saint Samarth Ramdas was painted on the walls of my school, '*Maraave pari keertirupi uraave*'. It means, 'When a person is no more, he should be remembered for his work.' We would get goosebumps singing songs in praise of Shivaji Maharaj, which taught us that to make our lives meaningful we needed to give back to society. We can divide people into three groups—the selfish, the goal-oriented and the saints. Saints are rare and being saintly is not considered smart these days. We find selfish people dime a dozen and these narrow-minded and self-centred persons live their lowly lives restricted to their holes. The goal-oriented ones are driven by positive energy. They have constructive and smart goals, which they strive to fulfil with full commitment and vigour. They do not get bogged down by obstacles and forge ahead untiringly. Once one goal is achieved, the next one is always ready! Their life journey is spent gathering the flowers of their meaningful achievements.

Someone had asked Gautama Buddha once, 'What is real happiness?'

Actions that purify our minds, our duties towards our family and society, and the deeds we do for the benefit of others are what give us true happiness. These help us develop an unbiased intellect. The ups and downs, or our problems in life will not determine our happiness. The greatness of our actions will be decided by the goals we have and not where and how we work. Police officers should be motivated by two goals. One, providing inspiring leadership to their co-workers; and two, developing their skills and capacity to provide excellent service to the public at large.

SMART policing

SMART policing is not a new concept and has been around for quite some time. Its objective is to bring the administrative and emotional aspects together and create an ideal work style. I had completed my degree—Master of Police Management, from Osmania University in Hyderabad—during my training at the academy. This degree is affiliated to the training at the academy and since half the syllabus was related to the training, I could complete the degree with special merit. I learnt subjects such as human resource management, finance, sales and office administration, apart from marketing, macro and micro economics, business law and organizational behaviour.

I decided to implement SMART policing by bringing together the knowledge I gained while doing this degree, the learnings from my training and my experiences on the job. Some obstacles did come in the way, some questions cropped up—but at the end of it, I was able to create a new framework for evaluating performance. I set goals for my co-workers based on that blueprint, which gave them a clear direction to work and an impetus for their administrative and professional abilities.

What does SMART mean?

'S' stands for strict and sensitive. Administration should be strict with discipline but sensitive at the same time. We should behave like strict fathers with our co-workers. While inculcating discipline and taking action, their improvement should be our primary focus. Caring for their well-being, tackling their professional problems and maintaining healthy communication with them are also equally important. We have to behave with extra sensitivity with the citizens who come to us with complaints. They often come to the police with blood and tears flowing. We should welcome them courteously and comfort them with our words. Empathy is always more effective than sympathy.

We must handle every complaint with the same sensitivity and cooperation that I would have expected from the police as a person in the same situation. This approach makes things really easy and I have a simple solution for this. Every day, I look at the daily crime reports and take feedback from the complainants by phone. I make it a custom to call the common complainant from the control room and ask them five questions:

1. When you went to the police station, how was the behaviour of the officer?
2. Did they try to reduce the nature of the crime? Did they delay filing your FIR?
3. Was any financial or other expectation made while filing the FIR?
4. Did you get a free copy of your FIR?
5. How soon after the crime did the officer reach the spot?

The complainant is in distress and generally doesn't tell lies. Hence, receiving positive feedback from the complainant would mean that we have achieved what is traditionally called 'customer satisfaction'. A daily report of the answers to this questionnaire is sent to the SP, along with the daily crime register. The result has been increased awareness among my co-workers and officers. They compete against each other to provide maximum satisfaction and comfort to the complainants. We have started rewarding the officer who receives the most positive feedback for the questionnaire for a particular case. In cases where we have received negative feedback or voices of displeasure, we have chided the officers responsible at first, but if the mistakes are grave, we have taken disciplinary action.

All these initiatives have led to an automatic promptness in filing FIRs. Instances of trying to reduce the seriousness of a crime and hesitation in filing simple NC (registering a complaint for a non-cognizable offence in the police diary) in case of dacoities, robberies and severe injuries have come down drastically and the police actions have become increasingly transparent. Officers have begun reaching crime spots immediately.

As a result of all this, the officer at the police station not only behaves courteously with complainants but has begun to offer them a glass of water as well! The officers have begun requesting complainants to give positive feedback if the complainants receive a phone call from the control room. A positive subculture has been created in the police department. Due to the daily stresses of work and excessive contact with the crime world, the behaviour of the officers naturally does get a little imbalanced, obstinate and rude. Hence, simple experiments also give us exceptional results.

'M' stands for modern. While developing modern and contemporary policing, every experience, domestic and global, comes in handy. I went to London for training two years ago. We studied the policing methods of several cities. 'Evidence-based policing' is being used all over the world these days. This method has been developed to reduce the operating costs of policing. It is not always possible to increase human resources in the police departments. Instead of that, the police have to control crimes in a scientific manner, and implement law and order professionally. That is why we need to use SMART methods in place of the usual methods and focus on preventive policing. We need to study different sections of society. This will allow us to get to know the population, geographical structure, economy, social situation and review the policing related problems and issues. We have to analyse the data scientifically, and based on the findings, we can decide the nature of policing that will be suitable for that area.

What does this really mean? We often don't diagnose the disease and give every patient the same medicine. Instead, we need to diagnose the disease properly and decide on the line of treatment. For example, some areas of the city have industrial colonies while others have educational institutions. Some areas have traders and others are middle-class localities. There are slums too. Every such locality has a different structure. Different problems need different solutions, to be effective. This needs careful planning to get all the required resources. We need to provide high-class training and eventually decide the policing procedure.

'R' stands for responsive. We need to *respond* to a situation and not *react* to it. I was listening to a talk by Sanjay Upadhye, where he explains the difference between the two beautifully. We receive the maximum number of calls on our helpline from senior citizens. Often, they take up a lot of time over trivial complaints, and we are forced to use blunt language with them, which they perceive as harsh and rude. What can we do? An old gentleman comes to the police station. His complaint is that his son has fixed an AC in his own room, while the fan in the gentleman's room is rickety and makes a noise. He is not able to sleep at all. The old man claims that he is being mentally tortured, and we should arrest his son. Or he may demand that we call the neighbours immediately as they play the TV loudly and it disturbs him a lot. But the fact is that there is no cognizable offence in either of these complaints. When we tell him so the old gentleman gets more annoyed; there is no point trying to explain it to him.

Upadhye suggests:

> Tell the man that the fan is a 'fan' of yours. Maybe such a funny pun will bring a smile to his face and his mood will get better. Then ask him to start talking to the 'fan': 'If it runs at speed one and makes a grr … grr noise, think of

> it as "grandpa go to sleep, grandpa go to sleep…". If you can't sleep even after that, increase the speed. Now the sound will say, "sleep now, sleep now…". If you can't sleep even then, put the fan on full speed, and hear its sound saying, "sleep, sleep, sleep, sleep…". Such a conversation can lighten the mood. If the neighbours play their TV too loudly, you watch the same channel with your own TV on mute! If someone asks you the reason, tell them you are watching TV on "surround sound". Uncle, don't *take* tension, give it to others!'

Truly, such light-hearted banter and conversations can make the stressful atmosphere of the police station happier and calmer. Both employees and complainants will feel a little unburdened, and their agony will be reduced. It is all about a change in perspective.

We tried an experiment in Nashik. We played soft classical music at our police station. Both the mind and the intellect were enraptured by the soft, soothing melody. Usually, people coming to police stations are sad, hurt and come in with blood and tears. Mostly, their fear of the police stops them from stepping into police stations. If we have to gain their confidence and trust, we have to change the surroundings within the police stations and our behaviour.

The usual appearance of a police station includes things captured from crimes lying around for ages, two-wheeler and four-wheeler vehicles parked outside, spit-stained walls, grimy cabinets and cupboards, harassed faces and agonizing screams. All of this goes to create a depressing atmosphere. Keeping the premises clean, record books, proper distribution of tasks, keeping things organized and in their right place and doing the designated tasks at the right time can remove this chaos and instil order. Accordingly, we cleaned our station premises, installed rainwater harvesting systems, brought in greenery with potted plants and trees, and painted the walls with colourful paintings related to spirituality and nature. We wrote inspiring quotes on the walls. We trained our personnel in organizational behaviour. Lo and behold! Our police station was transformed.

We also started implementing Six Sigma, Kaizen methods to improve the quality of our work. We evaluated the capabilities and strengths of our officers and other personnel, and gave them work that they were interested in and were capable of doing. We set individual targets and rewarded them if they completed the task on time. Work started happening fast because of our SMART goals. These help us to work precisely and provide justice effectively and on time.

'T' stands for technology. Robotics and artificial intelligence are now being used in policing and CCTV cameras are an example of this. These artificial eyes are proving to be a boon in controlling crime and identifying criminals. Even people who break traffic rules can be caught by these cameras. The movement of suspicious elements can be tracked using this software. The number plates of vehicles can be easily seen, and technology has made it possible to fight terrorism with ease. CCTVs have helped in reducing the number of policemen posted at different spots. The cameras are mounted on domes that have high-tech transmitters. These transmitters make it possible for the police to guide people in real time during emergencies.

We shouldn't work like donkeys, but work smartly and in an organized manner. We need to clarify our objectives and outcomes and plan accordingly. We should accept our failures open-mindedly and analyse the areas where we went wrong and need to improve. Life is full of ups and downs, successes and failures. When our ECG shows a straight line, it means death!

Our limbs go limp and the blood in our veins stops. Why should we then be afraid of failure? We shouldn't stop till we succeed.

Work without a break and fight till the end. There is no success without hard work, and no acclaim without success. No acclaim means no recognition and no acknowledgement of our work. If we desire to end corruption and bring in transparency, the officers and employees have to be appreciated for the work they do. Their skills and capabilities should be revealed to others. Such encouragement can increase the enthusiasm of the team, improve brotherhood, and inculcate healthy competition. They will compete to provide better service, behave amicably with people, and solve their problems professionally and in a timely manner.

Can assessment criteria for these parameters be fixed?

Performance assessment procedures

The 'A' in SMART obviously stands for accountability. How should the responsibilities of the employees be determined and how can their performance be evaluated? I implemented a three-month assessment cycle in every location where I was posted as police chief. This helped in deciding the responsibilities clearly, and these included every aspect of policing. The daily work of the employees was included in the assessment, with no separate end-of-quarter evaluation. There was no scope for manipulation.

The main tasks of the police are solving and preventing crime. We divided various types of crimes into different categories, as grade 1 to 5—violent crime, property crime, white-collar crime, organized crime, and consensual or victimless crime. We allotted 25 per cent marks for uncovering a crime and returning the stolen goods to the rightful owners. This led to an increase in the grading of cases of robbery, extortion, burglary, stealing of vehicles, chain snatching and led to a competition among the staff to investigate these cases and return the confiscated goods to the owners. The assets of the victims were returned to them at open, public functions. The confidence and trust of the common public in the police improved because of such initiatives.

The police force takes several measures for the prevention of crime. Visible policing, barricading, patrolling methods, night patrols, combing operations and conducting raids on suspicious locations are some visible policing measures. But compiling the profile of the criminal, initiating externment procedures, detaining offenders under the Maharashtra Prevention of Dangerous Activities Act (MPDA),[15] instilling fear among criminal gangs with the MCOCA and other such procedures are also constantly followed. Like crimes, even criminals are graded and records of habitual offenders are maintained. Special attention is paid to those offenders who have come out after completing their punishment.

The police get a *muchalka* from the district magistrate for the continued good behaviour of such offenders—a *muchalka* is a written agreement or bond taken by the DM from a miscreant, to bind him with an oath not to create any nuisance in society. Habitual offenders are declared fugitives. Hooligans and vandals who disrupt public law and order are put under detention in prison for a year.

We created a formula for the weightage of all these procedures: 50 points if one hooligan was externed; 25 points if his gang was history-sheeted; 200 points if action was taken under MCOCA; and 100 points for detention. All these actions take a lot of effort

---

15 The Maharashtra Prevention of Dangerous Activities of Slumlords, Bootleggers, Drug offenders, Dangerous Persons and Video Pirates Act, 1981.

and require a mountain of paperwork and documentation. We have to make innumerable trips to the courts. But once such assessment procedures were in place, the employees working detachedly in some corner of the police station gained hope and started working with a purpose.

Zero pendency and daily disposal

The biggest challenge in a police station is to complete different kinds of tasks—like crime investigation, checking applications, disposing cases of accidental deaths, and managing recovered assets lying for years—every single day. We created a simple system for this. We calculated the number of personnel needed, keeping in mind the total number of cases registered at the police station. It was a revelation. While one officer was handling forty to fifty cases, another was given only four or five cases. This was because the distribution of cases was based on the jurisdiction area of each police chowki or post. We stopped this system altogether. Instead, we took the average number of cases in the last four years and used that to calculate the number of cases each officer would be assigned in the forthcoming year. We evaluated the skills and abilities of the officer and assigned them cases that suited their skill set. For example, if an officer had a degree in Commerce, we assigned cases of financial fraud, embezzlement, and banking fraud cases. If some officers were trained in computers, we assigned them cases related to cybercrimes. Serious crimes were assigned to senior officers.

We noticed that those officers who disposed of cases fast were soon loaded with even more cases. We put a stop to this too and fixed the number of cases that an officer would handle on an annual basis. As a result, all officers started closing cases faster and since the distribution of cases was equitable, there were hardly any conflicts. We allotted 25 points for cases disposed and 100 if more cases were disposed compared to the previous year. This sped up our turnaround time.

We also classified all the recovered assets and items. The number of unclaimed vehicles was large. We auctioned the vehicles in a proper manner. When I was IG of Kolhapur, the then divisional commissioner, Chandrakant Dalvi, had organized a one-day 'zero pendency and daily disposal' camp. All the 186 station officers, forty-six DSPs, and five SPs were trained at the camp. Then we prepared for ISO certification. The IG office and 70 per cent of the police stations received ISO 9.0 certification within record time. The standard and the morale of the employees improved as a result.

The remaining 25 per cent marks were given to the pro public police administration. The people have to become the eyes and ears of the police. They need to control the police with both 'support' and 'pressure'. When there is an increase in unlawful acts and crime, the people must put pressure on the police. When the public stands with police in times of crisis and during man-made and natural disasters, the police automatically serve the people with enthusiasm and dedication. The main criterion for this is visible policing. We created a special QR code for every police station and its area, and created 'Nirbhaya Squads' for the safety of women.

Nirbhaya Squads

The whole country was shaken by the Nirbhaya incident in Delhi. When the Kopardi murder and rape case took place, Maharashtra erupted in flames. Such incidents shake the moral foundations of society, and we bow our heads in shame. I remember I was the IG in Kolhapur and had rushed to catch the 8.30 p.m. Mahalakshmi express after completing a meeting in Mumbai. I had a first-class ticket but since it was waitlisted, I wasn't sure which compartment my seat had been allotted in. I just hurriedly entered a compartment with my small briefcase in hand. A middle-aged foreigner sat in the compartment, and she looked worried and a bit scared. Dr Ansari, with his flowing beard, too followed me into the same compartment. The woman was really nervous but she gathered courage and introduced herself with a smile, 'Hi, I am Jennifer from the USA. Shall we take a selfie? I have to send it to my husband. It will help him identify my co-passengers.' We said yes and took the selfie for her satisfaction. She immediately forwarded it to her husband.

The police officer in me knew that she had posted the selfie for her own safety. She was scared to travel the night with two unknown Indian men. I introduced myself and told her that I am a police officer and assured her indirectly of her safety. Her worry seemed to have reduced a bit. In the meantime, the ticket collector (TC) arrived and told me that my seat had been confirmed in the adjacent B compartment. I took my briefcase and got up to leave, but the woman requested the TC to allot me the vacant berth in her compartment instead. The TC agreed and I continued my journey in the same compartment. Soon, the two of us got chatting.

Dr Ansari was a senior gynaecologist and worked as a visiting lecturer in a medical college in Miraj. The moment Jennifer heard that she pulled out a packet of sanitary napkins from her bag. She had worked in the United States Air Force (USAF) for twenty-five years and was now campaigning for the health awareness of girls and the usage of sanitary napkins in African and Asian countries. The napkins she showed us were washable, reusable and inexpensive. They were white and made of cotton.

She told us that these napkins had been a boon for girls from poor families.

I was tired after the day's work and went to sleep early. When I woke at six in the morning, the train had reached Sangli station, another person had entered the compartment and the three of them were chatting merrily. Seeing that I had woken up, Jennifer asked me an awkward question. 'Vishwas, what is your religion?' I told her I am a Hindu. Jennifer was elated hearing my answer. She said, 'I have met the whole of India in this tiny compartment! This is Mr Ravi, a Tamil Christian; Dr Ansari is a Muslim and has just finished reading his namaz. And Vishwas, the young police officer, is a Hindu and is protecting all of us. I am an American Jew and lucky to have witnessed India's unity in diversity personally. I am safe here. I bow down humbly to this great nation, which gives guests the place of god—*Athithi devo bhava.*' Jennifer was moved. We warmly took each other's leave at Kolhapur station and we are still in touch over email.

But, is this the real picture? Do all tourists who come to India return with the same sentiments? There was a considerable fall in the number of solo female travellers to India post the Nirbhaya incident. There were a lot of violent protests and communal polarization happened in the aftermath of the incident of rape. Laws changed and tough punishments were given, but the chain of violence against women from female infanticide to rape continues unabated. The safety of women and girls is a real challenge for the police, and even the public is extremely sensitive and strong-minded about the issue.

Several experiments have been tried regarding this issue across the country. The 'SHE' team has been implemented successfully in Hyderabad. It is but natural to feel safe in the presence of the police, but it is important to have a shield of safety in their absence. That is why a Nirbhaya Squad was set up in every area. This squad operates in plain clothes and carries hidden cameras. We make lists of the 'hotspots' in the city where women and girls come out in large numbers. These spots are assigned QR codes. The patrolling is planned in a clockwise and anticlockwise manner where jogging tracks, schools, and colleges are covered in the morning. Malls and multiplexes are patrolled in the afternoons, and markets and parks in the evenings.

Miscreants and mischievous elements that create trouble are watched, and their mischiefs are recorded in the hidden cameras as planned. Expert teams pounce on them and round them up. Cases are filed against the miscreants according to their crimes and appropriate action is taken. Cases are not filed against first-time offenders; they are sent to counsellors. If they are school or college going students, they are counselled in the presence of their parents. The delinquent actions of the children are shown to the parents on screen. It has been observed that 30 per cent of such offenders are married men. Such men are called in with their spouses and the impropriety of the husband is shown on film. There is no need for the police batons; the wife's wooden rolling pin does an effective job of punishing and restraining the husband.

In the backdrop of the Kopardi incident, we started Nirbhaya Squads in Western Maharashtra with some necessary changes. We ensure that chargesheets are filed in court within twenty-four hours in cases of sexual harassment. Even the courts have followed up and made sure that the hearings are hastened in certain cases and the offence is proven fast. The results of these initiatives are visible. For example, we are aware that women devotees who come to the Indrayani ghats take a dip in the river at the Alandi pilgrimage site. Lecherous men, rowdy youth and other such elements gather there habitually. We received complaints of such men harassing and teasing women. We sent members of a Nirbhaya Squad there and laid traps.

One of our young female police officers, dressed in jeans and a T-shirt and carrying a backpack, roamed the ghats like a college student. Soon enough, one of the rowdies came close and tried to get intimate with her. All his misdemeanours were being recorded in the hidden camera she was carrying. He asked her to come to a hotel with him on his bike. When she declined, he began to follow her wherever she went, lingered around her and gestured to her constantly. The moment the other Nirbhaya Squad members received her signal, they nabbed him easily. A case was filed against him under Section 354 of the IPC, which is about assault or criminal force used against woman with the intent to outrage her modesty. The chargesheet was filed in court within twenty-four hours. The biggest success was that the magistrate pronounced his judgement on the thirteenth day. The offender was sentenced to two years in prison and a Rs 5,000 fine.

Usually, school- and college-going girls who are eve-teased or harassed on the way, or working women who are sexually harassed at the workplace, hesitate to come forward and file complaints. The school and college students feel that if they do so, their parents will stop them from continuing their education and get them married. All their dreams will be shattered. The consequences are even more dire for working women. They are at risk of losing their jobs and livelihoods. We, the police, must firmly and proactively stand behind these girls and women and give them confidence. We need to take the lead and come forward to help women who desire not to disclose their identities and make sure they get justice.

Women are hired in 30 per cent of the positions at the deputy superintendent, police sub-inspector and constable levels in Maharashtra. They are full of energy and zeal. Most importantly, women officers are capable of handling all the frightening mental and physical crimes and problems faced right from birth to old age with empathy and sensitivity. With their active participation, the credibility of the department and its image has improved.

A girl student from a boarding school in Valava taluka in Sangli sent an anonymous letter to a police station, in which she had described in detail the sexual harassment by the head of the institution. The female employees of the school were hand-in-glove with the offender. The sealed envelope was addressed to the female sub-inspector who was the head of the Nirbhaya Squad of the area. The sender had clearly requested that the letter should be opened only by her and nobody else.

Our daring female SI made secret visits to the boarding school and assured the girls there. She took the parents into confidence. Owing to her efforts, girls who had been facing sexual torture for years were saved and the shameless head of the institution who was exploiting his wards and all his accomplices were handcuffed and punished.

Setting goals

We need to set our goals keeping in mind the welfare of the people at the grassroots and the weaker sections of society with sensitivity, and handle them using the SMART goal method. Once clear SMART goals are set, all confusions, uncertainties and conflicts vanish. Our self-confidence increases and we feel exceptionally secure. Energy flows through the body and keeps us going. We become unstoppable and nothing can distract us from our path. And yes, we must not allow any negative powers to come anywhere near us. We need to rein in the bitter memories and past failures, and the irrational worries about the future, as and when they raise their heads.

Everything in life does not happen as per our desire and expectations. We should not allow the crises in our lives to distract us from our goals. We should use every possible source of energy to give impetus to our actions and efforts. Our hands perform actions mechanically, but if we perform our tasks with commitment, creativity and vision, our work will be exceptional and completed successfully. The hands, mind and heart should work in tandem to create magic!

All successful people in the world are extremely focused and determined. They are aware of where to reach and how to go, because their goals are clear. And they reach their desired destination one way or the other. They make failures their stepping stones to success. But the questions still remain: How should our goals be? What should be their form? How should they be structured and how do we identify that they are our real goals?

Goal setting is a constantly evolving process and the necessary criteria are intrinsic to it. According to Maslow's hierarchy of needs, our material, physical, mental and spiritual needs have to be fulfilled. Even our goals are determined based on similar needs. The nature and form of our goals change, keeping a balance between our self-interest and the highest good. It keeps changing according to the times and circumstances. Nevertheless, there are certain important criteria or parameters for setting goals.

What do you want people to say about you in your absence? Create a personal sketch of how you want to behave with your spouse, what kind of ideals your children should see in you, and how your parents should be proud of you. How should your friends and co-workers remember you? What kind of reaction is received from society at the mention of your name? These are some of the questions you must ask yourself and write down the answers to. You will see your goals mirrored on that sheet.

This visualization will reveal the ideals you hold that are important subconsciously. You will see your unfulfilled desires and aspirations. Your value systems and upbringing will be revealed and the chains of selfishness will fall apart. The walls of narrow-mindedness that surround you will crumble; selfishness, malice, greed, envy, hatred and trickery will vanish. And then will emerge the 'ideal you' that you envisaged, which will give you your dreams, hope and resolve.

Your skills and talent will direct you towards your goal. Nobody can prevent you from reaching your goals any longer. Your self-confidence will be at its peak. Your inner fire will be inextinguishable and the words of dedication carved in your heart cannot be erased by anyone. You will be your own sculptor and you will be unshakable. How much ever people try to put you in trouble, you will come out dazzling like pure gold melted at high temperatures. Truth, service and safety are intrinsic to the motto of the academy. These are what helped us set our professional goals in the police service, but new goals crop up often in our personal and social lives. We must progress towards the ultimate goal in life by stepping on those goals and objectives. The journey that started in the village was colourful and complete. It had its share of ups and downs.

I was able to climb a peak in my twenty-third year. But I was now on my way to gather the knowledge and power to scale Mount Everest and expand my horizons. I could not see my goal clearly, but I was sure I would be able to see it clearly one day. Each one of us sees it differently, but all of us do have an ultimate goal in life. We have small milestones on the path to the same, just as we have to fight small battles before we can win the war. It is possible that we might ignore the milestones that show us the way to the ultimate goal, getting distracted by an easier and more comfortable path. There might be some pleasurable spots midway where we can relax, and the desire to stay back there distracts us from the goal. To avoid that, we need to be mentally strong, disciplined, vigilant and introspect deeply while crossing one stage after another. The journey towards the final goal is what gives us real happiness.

Like they say in Hindi, *'safar khoobsurat hai, manzil se bhi'*, which means 'the journey is more beautiful than the destination.' Crossing different points and reaching shorter milestones on the way makes the journey fulfilling, and we ultimately find our destination. There is an incomparable poem by Amrita Pritam where she describes the imaginary way in which she distributes the different objects of her legacy after her death. In other words, it is her Will:

> After my death, ransack my room
> Search each item that is scattered
> Unlocked, everywhere in my house.
> Donate my dreams, to all those women
> Who between the confines of the kitchen and the bedroom,
> Have lost their world, have forgotten years ago
> What it is to dream.
> Scatter my laughter among the inmates of old-age homes
> Whose children are lost to the glittering cities of America.
> There are some colours lying on my table
> With them dye the sari of the girl,
> Whose border is edged with the blood of her man
> Who wrapped in the tricolour was laid to rest last evening
> Give my tears to all the poets
> Every drop will birth a poem
> I promise.

My honour and my reputation are for the woman
Who prostitutes her body, so her daughter can get an education.
Make sure you catch the youth of the country, everyone
And inject them with my indignation
They will need it
Come the revolution.
My ecstasy belongs to that Sufi
Who abandoning everything,
Has set off in search of God.
Finally,
What's left…
My envy, my greed
My anger, my lies
My selfishness
These... simply cremate with me—

How inspiringly the poetess has expressed her life's purpose and ideals. If we must auction all our emotions and material possessions in life, we have to account for them when we are still alive. We need to accumulate this every day of our lives, the values and purposeful principles we desire to leave behind for our future generations.

My hard work at the academy had made me sweat and melted away the fat accumulated around my belly, and I became fit and healthy. It had given wind to my wings of knowledge and thoughts. These were going to stand me in good stead all my life. They would not be enough, but in abundance. Because I was going to gather everything I gained and ensure that my legacy never went empty.

9

Obstacles and Suicide

Life goes on with its ups and downs, and our emotions and feelings arise thick and fast depending on the situation. It is possible to channelize them in the right direction through mental training. Whenever we feel down and sad, we pray to God. Often when we are faced with a problem and gripped by sorrow, we start blaming our destiny and God. Sometimes we get trapped in a chain of problems and misery, and we take to superstition and rituals to find solutions to our problems. We also read self-help books to seek inspiration.

In times of really serious problems and emergencies, or when we are burdened with huge responsibilities, all our plans and strategies fall flat. Despite that we have to continue taking small steps every day to come out of the crisis. If we are falling into the trap of attachments, we need to give auto-suggestions to ourselves and warn our minds to come out of this trap. We have to consciously ensure that we become more mature with age and inculcate positive habits. Despite all these efforts, we fall prey to envy and jealousy. We do good to others and at the same time do unpardonable things knowingly and unknowingly, causing serious harm to others. This conflict between our personality, character and wisdom is constant in our lives. Our lives take new dimensions and our conscience changes form every day with our ambitions going in search of newer heights. This is what life is all about!

Change is the only constant in life, and that is why it is important for us to keep bouncing back, walking untiringly, unshakably towards our goal without being bogged down by the obstacles that come in our way. We should be optimistic and crush every impediment with confidence. This is the hallmark of a glorious life.

The conflict between mind and brain is constant. The brain is always quiet, practical and warns us of any danger. We are compelled to think about our future while taking any decision. On the contrary, the heart and the mind are mischievous and if something goes against them, it becomes very difficult to restrain them. We end up doing apparently dangerous things to keep our minds satisfied. This causes internal strife and creates a lot of conflict. If some injustice or discrimination takes place, the brain asks the mind to wait for the most opportune moment to complain. The mind then doesn't allow you to sleep in peace and keeps you agitated. As a result, your heart rate increases and the body begins to hurt because of stress.

At such times, the wisdom that has been enabled through training and our values wakes up and tries to mediate between the heart and the brain. In some challenging situations, if the brain wins you will achieve success prima facie, but there is a danger of compromise that may make you spineless. If you listen only to your heart constantly, your emotions get drained, and you may feel good for a while but later face practical difficulties. Your family and relatives get affected by your behaviour and the relationships get strained.

It is said that your heart should rule your home and your brain should rule your profession. This means that you should be more emotional at home and more professional at work, but there has to be a balance between the two. The wiser you are, the better control you have over yourself. When you commit less sins, your tension is also comparatively less. If you don't complicate matters, there will be no conflict between the mind and the brain. Harmony prevails and that is why people who pay back what they receive from society stay away from problems and difficulties.

Of late, many people seem to be committing suicides for trivial reasons. A youth in Nashik killed himself fearing that he would get COVID-19 and be admitted to hospital, administered saline and given injections. Several eminent personalities, successful entrepreneurs and talented artists give up their lives due to stress. I have witnessed the suicide of a supermodel and an actress at close quarters. I got a glimpse of the dark side of Page 3-depression. This model ruled the fashion world, but depression, disappointments, loneliness and unhappiness caused her to decide to take her life. The corporate world used and discarded her like a paper napkin.

In fact, this model was from a Marathi family that had migrated abroad two generations ago. She had won a national beauty contest abroad and had come to India to try her luck in the Hindi film industry. She reigned over the ramp world initially, but as her beauty began to wane with age, she fell prey to drugs. She then got into the Page 3 circuit and was exploited and used by people. The eyes of the son of a prominent businessman fell on her. He impressed her with his wealth and handsome personality. They went on a holiday to Goa, and she began dreaming of marriage.

She was four years older than him, and she went to a gynaecologist to check whether there would be any complications in having a child. The poor girl even sent her boyfriend's and her own horoscope to her mother to see if they matched. When her boyfriend took her home to meet his parents, his mother used the choicest of abuses, humiliated her and rejected her outright. The spineless boyfriend did not have the guts to go against his mother and dumped this girl.

She found it hard to take the humiliation and rejection. At the time when the Page 3 celebrities had gone home after partying late into the night, this drunk model took an overdose of sleeping pills, cut her wrist and collapsed. Nobody came to know what had happened for three days. Once the stench of the dead body spread, the neighbours informed the police. She had written the name of her boyfriend on the wall with the words, 'you killed me'. Owing to the lack of proper evidence, the boyfriend went scot free.

Miss you, Himanshu Sir

Himanshu Roy Sir was one of the people who had influenced my personality greatly. He was an achiever and had reached great heights. He had a dashing and impressive personality. I met him for the first time when he was the police commissioner in Nashik and I was the SP in Ahmednagar. We, the junior officers, had the opportunity to be guided by him while organizing the state-level police sports competition. A tall, heavy-set officer, Himanshu Sir was a wise, mature and distinguished man. He was extremely fluent in both Marathi and English, and we would be mesmerized by his English. There was not a single uncultured word in his speech, and I had never seen him gossip or indulge in small talk.

I had the fortune to work with him following the 26/11 attacks. Calm, affable and patient Himanshu Sir was a thorough professional. Often, his name was enough to control a situation, and he would eagerly come to the field to lead from the front and diffuse the trickiest situations. Once, during the visit of a former US President, the American security forces underestimated the Mumbai police and tried to wield their power. When I informed Sir about this, he immediately reached the Taj Hotel and told the Americans in no uncertain terms in English, 'The Mumbai police is committed and capable of protecting the American President. Please do not interfere with our work.' Sir's words instilled a lot of confidence in us.

Himanshu Sir was a living example of how a true leader should be. His decisions and instructions were always crystal clear and unambiguous. Once he made his decision, he never shied away from taking full responsibility for any untoward outcomes. Hence, there was no conflict between the officers and the police personnel. Once an association of the blind created a blockade during the peak hours in front of the Chhatrapati Shivaji Terminus (CST) station, to voice their demands. There was utter chaos and the main roads were jammed. The blind people lost their patience, and the protest turned violent as they started throwing chilli powder at the police and began hitting them with their white canes.

The police were taken by surprise by the sudden attack. I rushed to the spot immediately. The officer in charge there asked me for permission to use force. Using force on the blind protesters looked like the only way out to control the situation. I called Roy Sir (the Additional CP) and informed him that we wanted to lathi-charge the violent blind protesters. He refused to give permission and said not a single baton would be raised on the blind even if the traffic jam extended till Pune! He came to the spot and tactfully made the protesters understand and diffused the crisis. He was clear about what to do and what not to do. He was extremely knowledgeable and had friends in every field.

We both used to work out in the same gym. All weights in the gym were inadequate for his rippling muscles and beefed-up body. Roy Madam too used to come to work out in the same gym. Himanshu Sir would playfully lift her up easily. The chemistry between the couple was amazing. Himanshu Sir would talk freely with everyone in the gym and work out listening to classical music on his earphones. I have never seen anyone lifting heavy weights in the gym while listening to classical music! I have had the opportunity to interact with a host of Bollywood personalities in connection with the 'Umang' police welfare programmes. All of them held Himanshu Sir in high esteem. They spoke about him with regard and respect. 'We are only reel heroes; Roy Sir is the hero in real life,' they would often say.

He had excellent writing skills too. Once I had used the improper word 'bullshit' in annoyance while writing an unofficial letter to a junior officer. I had given a copy of the letter to Himanshu Sir. He called me and gave me valuable tips on writing formal letters and effective communication. I don't remember him ever issuing a memo or expressing his displeasure in writing. If a junior officer made a mistake, he would call them and take them to task in private. I have never heard of him having taken written action on anyone.

He would address police personnel as 'beta' or son and enquire about them with his hand on their shoulder. Even senior officers looked up to him as their elder brother, a guide and mentor. Such a versatile, consummate and multifaceted personality must have caught the evil eye! He was suddenly diagnosed with cancer. I went to meet him the moment I got the news. He calmed me down saying, 'Vishwas, we are fighters, and we will surely defeat this new enemy. No crying. It is time to fight.' Gradually, he became weaker with the chemotherapy, and we could see that his condition was worsening. He started exercising with the support of a walking stick. But when the end was certain in a few months, he defeated an impending painful death, and one morning he shot himself with his own pistol. His loss created a huge vacuum in our lives.

His painful exit raised a lot of questions within me. Why did such an inspiring and courageous person, who taught us how to live with hope and happiness and face challenges, get bogged down when his health was improving and then worsened for a traumatic end? How could God be so heartless to a man who defeated evil and the vermin of society, and who was mentally tough and physically fit? Why did such a handsome, charming and intelligent man with friends and acquaintances in every field, and a wife who loved him so much, shoot himself with a loaded pistol? Why did the man who sensitively cared for and supported his juniors and colleagues like an elder brother all his life, in the end leave us all so bereft? Why didn't Sir, who was so enthusiastic and lived with zeal, not take anyone into confidence before taking such a decision?

Viktor Frankl, a twentieth-century psychologist has written a book, *Man's Search for Meaning*.[16] He was one of those who came out alive from a Nazi concentration camp in Germany. Viktor narrated the story of a woman who called him on the phone at midnight and told him coldly that she was going to take her own life. Victor talked to her, refusing to cut the line. He explained to her how short-lived depression is and how

---

16 Viktor Frankl (1962), *Man's Search for Meaning*, translated by Ilse Lasch, Boston: Beacon Press.

valuable life is. Frankl kept her on the phone and talked her through her depression, giving her reason after reason to carry on living. Finally, she dropped her decision and gave Viktor her word that she would not take her life. When they met in person later, Viktor asked her what logic or argument made her change her decision, what had persuaded her. 'None of them,' she replied.

What then influenced her to go on living, he wanted to know.

Her answer was simple: it was his 'willingness to listen' to her in the middle of the night. A world in which there was someone ready to listen to another's pain seemed to her a world in which it was worthwhile to live. Often, it is not the brilliant argument that makes the difference but the small act of listening that proves the most valuable!

Swiss psychiatrist Kübler-Ross has propounded a psychological theory: Whenever we are faced with serious emergencies, bereavement, accidents or severe mental trauma, we go through five stages of grief—denial, anger, bargaining, depression and acceptance.

We are initially hesitant to face the crisis. Fear of the outcome makes us deny the event. We refuse to accept that we are in deep trouble. We withdraw into a shell and are in a state of denial. We realize the situation only when our back is broken. Then we become increasingly irritable and angry. We begin to hurt ourselves and then blame others for our sorrow. We talk to ourselves and have what-if conversations like 'if I had this, I wouldn't have fallen into this mess' and so on. We curse our destiny. Finally, we begin to see reality and depression follows.

The mind gets pulled apart and one becomes almost comatose. It is important to have someone at this stage to give us support and help us learn to accept the situation and fight the circumstances squarely. This will help us control ourselves and put the brakes on our depression. Human beings are basically strugglers and fighters. They need to just be protected during some weak moments. This is where friends and strong relationships come in handy and are extremely important. The close friends I made at the academy have stood as shock absorbers at every hurdle in my life. We IPS officers live our lives wearing a crown of thorns. Stress often scrapes us hollow from within.

One of my friends was one such versatile, happy-go-lucky man, like Rajesh Khanna in the movie *Anand*. Everyone wanted to be with him in the academy. After he joined the force, he had an impressive career and handled every tenure with success. He fought Naxalites during his tenure in Hazaribagh. He was seriously wounded when they attacked his house. He was airlifted to Kolkata by a chartered plane and luckily survived. But soon thereafter, he was diagnosed with renal cell carcinoma and our dear friend left us quietly. One who only spread happiness wherever he went, laughed heartily, cracked jokes—he never spoke about his illness to anyone.

Another batchmate of mine was the life of the batch during the foundation course in Mussoorie. She was very friendly, outgoing and took active part in social activities. She was an Indian Audit & Accounts Service (IA&AS) officer who had travelled the world. She put a full stop to her life all of a sudden. She was very active on Facebook and WhatsApp, but nobody knew what trauma she was going through. She didn't share her pain with anyone and took her own life.

Why do educated people who achieve great heights in their careers suffer so? What is life after all? You work hard and earn a living. Is that life? You go out and stand up for those who need you, improve other peoples' lives. You become a sponge that absorbs all the negativity and spreads positive energy. If some desired changes occur in someone's life because of you and your efforts, you spread light in someone's life, you help shape someone's future. Someone did not give up on life because of your support and did not lose hope because you were there—this is what makes your life meaningful and we understand what life is truly all about.

Making and breaking

We have all heard about IQ or intelligence quotient till now, but psychologists have said that not only IQ but even EQ, SQ and AQ are equally important for a meaningful life. Your IQ is an indicator of your analytical skills, memory, and your mathematical skills. Your EQ or 'emotional quotient' evaluates the strength of your relationship with people and the honesty of your emotions. Your punctuality, sense of responsibility, credibility, amiability and maturity are also included in the same. Your SQ or 'social quotient' is a measure of how social you are. Your friendships and your commitment to your relationships are discussed under this aspect.

We give unreasonable importance to IQ in our education, but it has been observed that it is people with high EQ and SQ who climb the ladder of success in life. We have often seen people with high IQ work under people with very modest IQ but excellent EQ and SQ. Your EQ is a measure of your character and mental health. Your SQ measures how pleasant and impressive you are as a person. Hence, we need to inculcate habits that enhance our EQ and SQ, along with our intellectual abilities, at the right age.

The fourth aspect that has come to the fore is AQ or 'adversity quotient', which is a measure of how effectively one tides over tough situations. This quotient is an indicator of your ability to fight an adversity and effectively come out of it unscathed. Negative aspects such as cowardliness, infirmness and committing suicide are also included in this. Your patience, resilience, self-confidence and self-sufficiency are also given appropriate weightage. We saw that a lot of successful people felt completely overwhelmed during the COVID-19 pandemic. We saw them get depressed and some went to the extent of taking their own lives. Let's take the example of Sushant Singh Rajput. It seems he lacked nothing in life. Yet he may have been dealing with some serious issues. The chocolate-boy hero of Bollywood, who was a champion in the Mathematics Olympiad, left us too early.

It is important that our children should know the real world, apart from their academics. We need to allow them to play games: let them get bruised and their knees sore. That is when they will learn not to be afraid if they see blood. Get them to appreciate art and make them understand the importance of physical labour. In the nineteenth century, Abraham Lincoln had written a letter to the principal of his son's school. If we understand its gist and implement it in our own lives and treat our students thus, there might be lesser number of suicides in the world.

> He will have to learn. I know that all men are not just, all men are not true, but teach him also that for every scoundrel there is a hero; that for every selfish politician, there is a dedicated leader .... Teach him that for every enemy there is a friend. It will take time, I know, but teach him, if you can, that a dollar earned is of far more value than five found .... Teach him to learn to lose ... and also to enjoy winning. Steer him away from envy, if you can, teach him the secret of quiet laughter. Let him

> learn early that bullies are the easiest to lick .... Teach him, if you can, the wonder of a book ... but also give him quiet time to ponder the eternal mystery of birds in the sky, bees in the sun, and flowers on a green hillside.
>
> In school, teach him it is far more honourable to fail than to cheat .... Teach him to have faith in his own ideas, even if everyone tells him they are wrong .... Teach him to be gentle with gentle people, and tough with the tough. Try to give my son the strength not to follow the crowd when everyone is getting on the bandwagon .... Teach him to listen to all men .... but teach him also to filter all he hears on a screen of truth, and take only the good that comes through. Teach him, if you can, how to laugh when he is sad .... Teach him there is no shame in tears.
>
> Teach him to scoff at cynics and to beware of too much sweetness .... Teach him to sell his brawn and brain to the highest bidders, but never to put a price tag on his heart and soul. Teach him to close his ears to a howling mob .... and to stand and fight if he thinks he is right. Treat him gently, but do not coddle him, because only the test of fire makes fine steel. Let him have the courage to be impatient .... let him have the patience to be brave. Teach him always to have sublime faith in himself, because then he will always have sublime faith in mankind. This is a big order, but see what you can do .... He is such a fine little fellow, my son!

Truly, these words make us aware of our own lives and behaviour. With time, for many of us, our attitude improves and we mature intellectually. But, truly, are we teaching our children such things in school and college? The top-ranking schools take ridiculously large donations and unaffordable amounts as fees; but what kind of value education and morals the teachers there are going to provide remains an unanswered, million-dollar question.

Every person in this world is unique, with their own individual talents and shortcomings. As parents and teachers, we must identify the passion in our children, our students and find out what gives them happiness. We should then help them on their journey to achieve that. All of us are used to judging how good a school is, based on the number of students who scored 90 per cent or more in the board exams and the pass percentage of the students. But we never evaluate how happy the students are. Is a qualification or degree acquired by rote-learning enough to make one capable and ready to face life? Education is beyond degree, marks and grades. Along with knowledge, students need to be taught values that can help them grow up into good citizens and live lives of dignity. They need to be constantly told that it is important for them to help others and try to make them happy.

The moment our child comes home from school, the first question we ask is, 'How many marks did you score?' If the marks are good our next question is, 'What is your rank?' And if the child stands second by any chance, madness follows. 'Why not first?' is our next question! We don't even bother about the condition of students who either fail or are not in the toppers list! As a result of this, the child firmly believes that they have to come first at any cost. Hence, by the time they complete their education and step into life's rat race, they have become self-centred and selfish. They think only about themselves and believe that they have to succeed by hook or by crook. Let the whole world go to hell! But the truth is that we parents and teachers are responsible for this moral degradation and devaluation. Our faulty system is responsible for it.

Parents aspire to give the best possible to their children. The moment the child returns from school, it is time for tuition classes. The child is forcefully pushed into IIT coaching, bharatanatyam, guitar, tennis and chess coaching. No one bothers about what the child really wants. Once the best is stuffed into them, the hunger in children for material success surges, and they fall into the trap of envy, inferiority complexes, fear, depression and laziness. These conditions can be called 'parent-inflicted'!

Those children who bear with injustice, torture and intense pressure during their childhood and formative years start throwing tantrums during their adolescence as a result. They are disinterested in everything and are constantly edgy and restless. They keep changing their goals and are confused when faced with career options. At this stage, parents begin to protect their ward saying, 'Don't worry, if you don't like this job, look for something else'. Now pampered and spoiled, the youth extract money from parents and go around unabashedly puffing cigarettes with their peers. Gradually, they get increasingly stressed, and soon enough, they are into addictions. From beer and whiskey, they graduate to weed and other drugs. If they do get a job, it doesn't last long and they get bored. If they get married, they don't get along with their spouse. They run to their parents for support. The parents on their part continue to protect them, refusing to let go. All this is a result of parents bringing up their children in such a way that the child doesn't learn to face even the slightest problem in their childhood (other than their pressure tactics).

It is great that you love your children and they are your life! But how can you constantly keep them clean and protected? How can you keep them away from pollution? When it is time for them to step into the real world, such dependent children who lack adequate immunity, break down in the face of tough situations and adversities. They begin to run away from any kind of hard work and opposition; they try to withdraw into their comfortable cocoons.

Parents—if you really love your children—allow them to live on their own strength. Many mothers wash the plates and vessels with sanitizer and rinse them with warm water before feeding their children, to prevent infections. Such hyper and overprotective parents must be told loud and clear that if they keep their children enclosed in such air-tight compartments, the child will feel choked! If parents want their children to face life and achieve something substantial in future, they must be allowed to face bullying, enmity, disappointments, pain, physical labour and fierce competition on their own. Of course, as parents we must be there for our children and support them whenever it is rightfully needed; but don't surround them with lifeguards and oxygen masks even before they have worn their swimming costumes and entered the pool. They will feel suffocated! Tell your children that they need to earn their own living, save money and not overspend. They need to hear the word NO and learn to digest it.

I once read a WhatsApp message that said, 'We seek the front seats when we go for a play but choose the back seats when we watch a movie.' One's status and place in life are constantly changing. We need oil to make soap, and the same soap is needed to wash away oil! Life is full of such contradictions. We see that small children and crazy people are the happiest in the world. That is why we need to madly follow our goals and once we reach them, we should enjoy them fully like small children. These are the simple mantras of life!

The mirror is the same: it shows us a happy face when we smile and sad one when we sulk! It is the same with life as well. It is we who decide how we want to look at life—as misery or a celebration! Schools and colleges teach us 'life sciences' but the 'science of life' is more important! Recognizing the language of the heart is more important than learning the grammar of language. We need to realize at the right time in life that it is not mathematics but our outlook towards life that helps us tide over crises and tough times. If we intend to change the system, we have to change our thoughts and mindset as well. When our children come home, instead of asking them their grades, we need to ask them if they helped anyone, if they smiled and spread happiness and were compassionate. When such children grow up, society changes and that, in turn, changes the country and the world. But, when the intentions of the citizens are pure, discrimination and divisiveness disappear. Stress vanishes and social harmony takes over.

Mobiles, relationships and mental health

I had memorized this abhang of Saint Tukaram, '*man kara re Prasanna, sarva siddhiche kaaran*' in childhood. It means, 'in this life, keep your mind (soul) happy, to achieve everything'. It gave me immense inspiration and strength, and kept me focused. It brought me back to my path every time I digressed or got diverted from it. However, things are so different today. The mobile and internet revolution has taken over our lives and has changed society, our children's minds inside out. This has beautifully described the frightening situation in a poem, in which the poet says:[17]

17 This is excerpted from a sermon 'The Paradox of Our Time' attributed to Dr Bob Moorehead, but which has also been variously attributed to many, including the Dalai Lama.

The paradox of our time in history is that we have taller buildings, but shorter tempers; wider freeways, but narrower viewpoints; we spend more, but have less; we buy more, but enjoy it less.

We have bigger houses and smaller families; more conveniences, but less time; we have more degrees, but less sense; more knowledge, but less judgment; more experts, but more problems; more medicine, but less wellness.

We drink too much, smoke too much, spend too recklessly, laugh too little, drive too fast, get angry too quickly, stay up too late, get up too tired, read too seldom, watch TV too much, and pray too seldom.

We have multiplied our possessions, but reduced our values. We talk too much, love too seldom, and hate too often. We've learned how to make a living, but not a life; we've added years to life, not life to years.

We've been all the way to the moon and back, but have trouble crossing the street to meet the new neighbour. We've conquered outer space, but not inner space; we've done larger things, but not better things.

We've cleaned up the air, but polluted the soul; we've split the atom, but not our prejudice.

We write more, but learn less; we plan more, but accomplish less. We've learned to rush, but not to wait; we have higher incomes, but lower morals; we have more food, but less appeasement; we build more computers to hold more information to produce more copies than ever, but have less communication; we've become long on quantity, but short on quality.

These are the times of fast foods and slow digestion; tall men, and short character; steep profits, and shallow

> relationships. These are the times of world peace, but domestic warfare; more leisure, but less fun; more kinds of food, but less nutrition.
>
> These are days of two incomes, but more divorce; of fancier houses, but broken homes. These are days of quick trips, disposable diapers, throw away morality, one-night stands, overweight bodies, and pills that do everything from cheer to quiet to kill.
>
> It is a time when there is much in the show window and nothing in the stockroom.
>
> What is the way out?

These words are so telling! On top of all this, access to mobiles and the internet has enraptured an entire generation. Once one is trapped in their grip, there seems to be no escape. We are seeing teenagers losing their minds due to this addiction. They are spending three to four hours on screen consuming useless information on social media. This has led to a lot of psychological problems. A game called 'blue whale' took so many young lives. Games such as PUBG, COD and Minecraft have wreaked havoc among youngsters. It is time for an open conversation on the harmful effects of such technology on families and parent-child communication, to assuage the fear that has gripped families.

Let's examine the effect of the mobile revolution on Indian society and the family structure. In the past few years, our communication has changed unrecognizably. We are stuck deeply in the muck of wireless phones. We are inseparable from our phones and, unlike the time when we had wired phones, our mobile phones have become extensions of our bodies. The internet has diffused into our minds and bodies so dangerously that we find it difficult to be away from it even for a minute. It has become a necessity for our survival, like oxygen! The twenty-first century has brought with it addiction of a very obnoxious kind. Addiction to drugs, sex, suicidal tendencies, depression and such other conditions are consequences of this new culture.

I had raided three rave parties and took action against a lot of young girls and boys. There was a lot of controversy as a result. The invites for all the three rave parties were sent through social media. Terror organization such as the ISIS has also influenced a lot of youngsters with their fundamentalist beliefs and trapped them in their poisonous net. There are thousands of toxic posts regarding caste, creed, religion, faith and language that are shared on social media every day. Communal tensions increase and riots take place because of these posts. All this is basically infectious and has spread rapidly, entered almost every home and is affecting the minds of everyone. There is a lot of discussion happening on how to control the electronic media and create codes of conduct keeping in mind age, education, social and cultural ethos.

Parents have handed this monster into the hands of little children. They calm down the moment they get mobiles: they don't argue, throw a tantrum or trouble their parents. They get lost in the world on the mobile screens like robots, and sit for hours on end mesmerized by the virtual world. I recently read an article by Mukta Puntambekar in which she talks about a young boy and his mother who came to her rehabilitation centre. The boy had become so addicted to the internet that he wouldn't realize he had urinated in his pants while being engrossed on the internet. This is a frightening example of addiction to mobiles and the internet.

These days, both parents go to work and are not able to spend enough time with their children. With nuclear families becoming the norm, children have no one to talk to. The usual games and sports that children used to play in school and in playgrounds are now a thing of the past. That is why these children take refuge in the virtual world of selfies, likes, sharing and comments to express themselves. It is a completely artificial, false and imaginary universe, totally disconnected from reality and rationality. Parents, too, just stuff a mobile phone into their children's hands when they throw a tantrum, are alone at home, or when they make a fuss during programmes or family visits. That is the only way the parents know to quieten their children!

The children play violent games on the net, which blunt their emotions and make them aggressive. The children lose their natural, inborn naughty and frolicking nature, and they become rude, hostile and violent. Their material demands grow constantly, and a sense of entitlement takes over. They upload their pictures unnecessarily on Snapchat, WhatsApp and Facebook and get attracted to all kinds of addictions. Many of these ignorant youngsters fall prey to sexual predators on the internet.

Everyone I talk to feels that there is only one solution to end this menace. Parents have to communicate more with their children and make the conversations increasingly constructive and active. They must give time to their children. It is not as if parents are not doing this, and several parents are not able to control the storm despite giving time to their children. Adolescence is an extremely explosive age.

There was a survey conducted in America that said that by the time children complete their twelfth grade, they would have spent 20,000 hours on the internet. During this time, they would have watched thousands of murders, suicides, rapes and innumerable pornographic clips.

This is the age when the frontal lobe of the brain is developing, and children are still not capable of differentiating between right and wrong and go through emotional conflicts. It is very difficult to understand children at this stage because they tell lies, hide their faults and, if the parents expose them, they throw an emotional tantrum. The situation gets complicated and goes out of hand. A police inspector's son slit his mother's throat when she repeatedly tried to make him understand something. He was apparently vexed with her nagging. Tolerance and patience seem to be vanishing from the personalities of our teenagers. It's a problem if we give them mobiles and a bigger problem if we don't. Their tantrums and mood swings have gone beyond our control.

When parents return from work these days, they both get busy on Instagram, Facebook and WhatsApp. Their child comes to them, sits around for some time, kisses them, tries to ask a few questions, but the parents are least interested. They are busy smiling at the comments on their phone instead of focusing on the child. The child is hurt at this indifference and goes back into their room disappointed. There the child opens an iPad and starts playing games online.

Parents create a ruckus about their children being addicted to the phone but don't realize that it started because of the time they spent hooked on it in the first place. Mobiles have had an adverse effect on the parent-child relationship, social and emotional behaviour of the children. Children of parents who spend a lot of time on their phones create a lot of tantrums in public places and annoy others. The mobile phone is the number one enemy of good parenting and upbringing. In homes where the mothers are constantly on the phone while working—and consider themselves multitaskers—patience and tolerance are lost and discord takes over. People don't realize where they are going while chatting on social media; misunderstandings become serious, marriages go haywire, trust is lost and families break. The cyber cell of the police is handling an increasing number of cases of marital discord caused by mobiles.

There are fathers who pretend to be busy on their laptops instead of spending time with their children. Such avoidable and dangerous habits have affected the concentration and focus of people. These habits have adverse effects on the brain and consequently lead to mental illnesses. Irritability, forgetfulness and lack of concentration are some of the primary symptoms and should be enough to remove the attraction for the internet from their eyes. It has become imperative for families to put appropriate and wise restrictions on the use of these digital appliances to ensure the physical and mental health of everyone.

When parents give unstinted and complete attention, the growth of children is healthy and holistic, and their self-respect and energy are automatically high. But those parents who are constantly on their mobiles will find that their children are often depressed, frustrated and express themselves in a reckless manner.

What is the solution to this serious problem? How can we manage our teenagers and control their behaviour? How do we make them aware of their responsibilities? I remember reading a letter a mother had written to her thirteen-year-old son while buying him an iPhone. It was like a contract between the parent and child. The mother had clearly expressed her expectations from her son while giving him the iPhone.[18] Here are excerpts:

18 Jannelle Burley Hofmann (2012), 'iPhone contract from your mom with love: Failure to comply with the following list will result in termination of your iPhone ownership,' *HuffPost*, 28 December. https://www.huffpost.com/entry/iphone-contract-from-your-mom_b_2372493

I hope that you understand it is my job to raise you into a well-rounded, healthy young man that can function in the world and coexist with technology, not be ruled by it. Failure to comply with the following list will result in termination of your iPhone ownership...

1. It is my phone. I bought it. I pay for it. I am loaning it to you.
2. I will always know the password.
3. If it rings, answer it. Say hello, use your manners. Do not ever ignore a phone call if the screen reads "Mom" or "Dad". Not ever.
4. Hand the phone to one of your parents promptly at 7:30 p.m. every school night and every weekend night at 9:00 p.m. It will be shut off for the night and turned on again at 7:30 a.m. If you want to call someone, use the landline at night.
5. It does not go to school with you. Have a conversation with the people you text in person. It's a life skill....
6. Do not use this technology to lie, fool, or deceive another human being. Do not involve yourself in conversations that are hurtful to others. Be a good friend first or stay the hell out of the crossfire.
7. Do not text, email, or say anything through this device you would not say in person.
8. Do not text, email, or say anything to someone that you would not say out loud with their parents in the room. Censor yourself.
9. No porn. Search the web for information you would openly share with me. If you have a question about anything, ask a person – preferably me or your father.

10. Turn it off, silence it, put it away in public. Especially in a restaurant, at the movies, or while speaking with another human being. You are not a rude person; do not allow the iPhone to change that.
11. Do not send or receive pictures of your private parts or anyone else's private parts. Don't laugh. Someday you will be tempted to do this despite your high intelligence. It is risky and could ruin your teenage/college/adult life. It is always a bad idea. Cyberspace is vast and more powerful than you. And it is hard to make anything of this magnitude disappear – including a bad reputation.
12. Don't take a zillion pictures and videos. There is no need to document everything. Live your experiences. They will be stored in your memory for eternity.
13. Leave your phone home sometimes and feel safe and secure in that decision. It is not alive or an extension of you. Learn to live without it. Be bigger and more powerful than FOMO – fear of missing out.
14. Download music that is new or classic or different from the millions of your peers that listen to the same exact stuff. Your generation has access to music like never before in history. Take advantage of that gift. Expand your horizons.
15. Play a game with words or puzzles or brain teasers every now and then.
16. Keep your eyes open. See the world happening around you. Stare out a window. Listen to the birds. Take a walk. Talk to a stranger. Wonder without googling....

Most of the lessons listed here do not just apply to the iPhone, but to life. You are growing up in a fast and ever-changing world. It is exciting and enticing. Keep it simple every chance you get. Trust your powerful mind and giant heart above any machine. I love you. I hope you enjoy your awesome new iPhone.

These words of the mother express a lot, and we all should understand and apply them in our lives. Children grow up really fast and their aspirations take flight rapidly. All these rules perfectly fit how the daily routine of a teenager should ideally be. Recently, I had the opportunity to felicitate Pranjal Patil, IAS. She was born blind, but blessed with tremendous vision. She used the mobile and internet to the fullest for her UPSC exam preparation. She listened to speeches on the net. She performed readings of Ramachandra Guha's book *India after Gandhi* on YouTube.[19] She downloaded innumerable audios of her lessons on her mobile. She studied hard, and this courageous girl featured on the merit list of successful candidates who made it to the IAS.

'Just disconnect' is the only solution for this monstrous problem. Scientists have predicted that this addiction to mobile phones is going to spread rapidly like cancer. The electromagnetic radiation emitted from cordless phones is dangerous for health. The closer the phone is to our bodies, the more dangerous it is. Our DNA gets damaged because of mobile use and free radicals are released, which are said to cause different kinds of cancer. While talking about the biochemical effects of mobile phones, only dopamine was talked about. Dopamine is called the 'happy hormone', but an excess of it is dangerous and leads to addictions. Mobile usage causes the release of dopamine in our body, which gets us hooked

---

19 Ramachandra Guha (2017), *India after Gandhi: The History of the World's Largest Democracy,* revised edition, New Delhi: Pan Macmillan India.

to our mobiles and we end up losing our minds. This is also because the mobile and its applications are designed like the colourful and attractive slot machines in casinos that trap us.

Cortisol, another harmful hormone in the human body, released due to mobile usage, is also a cause of worry these days. Cortisol is actually released in the body when we are faced with 'fight or flight' situations. It causes an increase in our blood pressure, makes us sweat, increases our heart rate and releases sugar into our blood so that we are prepared to fight the situation effectively. All this is fine when we are faced with danger, but the self-inflicted phone addiction has brought stress into our lives in the form of constant emails and messages that generate poisonous doses of cortisol. In the past, we would write letters only when we were at peace. But these days, we 'chat' using instant messages without a pause and have wreaked havoc on our relationships, friendships, affection and sense of belonging. It appears that chatting is the key reason for mental illnesses and cracks in our families.

On average, we spend four hours on our phones daily. They are always kept close to us, because of which we are automatically pressurized by different apps, social media, emails. This leads to an increase in cortisol levels that affect the frontal brain. It is this part of the brain that controls our decision-making abilities and discretion. This is the part that dissuades us from stupid and indiscreet behaviour. It may not be possible for us to avoid mobiles, but we can certainly put a lid on its intoxicating addiction.

The first thing we can do is to silence all unnecessary notifications and either put all those apps that keep distracting us into a folder or simply delete them. It is a good idea to spend one day a week completely away from our mobiles. We can start with small steps such as not using the phone while having meals, and then progressively increase our mobile-free time. We have to somehow find our own ways of reducing the use of mobile phones that have become an indispensable part of our lives and have taken over our minds.

Parents, please wake up at the right time and help the new generation to achieve their dreams. I know that all this is easier said than done and difficult to implement. Unfortunately, the truth is that errors, fraud, perversity and falsehood spread really fast, while it takes a lot of conscious effort to spread positive and constructive information. It is high time the parents, teachers, media, NGOs and government work together and come out with a road map to fight this dangerous storm. Some laws, regulations and codes of conduct have to be put in place so that we can stop this contagion from spreading. It is a welcome step that the government has set up cyber police stations, but it is my wish and prayer to God that the time when police have to investigate cyberattacks that destroy the emotional lives of our tender and innocent children never comes. I have only one prayer: 'Oh God, grant me the serenity to accept the things I cannot change, the courage to change the things I can, and the wisdom to know the difference.'

I believe that all of us have to consciously work towards bringing about this positive and constructive change. If we intend to establish a good society, we have to start with individual development. For that, the foundation is thought. Our thoughts get converted into words and words become actions; our repeated actions become our habits. Positive actions lead to good habits and bad actions become bad habits. Habits shape character and character shapes the future.

10

Youth Energy, Safety and Youth Parliament

The culture at the academy was steeped in tradition and discipline, but we were given ample opportunities to express our thoughts. The annual debate competition was one such occasion. In the ever-changing world, there is a lot of ideological churning at the national level and in changes in administrative procedures. Discussions took place at the academy on how changes in public safety and administration should be handled. With the evolution of technology and communication in the twenty-first century, we are faced with tremendous new challenges. In order to face them effectively, it is important for us to re-examine our ideologies. It is vital that we take systematic steps to protect our youth from the damaging influence of bohemian and self-destructive tendencies at all levels.

When I was the IG of West Maharashtra, I conducted a youth parliament debate on the lines of the debate competition at the academy. I had 146 police stations under me. We selected ten schools and colleges under the jurisdiction of each police station, and we finally invited 14,600 students from 1,460 academic institutions to speak on the police platform. Around fifteen lakh students attended these debates as audiences at various locations. We had selected topics and issues that are never taught in schools and are not discussed openly in colleges. Of course, some of the topics were related to the 'police department', 'crime' and 'law and order'! We had also chosen issues like 'sexual harassment of women and girls', 'internet and social media addiction', 'drugs', 'cybercrime', 'student suicides', 'fundamentalism', 'communal violence', 'corruption', 'domestic violence', 'good and bad touch', 'terrorism', 'traffic management'—to be discussed in a constructive and positive manner at these youth parliaments.

In the world we live in today, vices spread fast. Mobiles and the internet have taken control over the impressionable minds and intelligence of our youth. The adolescent minds are deeply affected by what is happening around us, because these children are very inquisitive. This is the time their minds are being cultivated and preparing the foundation for the personalities they will be in future. The fight against terrorism has become a fight of the minds. These young minds who should grow up to be social leaders, actually get poisoned by such principles and surrender themselves to antisocial elements. We have to irrigate these minds, influence these developing minds. Just parroting good values and thoughts in class is not enough. To inculcate good thoughts and values, the students themselves have to study, research, discuss and debate issues and come to their own conclusions. They have to decide the right path for their own future and for society, logically and rationally.

The youth parliament was a step in that direction. We, the police, work towards crushing the poisonous elements in society. Such elements that try to destabilize our society raise their heads from time to time in an organized manner. The large youth population in India works as ready fuel for them. Once such people are able to capture the minds of the youth and instigate them, they can make the youth dance to their tunes! Through this competition, we were able to change the minds and attitudes of the young people within our reach. They were exposed to the issues and problems that affect their world, country and society. They themselves came out with plans and solutions for these problems.

There would be four speakers each time. The first speaker would present the subject. The second speaker would speak about what they would do to solve the problem if they were the district magistrate or police commissioner, using bureaucratic processes. The third speaker spoke about the solutions they would find if they were a legislator, MP or CM. The fourth speaker would speak about how the youth could work towards solving the issue at hand. The speeches would be organized in this fashion, after which the judges would ask the panel questions. All the four speakers on the panel had to discuss and answer the questions. This brought about a sense of team spirit among the youth, and the creative and constructive role of the youth emerged from their answers.

They came up with simple and unique ideas. For example, a young girl said while speaking on domestic violence, 'Why can't we run a "ring the bell" campaign? Whenever we hear noises of domestic violence or fights from a house, we should patiently continue to ring the bell. This will certainly help in bringing a break to the violence, prevent any untoward incidents and also discourage such incidents in future.'

Another competitor said, 'If you want to prevent bomb explosions in public places, why don't you take the help of beggars and ragpickers? Why can't you make them the eyes and ears of the police?' And we actually implemented the idea and created 'eyes and ears committees' at different junctions and made them our friends. These friends of the police proved extremely helpful in nabbing petty thieves, chain snatchers and robbers.

Cybercrimes

The new generation today is riding on computers, and internet and mobile phones have become an integral part of their lives. There is a joke doing the rounds on social media: The groom's father asks a prospective bride's father, 'What does your daughter do?' The father answers, 'She is a heroine. On Tiktok! What does your son do?' The boy's father replies, 'He is a soldier, on PUBG!'

Jokes apart, we were able to realize the extent to which the cyber world had infiltrated our lives during the discussion on 'cybercrime' at the youth parliament. The young people unravelled the cyber world for us. Cyber literacy has become more essential than conventional literacy these days. The difference between urban and rural areas has disappeared with the spread of WhatsApp in the villages. All transactions are possible online, and there is an increase in transparency and ease. However, it has also bestowed on us the curse of cybercrimes.

Cybercrimes are of two types—one where the computer is the target of the crime; for example, hacking and website defacement. The second type of cybercrimes comprise those in which the computer is used as the medium. Frauds, mental harassment and defamation fall under this class of cybercrime. The government has passed the Information Technology Act, 2000, to effectively curb both these classes of cybercrimes. We are familiar with our conventional criminals, but we have no idea where the cybercriminals are located. We don't know whether they are in India or abroad, male or female. This anonymity gives the criminals a lot of confidence, and they are least afraid of the law. That is why it is a huge challenge for the system to control them.

It is important to develop some fundamental skills to fight these crimes. Your password is your only identity on the internet. You will be in deep trouble if your password gets revealed or gets shared by mistake. You can become a victim of financial fraud or your important data can get stolen. That is why it is important to change your passwords every one or two months. The password should not be simple and should not be easy to guess. Globally, 30 per cent of users have the word 'password' as their password or have passwords that are their names followed by the digits 1, 2 and 3! That is why it is best not to include vehicle numbers, the names of children, or birthdays in our passwords. Make your passwords complicated and include commas, apostrophes, exclamation marks, question marks and a mix of capital and small letters. Hackers keep attempting dictionary attacks and check all the names of your family members, adding 1, 2, 3 to their names. They also try checking your birthday. Hackers can make thousands of attempts using their latest computers, and if your password is easy, it can be cracked effortlessly. They can threaten someone on your behalf, post objectionable content on your Facebook page, and send emails in your name. It will be extremely difficult for you to prove that you have not posted or sent them.

Our generation learnt technology, but the new generation is born into it and learn the basics of computers very early in life. Their knowledge is vast and their learning constant. It is just that they lack awareness of digital security and maturity. They share everything in the virtual world. Parents should take the trouble to check what apps the children are using and who their friends are, because there are a lot of sexual predators online with false identities. They target profiles of minors. The apparently twenty-two-year-old user could actually be a fifty-five-year-old sexual pervert. Parents should open Facebook accounts even if they are not interested and insist on being on their child's friends list. This will restrict the child's privacy, but is worth it because it helps us protect our children from danger and guide them. Schools and colleges should make the students aware of the dangers of the internet and the cautions that need to be taken. Students need to be taught about cybercrime and the safe use of computers.

Parents and children need to sit together and create an agreement regarding the internet. This idea is being used in western countries where the family unanimously sets conditions on what kind of photos will be shared on social media, not using the camera behind closed doors, not sharing anything objectionable or hurtful to others, using the laptop on the dining table or in the living room where it is visible to everyone, and so on. We, Indian parents, too can try this strategy. Always keep your computer updated because the hackers are aware of the bugs and shortcomings of old operating systems. Computer hackers globally use these shortcomings as 'bots' for their dirty deeds. They can use your old system by remote control for internet crimes, and you will have no clue about it. It is important to install the latest antivirus systems and update your system periodically. As far as possible use original software or at least open-source free software because these can help prevent backdoor entries, the source codes are available and get updated automatically.

The mobiles we use are also mini-super computers. We do all our financial transactions using online banking. There has been a considerable increase in cases of banking and credit card fraud, but very few cases are actually reported. Banks and corporate houses don't come forward to report such cases, fearing for their reputation and credibility. To ensure that their name doesn't get sullied, the victims of fraud settle the matter by receiving compensation. This allows fraudsters to cheat fearlessly. We hear of cases where senior citizens are cheated using emails and credit cards. Such cases can easily be prevented if we take some simple precautions. The first step is to check your bank statements. There is an attack called 'Salami' in which only fifty rupees are debited from your account each time. That is why it is important to inform the bank if you spot any suspicious transaction and change your PIN immediately. We ignore such things because the amount is negligible, but if fifty rupees can be withdrawn, it is possible to withdraw fifty lakhs as well.

We should change our PIN numbers frequently. Do not discard any letters that come by post carelessly because these may have barcodes, your personal information, account numbers etc. Such information can be easily misused. It is always safe to do transactions using safe banking apps because the banks would have taken all the precautions regarding safety. They are linked to your mobile phone, and the OTPs are verified before the transaction is approved. Ensure that you do not perform any transaction from a public Wi-Fi or from a cybercafe; if you do, make sure that you log out properly.

A fraud called 'phishing' is very common these days. You will receive bank emails that look extremely genuine and will ask you to make some important updates and to click on the link provided in the email. Once you click on the link, you will be led to a cloned website that looks exactly like your bank website. The moment you put your login ID and password, your account gets robbed! Hence, please don't fall prey to such phishing emails and click on any such links. This should be your net banking mantra for safety. All banking websites that don't have https/ and the lock sign are dangerous. *'S' stands for 'safe'*.

Do not ever download any app blindly. The ISI of Pakistan had an app on Google Play Store called 'SmeshApp' that they used to steal information about all the movements and activities of the Indian Army.[20] This app used to steal call logs, location, messages and documents with ease. Whenever you upload an app on your phone, you allow it access to all photos, locations and contacts. You usually use only 5 per cent of the apps installed on your phone. Please understand that nothing on the internet world comes free, and there is a clear motive behind every app. They may not be stealing your information for fraud but can be used for advertising or surveys. Hence, please remove all the unnecessary apps from your phone. Do check the user feedback on Google Play Store, iTunes or apple store before downloading any app. In case you find negative comments and feedback, keep away from those apps.

There is a web series called 'Jamtara', which became very popular upon release. A case of fraud happened in Bihar exactly the way it was depicted in the series. A cyber fraud network was established in an inaccessible village in Bihar. The fraudsters set up call centres for their criminal activities. They call you saying you have won a lottery, your insurance maturity amount is due, you've got a bank bonus, won reward points and so on, and trap you. They provide you with all your genuine details and win your trust. Often it is the personal details that you share innocently on social media or on quizzes on bogus apps that get you into

20 Google removes SmeshApp used by Pakistan to snoop on Indian troops, News 18, March 2016, https://www.news18.com/news/india/google-removes-smeshapp-used-by-pakistan-to-snoop-on-indian-troops-1216294.html

trouble. They gather information such as your favourite colour, the name of your pet, your place of birth and such things that are used as security questions. They then cleverly extract your password and OTP from you during the conversation. In fact, your bank account is being hijacked during the conversation. Hence, be careful to not provide any such information on the phone. Such information is never sought by banks on the phone.

It is important to know the IMEI number of your mobile phone. You need to dial *#06# and you will receive the 10-digit IMEI number of your phone. In case your phone gets stolen, it can be traced using this number. iPhones and Google phones have a 'track my phone' feature, which you can use to lock your phone, destroy data, or create a loud ringing alarm that doesn't stop. Also always remember to remove memory cards from your phone before selling it or gifting it to someone, and format it six or seven times because any information or photo recorded on a computer or a mobile never gets deleted. All deleted information can easily be retrieved.

Cybercriminals constantly target essential services, security systems, and administrative offices. This is an unending war. Our computer scientists and technologists are among the best in the world, but we still have to be careful because our neighbouring countries create and spread messages that cause communal tensions, social discord, caste-based divisions and hurt religious sentiments. Such information is deviously used to spread unrest and create riots in our country. Such messages are spread through popular social media apps such as Facebook and Twitter. This is a daily happening and our cyber machinery works constantly to stop them. Despite these efforts, there are numerous people who fall prey to these offensive, inflammatory and objectionable posts, and share or forward them. They feel nothing can happen to them because they are committing their crime sitting in the safety of their homes, but that is not true. What is a crime in real life is a crime in the virtual world as well! Like you have an IMEI number for your phone, your internet connection too has an IP address, which makes it possible for the police to nab you easily. The admin of the WhatsApp group used for the objectionable activities can also be held responsible. Hence, all of us must be careful and avoid any suspicious groups.

When I was posted in Nashik, I was ordered to take action against eighteen boys. These boys had shared child pornography video clips with each other in their group. All these boys were from high-class families, and one of them was the brother of a very senior officer. Many parents came and pleaded with us, and even the boys apologized, but the law does not pardon ignorance. We took tough action against all of them and created such records that their lives and careers were badly hit. No visa, no passport, no government jobs! Such stains are never erased. It is very important to be extremely careful while stepping into the mesmerizing world of the internet.

Accidents and us

The discussion on 'traffic, accidents and deaths' during the youth parliament was an eye-opener for all of us. Over two lakh people lose their lives in road accidents every day in India. I have seen several such accidents up close and visited sites of serious accidents many times. There has been a lot of planning and many measures have been undertaken to put the brakes on the number of accidents, but not a day passes without newspapers bloodied with the news of people dying in road accidents.

When I was the additional commissioner in West Mumbai, a nineteen-year-old girl died in an accident in Juhu at midnight. Two friends with her were seriously injured. The three girls were going back home with six friends in their Hyundai car after partying in a pub. All of them were just out of their teens. It was around two at night, and they felt like eating something. They turned their car towards Chowpatty, but Rahul, who was driving the car, lost control and hit a rickshaw, a tree and then the divider. This girl sitting on her friend's lap was fatally injured and died on the spot. We filed cases on Rahul under Section 304, of culpable homicide not amounting to murder. He was in police custody for five days. I was, in the meantime, trying to assess whether Section 304 could be filed against the boy, Mani, on whose lap the girl was sitting. Everyone in the car, including Mani, knew that Rahul was drunk. When the accident happened, the girl became a 'shock absorber' and got sandwiched between the front seat and Mani, and lost her life.

I fail to understand how parents allow their children to drink excessively! How do parents allow 'drunk driving'? How are the children allowed to be in pubs till so late in the night? It is true that it is the police's duty to control 'drunk driving', but why isn't this menace getting controlled despite putting thousands of drunk drivers in jail? It is clear that drunk driving is still not considered a serious problem. I had recently read that an American NGO Called 'MADD' (Mothers Against Drunken Drivers) was started by a mother who lost her young son to drunk driving. She tried hard and succeeded in putting pressure on the government with her movement. As a result of her concerted efforts, she succeeded in forcing the US government to make changes in the Motor Vehicles Act to bring tough punishments for drunken driving offences. No one dares break any traffic laws in America today.

When I was the IG in Kolhapur, I witnessed a similar, serious road accident. Forty labourers were travelling in the open container of a dumper truck loaded with shovels, crowbars, spades, and other implements needed for construction. They had placed these appliances at the bottom of the container, covered it with a sheet of tarpaulin and were sitting on it. Night fell, and all of them went off to sleep. While travelling through the Western Ghats area, the driver lost his control, and the speeding dumper hit the railing on the side of the road. The sleeping labourers were thrown up in the air because of the impact and fell on the road. The sharp implements under the tarpaulin, too, flew up and fell hard on the labourers, piercing the bodies of women, children and old people. The police had to pick up the shattered bodies of twenty-five people and take them to the civil hospital in Satara.

Such fatal accidents happen not only on the road but in water as well. Only recently there was an incident at Ujjani Reservoir near Indapur when eleven drunk people drowned while taking a selfie standing on the edge of their boat. When I was the police commissioner in Pune (Rural), a boat capsized in Bhatghar Dam and twenty-seven people lost their lives. The boat had a maximum capacity of only twenty people, but thirty-five people had been loaded on to it. The boat toppled when it reached the middle of the dam. Seven people survived because they were expert swimmers. It took the police two full days to search and pull out the remaining twenty-eight dead bodies from the water.

I still can't forget the heart-wrenching scene to this day. Rigor mortis had set in, making the bodies rigid. A mother was holding her son's shirt-sleeve with her fist. When I saw the boy's body, he was without his shirt and his stiff hand was raised upwards. I could imagine the mother's struggle while desperately trying to save her son's life in her own last moments! She had gripped her son's shirt, but the boy must have slipped out and got pulled away. We hear of such tragic incidents every day. Many families are devastated by the accidental deaths of their earning members.

While I was the IG in Kolhapur, I insisted on strictly implementing the helmet rule, but the people protested furiously against it. In Kolhapur, our turbans are considered helmets! There were complaints like, 'Where will we keep the helmets once we stop riding? Wearing helmets for long durations causes neck pain. It is our life; why should the police bother? First stop incidents of chain snatching by helmeted bike riders.' Many such reasons were given to prevent the police from making wearing helmets compulsory.

During my tenure as police commissioner in Nashik, there were deaths due to road accidents every day. Young men and boys were dying because of their bikes hitting trees on the sides of the road. People started saying that the trees, which were over fifty years old, were hazards and should be cut down. I decided to put a stop to this chain of accidents. We put up barricades over weekends to prevent 'drunk and drive' incidents. I personally stood at one of the barricaded junctions and checked ten vehicles. A majority of them were families returning from parties. Nine of them were drunk drivers. How could these sloshed drivers spot dividers or trees? When I checked with the traffic police, I found that they had only four breathalysers while in a small city like Solapur, we had 120 machines. I requested the police DGP and got sixty machines. We began cracking down on drunk drivers with the help of these breathalysers. We started public awareness campaigns and implemented the helmet law strictly. We got a tremendous response with surprisingly optimistic results for our efforts. Compared to the previous year, the incidences of deaths by road accidents came down by 51 per cent. Even other crimes reduced considerably.

Change is expected and possible from new blood and that is why we chose the subject 'accidents and rules' as one of the topics for the youth parliament. Their analysis and conclusions on traffic and accident deaths were both surprising and shocking. Thousands of people who leave home daily for work or travel do not return home. Many of them fall victim to road accidents without any fault of theirs. Some drunk driver of a car, a bike or an overloaded truck, talking on the phone, becomes the cause of their death. Often, parents themselves allow their teenage children to drive to tuitions on motorcycles and scooters. The boys ride triples on the bike with their friends. Sometimes they get drunk, lose control of their bike and hit dividers or trees, resulting in severe injury or death. Parents have to live their entire lives mourning and repenting the untimely death of their only child. Two-thirds of all road-accident deaths are of youth between the ages of fifteen to thirty-five. Their numbers are many times more than the number of soldiers who died in battle.

The number of trucks driving on roads at night is 30 per cent more than during the day, but the number of accidents at night is 70 per cent more than during the day; 80 per cent of the victims are either bike riders or pedestrians. Often, people damage or remove dividers for their own comfort or for expanding their roadside businesses. This leads to fatal accidents because of the blind turns that get created. Frequently, tractors, bullock carts, vehicles without reflectors, trucks carrying sugarcane, stationary vehicles parked on the roadside without blinkers are open invitations for accidents. We follow no lane discipline, and overtaking is the most common cause of accidents.

We Indians consider three people on a two-wheeler, driving without a licence, talking on the mobile while driving, and drunk driving our birthright! We consider the traffic police—that strictly enforces the wearing of seat belts, helmets, prevents overloading, triple riding, tows away vehicles parked wrongly, disallows jumping signals, and driving on the wrong side—

corrupt and authoritarian. We start looking for justifications for breaking all traffic rules. The easiest is to blame the system and the government. We start finding faults—street lights are not working, signals are in bad shape, signages are improper, there is a lack of parking space, and so on. We blissfully ignore our own indiscipline and lack of civic sense. We are incapable of being disciplined even for our own sake. Till we have this mentality, people will continue to die on the streets and the number of deaths due to accidents will continue to rise year on year.

Change has to begin at the individual level. We cannot change the world, but we can certainly remove as many obstacles as possible. All of us have to take the responsibility of building awareness of traffic rules, educating the public, implementing the rules and working hard to ensure traffic discipline. The first step is to conduct a safety audit of all the city roads and highways and then create a blueprint for traffic management. The police should have a highway beat system in place, where policemen are given a 10–12 km range for cross patrolling.

Highways are like the key arteries of our body, and the highway beat staff should be responsible for their smooth functioning. A survey could be conducted with the aid of traffic engineers, engineering and architecture college students and NGOs. The traffic density and flow can be traced using drone cameras. The key traffic crosses in the city should have CCTV cameras with their monitoring done from the police control rooms. The police should not issue challans to offenders on the road. Instead, they should focus on ensuring that rules are followed.

These days high-tech CCTV cameras are available that can automatically identify number plates and vehicles that break traffic signals. These cameras should be used to catch traffic rule violators and send them their e-challans. Synchronization of traffic signals is a must. Points with frequent traffic jams, and accident-prone locations must be identified. Measures must be taken and implemented in a scientific manner. If someone is lying injured in a road accident, the vehicle driver's blood and urine samples should be tested, and in case they are found drunk or intoxicated, they should be slapped with cases of culpable homicide. A law should be made under which parents who allow underage wards to ride bikes should be named co-accused. The illegally damaged dividers should be repaired, and cases should be filed against the offenders under the Prevention of Damage to Public Property Act, 1984. Systematic collective efforts can surely bring about far-reaching change.

The campaign should actually start with schools and families. Our youth are still under the false impression that driving licences can be acquired illegally through agents. Rules to acquire a driving licence should be made more stringent. As in western countries, we should bring in rules that allow us to revoke a driving licence for specific violations.

Movement in traffic is a science and should be taught in schools and colleges as a subject. If the children are made aware of what the rules are and why they are needed, in a logical manner, they will question their parents when the parents break any rules. We should set up 'traffic parks' to impart such knowledge. Changes have been made in the Motor Vehicle Act, 1988, recently, and once the new rules are enforced, traffic discipline can be imposed more effectively. The government too should make it a priority and take policy decisions on the number of vehicles, the state of the roads and public transport from time to time.

Look at the pollution levels in Delhi: they have reached alarming levels and all departments have given up. Once the right opportunity is lost, all efforts go in vain. We have seen from history that a small error by someone can have catastrophic consequences, wherein generations to come are forced to pay the price. We have committed grave mistakes with regard to environmental issues and played with nature constantly with disastrous results. It is certain that the future generations will not pardon us.

There is a small inspiring poem that describes how an empire can be lost for minuscule reasons:

> For want of a nail the shoe was lost,
> For want of a shoe the horse was lost,
> For want of a horse the rider was lost,
> For want of a rider the message was lost,
> For want of a message the battle was lost,
> For want of a battle the kingdom was lost,
> And all for the want of a horseshoe nail.

We must repair the horseshoe of our horse. Like Gandhiji said, 'You must be the change you wish to see in the world'.

By doing this, tough situations get resolved, our path gets cleared, lives can be saved, and we can save families from falling into disaster. If what the youth discussed in the youth parliament is true, all this has to be included in our education system.

Harassment of women and children

We had chosen 'harassment of women and children' as the last topic of the youth parliament. The discussion on the topic was so intense and deep that one could write a complete PhD thesis! A lot of concrete and appropriate measures and plans emerged from the creative thoughts of the youth. If clever people know how to come out of danger, the wise know how to keep away from danger. That is the mantra the girls shared with the other women in their families.

The first step is safety, and avoiding getting into danger. How will you know that you are in danger? When the attackers are armed, outnumber you, are stronger, and when the location and time are conducive for them to attack you, the monsters in them awaken. When you get these signals, you must find a way to get out of that place. If slipping out is not possible, call the police or your near and dear ones, and tell them your location. Also, you should keep away from friends and acquaintances who seem addicted to drugs, alcohol and illicit sex. If you have no option, at least be with friends who will care for you when you are in trouble.

The second step is being alert. What kind of safety measures and barriers can you create to keep attackers away? The doors and windows of your house should provide double layers of safety. A grill gate outside the door is a must. In case you live alone, install an alarm bell or have a pet dog if you can. Trim the shrubs of your garden so that the attackers cannot hide behind them. Have curtains on your windows to obstruct the view into your house.

These days, online dangers are proving fatal. Learn about the privacy settings of social media platforms such as Facebook or Instagram, and instal appropriate filters. Do not share your private photos, personal information, and location with everyone. Have a good antivirus installed on your system. Create as many hindrances between you and any potential danger. Please remember that criminals and offenders never reveal their real identities on the net. But they can easily find out if you are alone, mentally or emotionally disturbed while chatting, and that is when they trap you and you fall straight into their nets.

The internet is a virtual world and is not what it appears to be. You make friends with unknown people on dating websites such as Tinder. A person who looks trustworthy, honest and has an impressive profile might actually turn out to be a lustful, dangerous maniac in real life. Hence, never send signals that you are weak and helpless. Your signal should be loud and clear—'Don't mess with me, or you will get it back in the same coin.' Attackers are on the lookout for vulnerable and easy prey. If you too are soft and gullible, change your body language. Once the criminal realizes that he will have to fight you or he will get into trouble, he will back off. Hence, self-belief and a powerful body language make for a safety mantra. Your shoulders, back and neck should be straight. Even if you are afraid or nervous, it should not show on your face. Make direct eye contact but don't stare. People who are guilty hesitate to make eye contact. Eye contact can give you the right signals at the right time. Avoid either overconfident or naive.

Walk confidently, with a straight posture and a strong gaze—these form the three pillars of self-confidence. Always be aware and alert about the behaviour of the people around you. The alarm bells should ring before the danger appears. Your antennae should be alerted whenever you spot anything unusual or unexpected. For example, change your path if you see men sitting in a stationary vehicle at an isolated street corner, or bike riders sitting on bikes wearing their helmets. Don't stay lost in your mobile or your iPad when you are outside alone. You may be hit hard anytime, and your carelessness could land you in deep trouble. Predators are always looking around for lone and careless victims.

Whenever some untoward incident happens, either run away or be ready to fight. If your instinct and gut feel sends you alarm signals, just slip away. You don't have to be inoffensive, sweet and simple under dangerous circumstances. Your language has to be aggressive and strong. If that is not possible, make an excuse about needing to make a phone call and get away. People and events that mesmerize you could be a deception, because most of the time, murderers, rapists and child abusers are two-faced and phony. They pretend to be cultured and friendly, and trap the unsuspecting victim. You need to draw the line and ensure that the predator doesn't cross it. They can strike casual conversations by asking for some address. If someone tries to come too close for your comfort, tell them firmly to stay six feet away. If the person still tries to cross the line, you will have the time to take some preventive action. Only harsh, rude and threatening language can stop drunk and prurient individuals.

All these aspects have to be taught to young girls. Little girls get confused when familiar people play dirty with them. All girls need to be taught the difference between good and bad touch. In short, our message has to be clear and precise.

Many people falter when they are in danger. Their limbs go weak, and they get into a defeatist mindset. Fear and terror crush them, and such people fall easy prey to predators. It is important to be able to be aware of the situation and evaluate the danger. This can be achieved by proper training and education.

I could cite my own example of the time when I was the IG in Kolhapur and was able to come out unscathed from a serious accident. I was on my way to the airport to meet the CM when my speeding car skidded at a tricky turn and fell into a ditch. I was saved because I was wearing a seat belt even while sitting in the back seat. My gunman and driver, too, were wearing seatbelts. That is why despite the car falling into a ditch, our heads did not hit the surface in front (in my case, the front seat) because of the impact, and we did not suffer any serious injury.

Secondly, my reflexes prevented me from hitting the glass of the window on the side, or its edge.

We should always be aware of our surroundings: the moment our car swung unexpectedly, my mental guards got alerted. I realized that our car was going to meet with an accident but I was unfazed. I strengthened my grip on the handle on the left and prepared my body to face the danger. As the car skidded into the ditch, I pulled my body in the opposite direction. The grip of the handle got ripped off under the pressure. I had the presence of mind to hit the cushion on the side instead of the glass window and the handgrip hit me on the middle of my forehead. In short, I was saved thanks to my discipline of wearing seatbelts at all times, and because of my presence of mind and trained body. I wasn't hassled even for a moment. I came out of the car with the help of a young farmer who rushed to the car. My uniform was crumpled at the knees. I brushed down my trousers and set off on my duty.

Most times, when lightning strikes or a non-venomous snake bites people, they die because of heart attacks. I have seen many people panicking on seeing their COVID-19 test results come positive. Such fear reduces the immunity of the body and refuses to fight the virus. The training at the academy is primarily focused on preparing us to keep our bodies alert and minds strong during times of serious danger. That is why it is vital to teach our girls the basics of self-defence using simulation techniques.

Fear is the root cause of all disasters. Fear is the refusal to accept that something is not in our control or is temporary. Once we accept this, fear turns into courage. For that, one needs presence of mind, preparedness, and a trained body and mind. Half the battle is won when the attacker realizes that you are not weak and vulnerable. While being attacked, the best option is to free yourself and run as fast as you can. Change direction rapidly while running. It will be easy to deceive the attacker if he is drunk. Run towards a crowded place if possible and attract peoples' attention.

Most times, even others don't know what to do, and they don't come forward to help because they want to avoid getting into any unnecessary trouble. Don't be under the impression that people will come to help seeing you in trouble. When you are panicking, you don't know what to say, and you are lost for words. Instead, seek help and shout loudly and clearly using words like, 'Go away!' 'Help!' and 'Rape!' This will help alert people nearby. We must teach these tricks to our children. Children must also know their parents' mobile numbers and their home address by heart. Teach your children to bite and run away from anyone who tries to touch them inappropriately or tries to be intimate.

Many women believe that they are helpless and cannot fight the attacker. Just imagine, if your wife or daughter is being sexually molested in front of your eyes, will you remain a mute spectator? The strength of ten elephants will course through your body, and you will become as fierce as a tigress and agile as lightning. You will squeeze the attacker's neck, use your teeth and nails as weapons, and try to tear him apart. So don't be fearful when something like this happens to you. Use your handbag or a chair lying around as a shield. Use a broom or an umbrella as a stick. Use a fork, kitchen knife, pen or scissors as weapons. Keep your eyes open and look for things like paperweights, glass items, vessels and use them as stones. Spray mud, sand, alcohol or deodorant directly into the attacker's eyes. Transform yourself into a fighter—kick, punch, scream and scratch!

Our physical strength increases tenfold when we are faced with danger. We become like the fawn that outruns the cheetah to save its own life in the jungle. It is a matter of life and death after all!

I had invited Dr Amol Kolhe for the closing of the youth parliament competition. He cited an example whilst giving his speech:

> Two brothers had gone to the fields. The fourteen-year-old elder brother was fat and the ten-year-old younger one was thin and wiry. Both didn't know how to swim. They were pulling water from their dilapidated well when the older brother's leg slipped, and he fell straight into the well. The younger brother, seeing his brother drown, threw the rope into the well and fortunately the rope fell into the older brother's hands. The half-dead boy somehow managed to tie the rope around his waist, and the thin brother started pulling his heavy older brother up with all his might. He used every ounce of energy in his body and managed to save this older brother's life.
>
> When the news of this incident spread in the village, people refused to believe it. They believed that the brothers were lying and cooking up a story. How was it possible for a boy weighing 37 kg to pull up his brother who weighed 70 kg, 30 feet up from a well? There was a discussion in the village square that evening and people gave their own logic and reasoning.
>
> Finally, the village school teacher stood up. The villagers had a lot of respect for him. The teacher said, 'This is possible. Because no one had told the ten-year-old boy that he couldn't pull his heavy brother, weighing 70 kg, up.'

We ourselves create limits for our strength and capabilities. We consider our surroundings as our world and create boundaries. The horizon we see is an illusion. Columbus said, 'You can never cross the ocean unless you have the courage to lose sight of the shore.' Everyone nodded in agreement. They had found the answer to their question. And yes! It is indeed possible if your driving force is unlimited passion, life-threatening fear or intense attraction! A normal human being can transform into 'Hulk' and perform seemingly impossible tasks successfully.

The academy makes an effort to bring out this hidden mindset and skills from within us. We have seen police officers such as 'Singham' knock down ten people singlehandedly. This is impossible in real life, but SPs can brighten the lives of lakhs of people with their impressive personalities. They can defeat every illegal and unlawful activity and mentality in their jurisdiction. This is possible if the responsible officers use their wisdom and intelligence for the benefit of society. We need to find ways of bringing the gems of wisdom that we received at the academy to the youth at large. We must be able to use the ideas and teachings learnt during the rigorous training at the Hyderabad academy, for the general good. I had always kept awareness and advertence in my mind at all times during the training.

11
Head Held High

The countdown to the end of the ten-month training had begun. The practice for the passing-out parade drill had started. The passing-out parade is a grand, solemn and spectacular ceremony. We were supposed to join our appointed state for the field training after the parade. We practised for the parade twice a day in the sweltering heat, dressed in our starched uniforms. We were not allowed the slightest movement while standing at attention or at ease. All the trainees had to stand motionless, all our steps had to be in sync during the parade.

We were given tips on how to march with our rifles, and to stand still during the chief guest's speech. Care was taken that none of us fainted during the parade. We were taught how to move our toes when our boots got too hot, instructed to look ahead and only move our eyeballs and not our heads, and to control sneezes by biting our lips. We worked really hard to ace the final challenge of the passing out parade and were excited about our field training stint.

Finally, the day arrived and the academy was brimming with the parents and relatives of the graduating batch of trainees.

Parents, in-laws of newlywed trainees, and friends were waiting eagerly to watch their dear heroes marching in the parade. All the guests were seated at their designated seats an hour before the start of the ceremony. The senior officers and their spouses were seated in a special enclosure.

It was time for the chief guest to arrive. We stood waiting with our rifles, behind a wall that resembled the rampart of a fortress. All of us were dressed in starched uniforms, sparkling, polished boots and cross belts. Our trainer was motivating us with his invigorating words in Hindi, '*Yahi imtihan ki ghadi hai saheb, poori himmat, phurti aur hausle ke saath kavayat honi chahiye. Apna best dena saheb, 51 RR ki ijjat ka savaal hai.*'

Energy cruised through our veins, and our eyes sparkled with determination. We chanted aloud, '*bas ab kar dikhana hai! Hausla buland hai aur seene me junoon hai! Bharat mata ki jai! Bharat mata ki jai! Bharat mata ki jai!*'

The atmosphere was electrifying and the bugle sounded. The command for us to enter the parade ground was given. We followed the rhythm of the police band dressed in pristine white uniforms and marched in. Eyes forward, spine erect, we marched with our arms swinging in tandem, platoon-wise, into the ground and reached the centre. The parade commander ordered, 'Parade! Tham!' We stopped to loud applause from the visitors' gallery in appreciation of our march. Now we eagerly waited for the chief guest to arrive. The chief guest was Union minister of state for home affairs, Shri Vidyasagar Rao. We welcomed him with a salute. At the request of the parade commander, he reviewed our parade, riding a decorated jeep. Everyone saluted the flag.

All those present were mesmerized by the presentation of the parade. Our marching in synchronized steps to the command of 'Dheere chal!'—a slow and rhythmic march, taking each step with deliberation—was a delight to watch. The parade ground resounded with applause.

Each moment was one to be savoured, moving at its own pace. The display at the parade was a culmination of the efforts we had put in for the past ten months. My father and mother, watching from the spectators' gallery, observed the parade, their eyes moist, absorbing each moment for posterity. How proud they must have been! The little boy who would clatter off in wooden chappals to the village school on the temple premises, today marched across the parade ground with confidence and honour. Their son, who hailed from an obscure village called Kokrud, today walking with royal confidence, his head held high on the NPA parade ground in Hyderabad, waiting to take his oath as an IPS officer. The very thought of the feelings my parents would be going through overwhelmed me.

I was going to take an oath today that was going to change the course of my life, my values and my dedication. An oath is a verbal pledge, the highest promise one can make. Today was a day when we were going to bind ourselves to this lifelong commitment. The words of this pledge are our weapons and our shields! They express our service to the nation with our bodies, minds and spirits. There are two stories that will tell us how what we decide to do today impacts our own future and the lives of generations to come. The first story! Al Capone was a dreaded don in Chicago in the first half of the twentieth century. He established an illegal and illicit business syndicate and ruled Chicago. He was the undisputed king of the underworld of murders, robberies, flesh trade, and drugs. Al Capone had committed every possible crime we can think of but was able to evade the law and escape every time with the help of 'Easy Eddie' a lawyer who was a master at bending the law at will.

In return for his services Eddie received handsome amounts of money, luxurious homes and every possible luxury.

Easy Eddie had only one son, whom he kept far away from the world of crime. He taught his son the difference between right and wrong, discreet and indiscreet, and other values in life. He wanted his son to grow up into a person who could make a respectable place for himself in society. He knew that despite having all the wealth in the world, he could not give his son a reputable name and thus couldn't be an ideal father. This was extremely distressing for him. One day, not able to take this anymore, Eddie decided to quit Al Capone's company. He knew he would have to pay a heavy price because he was going to go against the biggest don of Chicago.

Eddie revealed all the details and evidence about Al Capone's crime to the police and tax authorities. The result of his actions was disastrous, as Eddie was soon shot dead in broad daylight. But he had managed to leave a positive and inspiring example for his son. Even life can be lost for the sake of truth. Eddie sacrificed his life to teach his son the lesson that 'truth prevails at any cost.' The police found a poem and rosary in Eddie's pocket, which read: 'The clock of life is wound but once, and no man has the power to tell just when the hands will stop. Now is the only time you own. Live, love, toil with a will. Place no faith in time, for the clock may soon be still.'

The second story is about one of the heroes of World War II. Butch O'Hare was one of the most daring American fighter pilots and was posted on the naval ship USS Lexington in the south Pacific. A powerful, fully loaded Japanese squadron was progressing towards his warship. With its own squadron already out of range, the American warship was vulnerable and weak. There were no aircraft to protect it.

Butch's fighter had no choice but to fight the Japanese squadron on his own. That option was dangerous, but Butch entered the Japanese formation without a moment's hesitation using the limited weapons and ammunition he had. On his way down to land on the USS Lexington, Butch managed to destroy five aircraft of the Japanese squadron before he landed safely on the warship. Butch's heroics had been recorded on the camera in his aircraft. Everyone praised him for his extraordinary guts and presence of mind. For his heroic deeds on 20 February 1942, he became the 'First Fighter Ace' of WWII and was honoured with the Medal of Honor. The young, twenty-nine-year-old war hero was martyred the very next year in another air mission. The people of Chicago couldn't forget their hero and immortalized him by naming the Chicago international airport after O'Hare. There is a statue of Butch O'Hare installed between terminals 1 and 2 at the airport.

Now, the question that arises is this: What is common to both these stories?

The amazing answer is that Butch O'Hare was Easy Eddie's son!

But what has that got to do with the passing-out parade?

The answer is that irrespective of your background and your adverse circumstances, life gives you opportunities. Your willpower and determination take you to your goal. You may feel totally broken, defeated and believe that everything is over, but things are never over. For us, in the IPS, that is when the oath taken at the NPA gives us strength and energy. Our fortunes turn for the better, and we are able to land our knock-out punches. It was time to take the pledge—to give my all for my nation, my land, my people. Eddie passed all the power and positivity to his next generation with his rosary and the lines of poem that was found on him. Those pure emotions and holy thoughts made O'Hare's legacy immortal.

'*Vedaat Marathe veer daudale saat*' Here is a similar story of valiance! Prataprao Gujar, a general in Shivaji's army, had been sent to deal with an invading force led by the Adilshahi general, Bahlol Khan. Prataprao's forces surrounded Bahlol Khan's camp and captured him. In spite of specific warnings from Shivaji Maharaj, Prataprao released Bahlol Khan when he promised not to invade Maratha territories again. Soon after his release, Bahlol Khan started preparing for a fresh invasion. Incensed, Shivaji Maharaj wrote an angry letter to Prataprao, refusing to see him till such time that Bahlol Khan was re-captured.

Prataprao now learnt that Bahlol Khan was camping near Nesari, with 15,000 troops. In a fit of rage, he rode away alone to capture Khan. Seeing their leader heading certain death, six other Maratha sardars joined him in the charge. The seven warriors attacked the enemy camp and killed hundreds of enemies, but were slaughtered eventually. Despite knowing that death was certain, they didn't step back. The legend of these seven warriors is famously sung as '*Vedaat Marathe veer daudale saat*'. The seven adored Shivaji Maharaj so much that the oath they had taken for swarajya and the strength of their loyalty gave them the power to lay down their lives for their king and their country! It was now our turn to take a similar oath for India.

The untiring efforts of the academy had turned us into silver if not gold! Silver is heated in fire till it loses all its impurities. Even if it is heated a second longer, it gets ruined. The moment the silversmith can see his face in the piece of silver, he removes it from the fire. We too had reached our melting points and could see our moulded, sculpted, fiery faces. This was the pinnacle of our training. The academy was a furnace in which we had been heated and moulded for the future. You have to willingly allow yourself to face heat until you melt in the furnace; only then will you get moulded into the shape the silversmith or goldsmith desires. Your soul is your teacher. Like the horse that is led to the river to drink, other people guide you towards the reservoir of knowledge and skills, and it is you who has to receive it.

The chief guest spoke about the challenges of the future and expressed his optimism towards our capabilities to handle them. He began by praising our impeccable parade wholeheartedly. There were no errors or shortcomings in the parade, and all the commands were followed with precision. The uniforms were stiff, the steps in sync and on the beat! He was most impressed with our body language. He said:

> My officers, your self-confidence shone through your body language, your eyes reflected your vision and farsightedness and your dreams. Every step of yours clearly showed your preparedness to work as a team towards making your service and our country prosperous and great. As an IPS officer, you are going to witness and experience a world that is very different from what you have seen till now. All of you have come here from varied educational and cultural backgrounds. This academy has integrated all of you into the IPS, which has a glorious history and tradition. In fact, today all of you are entering a new life, and it is the most important day in your life as an IPS officer. The second most important day will be the day you retire from the service with honour. You are starting your career today. Your values, ethics, beliefs, attitude and the culture of this land will decide the course of your life.
>
> The world is changing, and it is certain that India is going to lead the world. The NPA has created leaders

for the police service of a bright India. You will have to implement practically in real life the theories you have learnt till date. Modern guerrilla warfare and the field tactics you have learnt here will stand in good stead and help you overpower and fight the terrorists and Naxalites successfully. Apart from security, you must have a sensitive and empathetic attitude towards society at large and have a positive and appropriate outlook towards their human rights. The world of the future is going to be transparent. You will have to fight casteism, communalism, 'linguism', regionalism, sectarianism, naxalism, terrorism, extremism and several other 'isms'. Working with traditional, outdated and feudalistic mindsets will not be effective at all.

You will have to prioritize women's empowerment and security. You have to befriend society to ensure communal harmony. Being alert, aware and sensitive about the needs of women, children, the elderly, Dalits and minorities has to be your dharma. You will have to be patient and mature while handling protests by farmers, students and workers. Although the safety of the good and punishing the evil is your duty, your priority has to be the securing of law and order. The criminal justice system is like a relay race in which the police start the race and pass the baton to the prosecution and courts, which then hand it to the prison system. For this to happen successfully, there has to be proper coordination and balance between all departments. There is an old philosophy in Africa called 'Ubuntu', which says, 'I am because you are'. Man cannot live in isolation, and we cannot imagine a life where we are separated from each

> other and are self-centred. What we say or do affects others. When we do good deeds, they spread wide.
>
> Trainee officers, that is why you are leaving this academy today fully trained, equipped and enriched. I expect all of you to use your power, authority and skills to provide justice to the weak, the needy, and the aggrieved. You will always be committed towards the creation of a strong and safe India.

The inspiring speech of the chief guest ended with thundering applause from the audience.

Every speech by the chief guest at the passing out parade is crisp and filled with motivational words. Recently, the national security advisor, Shri Ajit Doval, was the chief guest for the 2014 batch. I had the fortune to listen to his exceptional speech. Every word he spoke reflected his experience, wisdom, professionalism and dedication. He said:

> I, too, had come out of this academy after receiving training as an IPS officer forty-seven years ago. This is a great alma mater. I am still grateful for what I received from here. You and I are bound by a unique camaraderie of this service. I was actually confused about what to say to you. I was not sure whether I should use flowery words and show off, or talk about how I feel looking back at my journey ever since I graduated from here. I am going to talk about how this academy benefitted me in my life, and how the training transformed my views, value systems and attitude. The training has two parts: one the hardware part which includes PT, horse riding, forensics, knowledge of law, parades and all

aspects of indoor and outdoor training. But honestly, these weren't very useful for me. However, there was a specific rationale and spirit behind every aspect, which was automatically rubbed into you and became a part of your system.

If I was working out hard on the PT ground and sweating it out every day, it taught me that a police officer has to be physically fit. When you are physically fit and healthy, you will be mentally healthy as well. That is why, make this your mantra for life. If you intend to achieve great things in life, take good care of your health. Parade teaches you team spirit. It teaches you that you can march together, work together, and coordinate with each other. You imbibe the three roles of being a leader, co-worker and student from parades. You learn to lead and follow a leader. You learn to unhesitatingly take orders and follow them to the T.

The second gift I received from here are my batchmates, my comrades for life! These companions stood by me firmly in times of professional and personal need. Hence, make sure you respect this friendship and protect it. But the most valuable aspect is something different, and I will tell you about it after I narrate a story from Buddha's life. When Buddha was on his deathbed counting his last breath, all his disciples gathered around him. Everyone was worried and sad. Each one had only one question to ask Buddha, 'What will happen to us? Who will guide us? Who will show us the right path?'

Buddha said in his last moments, '*Attadeepo bhava*' meanings, 'Be your own guiding light.' Similarly, what you have learnt here will make you competent enough to be your own guru and guide. This is the biggest contribution of the academy. All of you must leave this place pledging to train yourself every single day of your life. Today and from tomorrow onwards, you are both the player and your coach, you are both the trainee and your trainer if you decide to do so. But, if you think that this is the time .... [that] the training is over and it's all laurels .... you can just go around and be a big man in your district, you will be having lot of honour, privileges and sometimes some problems .... then you have just stagnated there, and you are adding nothing to your physical, mental and professional capability. You will stagnate, and you will not grow—that is why, '*Aatmadevo bhava*!' or 'Be your own God!'

The academy has made you capable and created a network for you. These skills and your constant training will make you capable of handling all the different challenges in future. I don't think you need to learn anything more after this. A lot of tough challenges will come your way, but you will handle them with ease! Trust me, these may not even be noticed, but one mistake, and you will have to pass through a trial by fire. Be prepared for such testing times! You have to train yourself continuously to serve the police service, the nation and yourself.

There are multiple challenges you face. Internal security, cybercrime, organized crime, communal strife, and the rights of the marginalized are some of them you will face every day. In the post WWII period, thirty-seven countries have failed or have degraded themselves. Of these, only nine were due to external aggressions while twenty-eight degraded themselves or became a failure because they could not manage their internal security. Pakistan that couldn't handle East Pakistan, Yugoslavia, Czechoslovakia, or the balkanization of the erstwhile Soviet Union, are all examples of such failure. That is why internal security is most important. Wars have changed form.

You are now in the phase of a fourth-generation war and this is a very, very difficult war. It is warfare with an invisible enemy ... It's warfare in which civil society is both the battleground as well as the ground and the people that you have to protect. Despite the force, material resources and technology, a superpower like the United States faced defeat in Vietnam, while the Soviets failed to achieve their strategic or political objective in Afghanistan. Because this war cannot be won by armies. This is the war of a policeman. If you win the country wins, and if you lose the country loses. It is not warfare for the land or terrain. If your intelligence agencies are very good, your awareness and connection with the people very high and if you have got the skills, you are the master!

When you retire after twenty-five or thirty long years of service, the country would have changed. India would have become an economic superpower. Along with prosperity will come problems of internal security. If you do not handle these problems in a professional and skilful manner, then despite all the prosperity, our country will be weak and become vulnerable to enemy attacks. Internal security is the responsibility of the police, and the leadership of this force is in your hands. Train yourself to become powerful intellectually, emotionally and spiritually, as strong as possible you can.

You have to master ever-changing technology. The biggest challenge will be now. If you have to fight and win this fourth generation of warfare, whether it is organized crime, terrorism, bank frauds, insurgency or foreign powers trying to meddle in your internal affairs, you have got to be demonstrative and tackle them using technology. The criminals will always be two steps ahead of you.

Now I come to the final dose of this brief discourse! You have to build capacity and systems to solve disputes, controversies and conflicts. You will have to gather all the information, knowledge, material and skills needed to do so. There is no other service that poses more challenges of personal and professional conflicts of interest, than the police service. When President Bush was addressing the nation after the 9/11 attacks, he made a very important point. He said, 'America always advocates freedom and independence, but at the same time protects the highest national interests. If a conflict arises between the two, national security and interests will be paramount.' You, too, will be faced with such conflicts on a daily basis. The law will say one thing, and someone else will pressurize you not to follow the law. You will have to handle communal riots while there is a family celebration happening at home. Terror attacks may take place when you are exhausted or unwell. There will be a conflict between natural justice and the law. A troubled and tormented person may commit a crime, and you may hesitate to punish him. At times, scandalous misinformation may be deliberately spread about you, and the media and political system may believe them. You will have to face several conflicting situations like these in your career.

There is a very effective remedy for this. Brand yourselves! Earn the reputation of being a credible, determined and honest officer. Inculcate courage, resilience, and loyalty. Learn the law and feel proud of your police force. Go beyond caste, religion, language, and region. The golden letters IPS are etched on your uniforms. The uniform has given you a brand. If you protect your brand with integrity and honesty, the pressures on you will automatically come down and conflicts of interest vanish. If your decisions are based on values and honesty, people will respect you and be afraid of you at the same time! Your brand may not be the answer to all your problems, but you will never be indecisive and uncertain. You get conflicted when you do something and your conscience starts ringing alarm bells. Whenever you do something out of fear, pressure, prejudice or repentance, problems are bound to happen.

The IPS is a great service and you are stepping, into a bright career with dreams and hope. When you look at the mirror tomorrow morning, test your brand. How do you want your close family members, relatives and friends to think about you? How do you want your juniors, seniors, peers and the public you serve to see you? When you retire after your long career, and you go to hand over your baton, the satisfaction and contentment on your face will tell you that 'my life in the police service has been a success. I have served my country and society with dedication and devotion'.

The chief guest's speech ended. He had given us the mantras for a conscientious and efficient life in very simple words. It gave us goosebumps to think of such service to the nation, and we felt the tingle of the IPS brand in our heads. The parade commander took permission to dismiss the parade. The flag squad left first. Everyone stood up out of respect for the flag. The parade commander roared in Hindi, '*Deekshant parade nishkraman ke liye char char ki baaree me dahine baayen ko dheere chal.*'

We marched slowly and steadily from the historical parade ground towards the field of our life. The last step that we had to cross, to venture out, had words written on it that are etched deep in our hearts and souls, 'THE FIRST STEP IN SERVICE TO THE PEOPLE'.

What is, after all, the duty of a police officer? What is our responsibility? At times when a person is in danger or when a person's life or property is in danger, I will stand firmly behind them. My uniform will not be my identity; I will give identity to my uniform!

I was overwhelmed and had dreams in my eyes. My heart was beating fast, and energy coursed through my body. When I placed my foot on that last step, it was a divine sensation. It was the moment for which I was born. It was the moment for which I had worked so hard, given my all. The sweet, innocent, carefree times in my life were over. It was now time for duty, for action. Every step I took henceforth would not be for me, but my country.

What do you need to compose a song? You don't need a great voice; you don't need to know how to play many instruments. You don't have to be a music expert either. All you need is a soft heart that is sensitive and can understand the pain and sorrow of the people around you. A beautiful melody will surely originate from there. As I stepped on to that last step, I pledged to have a similar sensitive and empathetic heart—all my life and for my service. The Namdev step at Pandharpur and the step at Alandi Haibat are symbols of the devotion and surrender of the Warkari sect. The step at Hyderabad symbolized public service and patriotism, and set my goal for life.

I had read somewhere that the Bhagwad Gita mentions two kinds of actions: kriya and karma. The actions we perform on a daily basis for our living fall under the kriya category. We earn a living, take care of our children and parents, and buy daily needs. All such activities that we do for our family are kriyas. Even animals and other species perform similar actions to some extent. However, karma means actions that are dispassionate and detached. We must have a healthy balance of kriyas and karmas in our daily life. We do not receive any remuneration or reward for our karmas. Karmas bring meaning and satisfaction into our life.

Sant Kabir, Sant Tukaram and Sant Gyaneshwar tried to instil this aspect into society during their time. When Gyaneshwar completed writing the *Gyaneshwari*, he prayed to God saying:

> 'O Parameshwara, if you are pleased with my conceptualization and songs, bless me so. *jekhalaanchivyankatisaando/ tyaasatkarmirativaadho/ bhootanparasparepado/ maitrajeevanche.*
>
> Lord, this is what I ask from you; destroy the negative tendencies from people. No one is inherently bad. He may have negative tendencies. Just remove them and, once they are removed, let them grow towards positive living. If you do this, all people in this world will live happily and with love.

> *Duritaanche timirajaavo/ vishwasvadharmasuryempaho/ jevaanchchitaatelaaho/ praanijaata.*
>
> Sin exists in this world only due to the darkness of ignorance. Let the sun of practising one's own duty disperse this darkness. This world of practising one's duty is not defined by Hindu, Islam or Buddhist religions, but it is one where humanity defines it. The essence of it is in the three tenets: to love, to help and to do one's duty. If one follows this dharma, everyone will be able to get what they want and wish for.

When we assimilate this ideology, our views about our profession become more humane and purer. What could be the highest point of our profession? We would have reached the pinnacle of our profession when it loses meaning or its purpose is solved. For example, when a doctor pledges to remove all disease from society or the police are able to root out crime completely, a society of their dreams comes into being. These thoughts may seem far-fetched or illogical, but it was the carefree madness of youth that made us take such impossible oaths. That was the time for unthinkable dreams and to toil day and night to make them come true. Our self-search had begun, and we had left despair and pessimism far behind.

My determination was at an all-time high and was getting pulled towards my future: I will melt all chains and fetters that bound me so far and make them my weapons that I will use to face every challenge. I am filled with enthusiasm and energy; my intentions are pure and I have strength in my arms; why should I be bothered by anyone? I march fearlessly towards my goal, just like Shivaji Maharaj's followers!

Like they say, one who can't leave the safety of the shore can never dare venture far into the sea. In a way, in the last thirteen months, I had dived deep into the ocean of my personality. During the tough ten-month long training at Hyderabad, I had challenged myself and developed my skills and capabilities. The academy had taught me to fight fear and danger. Be it the fear of mountains, water, horses, public speaking—our alma mater inspired us to overcome every such fear.

Sant Kabir said, *'Man ke hare haar hai, man ke jeete jeet'*, which means, 'One who is defeated by the mind, sees defeat; one who conquers the mind, sees victory.' I had experienced this first hand during the ten months at the academy. The long, rigorous days of training had filled me with resilience and given me the patience to face challenges strongly. I learnt modern techniques that would help me fight problems defiantly in the future. I learnt the fundamentals of policing, fighting crime, the law, intelligence gathering, and maintaining law and order. I had gained knowledge about how the policing style has to adapt to the changing times.

Policing can no longer be detached from society: we have to take society along and create systems that would be beneficial to it. The line by Robert Peel is etched deeply in my conscience, 'The police are the public and the public are the police.'

We have to hold the needs of the public in the highest esteem while policing. If we keep people with us during peace times, we will get their unstinted support during times of crisis. We have to forge a strong public-police partnership and sustain it at all times. It is our oath to use every skill learnt at the academy for nation building, empowering society and providing security and safety to everyone. We have to go out and give back, with interest, whatever we received from society. We will be dedicated to 'Satyam, Seva, Surakshanam'—the motto of the academy.

Chatrapati Shivaji owned the Sahyadris and began the earnest task of building his kingdom with an oath of sacrifice to Shambhu Maharaj. My own inner voice was now rousing me to wake up, get up and follow the ideals of the great king. It challenged me to dedicate myself to my duty with a sense of sacrifice. It was telling me, 'Reach for the skies with your dedication, and you will see how the world will fall at your feet.' Now I had to walk without getting tired, without stopping. The path would be difficult, but my penance would be no less. I was going to return, with gratitude, what I had been given by the Lord. I was not to take, but give! To give everything I had—for my country. I had to break free of all bonds and throw away the armour that protected me. It was a bold, new confidence that needed a new outlook.

My identity is not based on my caste, religion, language, or the place where I came from. I am Indian. My life, my soul, my loyalty—they all are for my motherland. So that when I die and stand in front of my Lord, I will have only one thing to say, 'There is only one identity I have—I am an Indian, and I am the son of my mother India!'

Jai Hind!

About the Author

Vishwas Nangre Patil is a 1997 batch Indian Police Service officer. He is currently posted as the joint commissioner of police (Law & Order), Mumbai City (2022). In 2015, he received the President's Police Medal for Gallantry for his role in the counterterrorist operations during the 2008 Mumbai terror attacks.

He has a strong passion for writing and loves reading books.

About the Translator

Subha Pande is a multilingual translator and has translated Kaajal Oza Vaidya's *Krishnayan* into English (Eka, 2021), Kavita Kané's *Sita's Sister* and *The Fisher Queen's Dynasty* into Hindi. She has also translated six novellas and a short-story collection by Sivasankari into English. Her English translation of Girish Kuber's Marathi book *Yuddha Jeevanche* will be published by HarperCollins in October 2022. Subha is also a certified Yoga instructor. She lives in Vadodara with her writer husband, Vikrant Pande.